WEEK

Analytical Methods of Electroacoustic Music

STUDIES ON NEW MUSIC RESEARCH

Series Editor:
Marc Leman
Institute for Psychoacoustics and Electronic Music
Department of Musicology
University of Ghent, Belgium

Signal Processing, Speech and Music
Stan Tempelaars

Musical Signal Processing
Edited by Curtis Roads, Stephen Travis Pope,
Aldo Piccialli and Giovanni De Poli

Rhythm Perception and Production
Edited by Peter Desain and Luke Windsor

Representing Musical Time: A Temporal-Logic Approach
Alan Marsden

Musical Imagery
Edited by Rolf Inge Godøy and Harald Jørgensen

Notes from the Metalevel: An Introduction to Computer Composition
Heinrich K. Taube

Rhythm, Music, and the Brain: Scientific Foundations and Clinical Applications
Michael H. Thaut

Analytical Methods of Electroacoustic Music
Edited by Mary Simoni

Analytical Methods of Electroacoustic Music

EDITED BY

Mary Simoni

Routledge
Taylor & Francis Group
New York   London

Use of the "Sybil" toolbox and Harvey Analysis Model is by permission of the University of Huddersfield.

Use of sketches and sound sources for *Mortuos Plango, Vivos Voco* by kind permission of Jonathan Harvey.

Excerpts from *pipe wrench: flute and computer*, Elizabeth McNutt, EMF Media 2000, used by permission of the artist (www.emfmedia.org/catalog/em125/index.html).

Excerpts from *Jupiter*, music: Philippe Manoury, © by Editions Durand, used with permission.

Excerpts from *Riverrun* used by permission of the composer and Cambridge Street Publishing (www.sfu.ca\~truax\csr.html).

Excerpts from *K...*, libretto: Bernard Pautrat and André Engel, based on the work of Franz Kafka; music: Philippe Manoury, © by Editions Durand, used with permission.

From Kafka to K... A Multimedia Exploration of Philippe Manoury's K was originally released by IRCAM, the Institut de Recherche et Coordination Acoustique/Musique.

Published in 2006 by
Routledge
Taylor & Francis Group
270 Madison Avenue
New York, NY 10016

Published in Great Britain by
Routledge
Taylor & Francis Group
2 Park Square
Milton Park, Abingdon
Oxon OX14 4RN

© 2006 by Taylor & Francis Group, LLC
Routledge is an imprint of Taylor & Francis Group

Printed in the United States of America on acid-free paper
10 9 8 7 6 5 4 3 2 1

International Standard Book Number-10: 0-415-97629-4 (Hardcover)
International Standard Book Number-13: 978-0-415-97629-9 (Hardcover)
Library of Congress Card Number 2005014484

Library of Congress Cataloging-in-Publication Data

Analytical methods of electroacoustic music / [edited by] Mary Simoni.
    p. cm.
  Includes bibliographical references and index.
  ISBN 0-415-97629-4 (hardback : alk. paper)
    1. Electronic music—History and criticism. 2. Computer music—History and criticism. I. Simoni, Mary Hope. II. Title.

ML1380.A53 2005
781.2--dc22
                         2005014484

Taylor & Francis Group
is the Academic Division of Informa plc.

Visit the Taylor & Francis Web site at
http://www.taylorandfrancis.com

and the Routledge Web site at
http://www.routledge-ny.com

Contents

Acknowledgments

The impetus for this book came from listening to numerous concerts of electroacoustic music at conferences of the International Computer Music Association (ICMA) and the Society of Electroacoustic Musicians in the United States (SEAMUS) as well as a wide variety of recordings from the last few decades. I was intrigued by the fact that the depth of analysis and critical essay enjoyed by classical music did not accompany electroacoustic music. Due to the comparative youth of electroacoustic music, many composers are living in our midst during a period of cataclysmic change. It seemed prudent, if not essential, to document this vibrant genre of music-making through analysis in direct consultation with the composers. After frequent discussions with several of the authors regarding our own approaches to the analysis of electroacoustic music, I decided during the International Computer Music Conference 2002 held in Sweden to compile this edited volume. This book would not have been possible without the dedicated commitment of the composers to advance the art and the relentless energy of the contributors to fully describe and document the art through analysis. I owe a debt of gratitude to Karen Siegel for her patient and careful reading of the book and to Scott Jaeger for creating the accompanying DVD. I am tremendously appreciative of the resources and staff of the University of Michigan School of Music that made this volume possible.

This book would not have been possible also without the support and encouragement of Richard Carlin, acquiring editor, and Devon Sherman, editorial assistant, at Routledge; Julie Spadaro, project editor, at Taylor & Francis; and Lynn Goeller, project manager, and the team at EvS Communication Networx, who worked cheerfully with great dedication throughout the production process. Finally, this book would not have been realized without the dedicated support of my husband, Kevin Dowd, and my daughters, Shannon and Sarah Dowd.

1

Introduction[1]

MARY SIMONI

The evanescent nature of music and humanity's duty to preserve creativity have led to various representations of musical abstractions. Since the eclipse of the oral tradition with the advent of the scribes, we have struggled to bridge the abyss of lost meaning between representation and intent. Just as the written word alone does not exclusively impart meaning, musical representation does not solely communicate compositional intent. Whether the musical representation consists of neumes, notes on a staff, or graphics, we are obliged to look beyond these visual artifacts and listen carefully to fully understand the music. The visual artifacts are, after all, nothing more than a means to harness the intent of some musical abstraction. This practiced balance among representation, compositional intent, and human perception is why music analysis is truly an art about an art.

1.1. The Four Basic Elements of Music

Many texts on the theory of music describe music in terms of four basic elements: pitch, duration, intensity, and timbre. Pitch, the highness or lowness of a note, is human perception of the physical phenomenon of frequency—the number of oscillations per second of a periodic waveform. There is a logarithmic correlation between a frequency measured in Hertz (Hz) and our perception of that frequency described as a pitch. Pitches are identified as members of the musical alphabet—A, B, C, D, E, F, and G. Human perception of 220 Hz is usually correlated with the pitch A. The A an octave higher has twice the frequency, or 440 Hz; whereas, the A an octave below has one-half the frequency, or 110 Hz. Arabic numerals are used to designate the octave of a pitch. The convention used in this book is that the pitch A above middle C has a note name and octave designation of A4.

Duration is the length in time of a musical event and may be described in terms of relative or absolute time; for example, "one event is twice as long as another," or "an event is precisely 50 milliseconds in duration." An elaborate system of notation comprised of such objects as eighth notes, quarter notes, half notes, and whole notes delineates relative durations. These relative durations may be interpreted as absolute duration with the inclusion of a time signature and a tempo marking. For example, a time signature of 4/4 indicates four beats in a measure, with a quarter note receiving one count. If this time signature appeared with a metronome marking of a quarter equals sixty beats per minute, the absolute duration of a quarter note would be one second.

The intensity of a musical event correlates with the listener's perception of the loudness of a sound. Human perception of intensity is nearly logarithmic. The decibel (dB) is the logarithmic unit of measurement used to compare the intensities of two sounds. One sound played with twice the intensity of another is roughly equivalent to an increase of three decibels. Musicians have developed notational systems to represent intensity. Italian terms such as piano (soft) and forte (loud) describe the intensity or dynamics of a musical passage. Representations have been developed to vary dynamics over time using terms such as crescendi (to gradually get louder) and diminuendi (to gradually get softer). These terms are by no means absolute measurements of intensity and vary in performance according to any number of factors—the range of intensities that may be physically produced by an instrument in relation to other instruments in an ensemble, the character of the music, or the acoustics of the performance space, for example.

Timbre is defined as tone color: it is the element of music that differentiates two sound sources sounding the same pitch for the exact same duration at the same intensity. A timbre may be characterized by its spectrum—the frequencies present in a sound and their corresponding intensities over the duration of the sound. Partials are the building blocks of timbre. The lowest frequency is considered the first partial, or fundamental. Partial numbers increase for each frequency component sounding above the fundamental frequency. A spectrum may be categorized as harmonic or inharmonic. A harmonic spectrum contains partials that are integer multiples of the fundamental frequency. Conversely, an inharmonic spectrum contains partials that are not necessarily integer multiples of the fundamental. Being able to characterize a spectrum as harmonic or inharmonic is useful in categorizing timbre. Traditional acoustic instruments that produce a focused pitch, such as the violin or clarinet, produce predominantly harmonic spectra. Instruments, such as the snare drum or glockenspiel, that have a percussive, noisy attack produce inharmonic spectra.

Throughout music history, representations of musical abstractions have been a double-edged sword: a representation allows us to create, disseminate, and preserve a musical abstraction; yet, these representations may lead to interpretations that are inconsistent with the composer's intent or, worse yet, constrain human creativity to the paradigm imposed by the representation. Consider the interpretations of the score of the unaccompanied cello suites by J. S. Bach performed by Yo Yo Ma (1983) and Mstislav Rostropovich (1995). These performers introduce subtle nuances in tempo, phrasing, character, and dynamics that illuminate the listener's understanding of the composition several hundred years after the composer's death. Next, consider the work of Arnold Schoenberg. The technique of twelve-tone composition exalted the organization of pitch and, thus, extended music composition within the constrained paradigmatic representation of the musical staff (Brindle 1966).

Figure 1.1, an "Alleluia" from the *Liber Usualis*, demonstrates the musical notation of Gregorian chant—a Roman chant codified by Gregory I during his papacy from 590 to 604 AD. The neumes embed compact meaning for the interpretation and performance of pitch, duration, intensity, and timbre. The four-line staff begins with a clef sign denoting C5. As seen in the transcription from Gregorian chant to contemporary staff notation in Figure 1.2, the neumes depict the pitch sequence, the rhythmic grouping, and how the pitches should be articulated in relation to the accompanying text. Despite the potent economy of neumatic representation, the Benedictines of Solesmes (1961) are compelled to augment this musical representation with a textual description stating that the ictus, or strong beat of a rhythmic grouping, may be accompanied by an increase in intensity and further intimated by a change in the timbre of the voice. Although this textual description extends understanding of the performance of the neumes, a significant range of possible interpretations remains: Should each ictus have the same intensity? Should the change in timbre be bright or dark?

Figure 1.3, a spectrogram, is yet another representation of the same "Alleluia." To create the spectrogram, a recording of the sung "Alleluia " was analyzed using the Fourier Transform, a mathematical procedure used to analyze the frequency and amplitude of a signal over time (Moore 1978, 38–60, see chapter 2). The changes in pitch in Figure 1.2 correlate to the

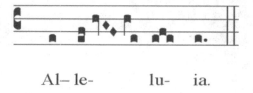

Fig. 1.1 "Alleluia" as notated in the *Liber Usualis* (Benedictines xxviij). (DVD reference 1)

Fig. 1.2 Transcription of "Alleluia" from the *Liber Usualis* using contemporary staff notation. (DVD reference 2)

changes in frequency on the vertical, or Y-axis in Figure 1.3. The relative durations of Figure 1.2 are denoted as a sequence of absolute durations on the horizontal, or X-axis in Figure 1.3. The relative darkness of frequency or frequency regions in the spectrogram indicates the intensity of a partial. The timbre of the sung "Alleluia" is quantified by its partials. An analysis tool such as the spectrogram provides an objective representation of the change in timbre over time for this particular performance of the "Alleluia." If the Benedictines of Solesmes had included a recording to accompany the spectrogram as a supplemental representation of the "Alleluia," the likelihood of misinterpretation in the performance of Gregorian chant would be greatly reduced.

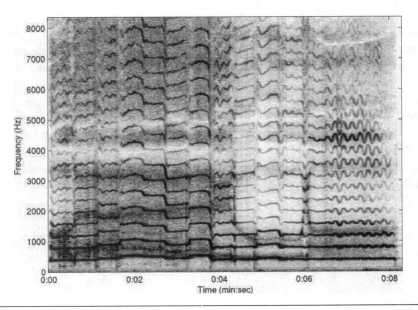

Fig. 1.3 Spectrogram of "Alleluia" from the *Liber Usualis* sung by a female cantor. (Kosmicki 2005; DVD references 3–6)

In Figure 1.3, the timbre of the sung voice on the initial syllable of alleluia, or "ah," is sung on the pitch G4. The pitch G4 has a fundamental frequency of 392 Hz. The next two frequencies sounding above the fundamental are located approximately at integer multiples of the fundamental frequency. These three partials are in an integer relationship with the fundamental, so they are said to be harmonic. Vowel sounds such as "ah," either sung or spoken, have increased intensity or resonances in certain frequency regions. These resonances are in predictable locations in vowel formation and are known as "formants." The location of the formants contributes to our perceptual recognition of vowel sounds (Sundberg 1989, 45–56).

Figure 1.4a is a Csound orchestra (.orc) file used to realize the timbre of a synthetic bell based on an algorithm derived from research by John Chowning (1973, 526–34). Csound is a sound synthesis language developed by Barry Vercoe and R. Karstens in 1986 (see Boulanger 2000), and is derived from the Music-N sound synthesis languages (Mathews 1969) that developed in the 1950s. Figure 1.4b is a score (.sco) file used to realize the note events of the "Alleluia" in Figure 1.2. During a Csound compilation, the score file is passed to the orchestra file so that the synthesis algorithm encoded in the orchestra may render the events in the score. The result of the compilation is a sound file. Each note event in the score file begins with the letter *i*. Assuming a tempo of a quarter note equals sixty beats per minute, the onset of each eighth note commences every one-half second and has an absolute duration of fifteen seconds. Due to the relationship between the start time and the absolute duration of each event, events will overlap in time, resulting in a dense and complex spectrum.

```
sr=44100
kr=441
ksmps=100
nchnls=1
instr 1
    i.dur = p3
    i.amp = p4
    i.car.freq = p5
    i.mod.freq = i.car.freq * (7/5)
    i.max = p6
    a.amp.env oscili i.amp, 1/i.dur, 1
    a.mod.env oscili i.mod.freq*i.max, 1/i.dur, 1
    a.mod oscili a.mod.env, i.mod.freq, 3
    a.car oscili a.amp.env, a.mod+i.car.freq, 3
    out a.car
endin
```

Fig. 1.4a Csound orchestra file used to realize the timbre of a synthetic bell.

```
f1 0 1024 5 1 680 .0001 344 .0001
f3 0 1024 10 1
```

; instr	start	dur	amp	freq	imax
; p1	p2	p3	p4	p5	p6
i1	0	.5	0	0	0
i1	.5	15	13000	980	10
i1	1	15	13000	980	10
i1	1.5	15	13000	1100	10
i1	2	15	13000	1308	10
i1	2.5	15	13000	1234.75	10
i1	3	15	13000	1100	10
i1	3.5	15	13000	1308	10
i1	4	15	13000	980	10
i1	4.5	15	13000	980	10
i1	5	15	13000	1100	10
i1	5.5	15	13000	980	10
i1	6	15	13000	980	10
e					

Fig. 1.4b Csound score file used to realize the note events of the *Alleluia*.

Figure 1.5 is a time-domain representation of the sound file resulting from the Csound compilation of Figures 1.4a and 1.4b. The time-domain representation depicts time as the horizontal, or X-axis, and amplitude as the vertical, or Y-axis. Intensity is proportional to the amplitude squared (Yamaha, Davis, and Jones 1989, 19–21). The onset of each event is clearly evident in this time-domain representation due to the temporal increase in amplitude.

Figure 1.6 is a spectrogram derived from the sound file from the Csound compilation of Figures 1.4a and 1.4b. The timbre of the synthetic bell has a noticeable blurring of frequency, indicating a complex inharmonic spectrum. The mathematics of frequency modulation synthesis implemented in the

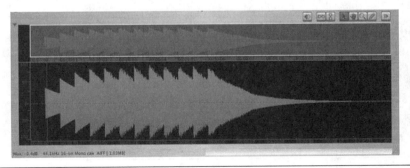

Fig. 1.5 Time-domain representation. (DVD reference 7)

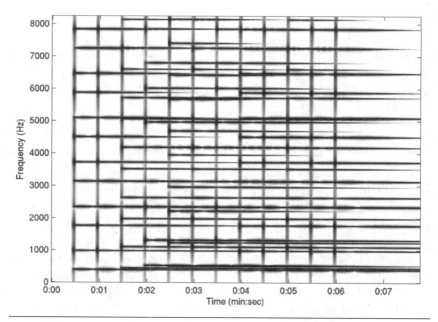

Fig. 1.6 Spectrogram of the "Alleluia" played by a synthetic bell. (DVD references 8–11)[end]

orchestra results in a spectrum with a fundamental frequency of 392 Hz. The next two frequencies sounding above the fundamental are located at 980 Hz and 1764 Hz—2.5 and 4.5 times greater than the fundamental frequency. Since these frequency components are in a noninteger relationship with the fundamental frequency, these partials contribute to an inharmonic spectrum.

As demonstrated by neumes, contemporary staff notation, Csound orchestra and score files, time-domain representations, and spectrograms, the four basic elements of music—pitch, duration, intensity, and timbre—may have any one of a multitude of representations. Learning to read, write, and interpret these representations in relation to our perception of music is a skill acquired through study and practice. Musical abstractions, once harnessed by some representation, are invariably cheated of some aspect of their meaning. The neumes on a staff indicate pitches and relative durations but are noticeably devoid of intensity and timbre. Parameter lists such as those in Figures 1.4a and 1.4b can describe an infinite number of values for an immeasurable number of parameters, but the overabundance of textual information renders interpretation exceedingly complex, sometimes to the point of being meaningless. Time-domain representations depict the amplitude for any moment in time but are devoid of pitch and timbral analysis. Spectrograms demonstrate remarkable detail about timbre by showing the frequency of partials and their intensity in time, but perception of the fundamental pitch is often impalpable. For these reasons, this book advocates the exploration of multiple representations to assist in the analysis, understanding, and appreciation of electroacoustic music. Just as a scientist knows what information is revealed using tools such as a calculator or a microscope, so too should musicians understand the merits and limitations of a wide variety of musical representations.

1.2. The Influence of Representation on Music

The initial motivation to develop representational schema for music were to assist with the preservation and dissemination of cultural and religious traditions. Notational representations such as those in the medieval era captured the essence of music making of the day: vocal monophony based on a sacred or secular text. During the rise of instrumental music in the Renaissance period, new representational schemes such as tablature, part books, and notational enhancements emerged to support and sustain the development of new instruments, consort playing, and improvisation. By the Baroque period, notes on a musical staff, referred to as "the score," created a paradigm that nurtured the development of melody, harmony, rhythm, and counterpoint. It is strident testimony to the wellspring of human creativity that the blossoming of our musical heritage is couched in such a terse representational scheme as notes on a staff.

The development of musical notation contributed to the specialization and delineation of the roles of composer, performer, and conductor. A score could adequately represent compositional intent, so it was no longer necessary to have the composer present to realize the music. The role of the performer or conductor became that of interpreter of the composer's intent as conveyed through the score. This division of labor in music making is manifest in the evolving organizational structures in our schools and conservatories: we have curricula devoted exclusively to performance on a particular instrument; specializations in vocal, symphonic band, and orchestral conducting; and separate compartments for composition and music theory.

Within and beyond the boundaries of schools and conservatories, a growing number of composers are experimenting with electronics and computer technology as a means of extending their creativity through the development of new instruments, timbral extensions of existing instruments through digital signal processing, or the creation of computer programs that foster new paradigms of representation. The information age in music making has flung these composers squarely back to a period in human creativity that rivals that of the medieval period; musical instruments are not standardized, representational systems for music are emerging, and the roles of composer and performer are once more blurred to the point of near unity.

Imagine that we could chart a multitude of trajectories from the medieval to the present that would span the development of the four elements of music. These trajectories might include the submission of monophony to homophony and polyphony, the manipulation of pitch organization from the church modes (Apel 1972, 165–68) to set theory mathematics (Forte 1977), the increasing complexity of rhythm from the rhythmic modes (Grout 1973, 82–83), to metrical modulation (Pressing 2002, 285–310), and the expansion of consorts to the Wagnerian orchestra. Is it possible that the elements of music can continue to increase in complexity? Is it possible that this complexity increases in scale beyond human perception?

As we sit suspended over the threshold of the twenty-first century, it is apparent that the singular element of music that beckons further exploration is timbre. No longer are composers bound to the physical manifestation of an instrument, with its inherent beauty yet idiosyncratic personality. Theoretically speaking, the computer may be programmed to represent any timbre imaginable, provided we master the parameters used to create that timbre. Early pioneers of electroacoustic music such as James A. Moorer and John Grey demonstrated through analysis that timbre is the ultimate nexus of the other three elements of music: timbre is essentially the amalgamation of frequency and intensity in time (Moorer and Grey 1977a, 1977b, 1978). The composition *Mutations* by Jean-Claude Risset (1987) brilliantly mingles pitch, intensity, and duration into the phenomenon of timbre by the graceful

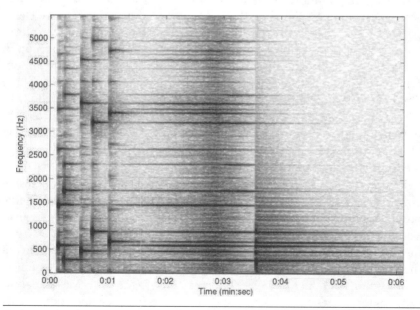

Fig. 1.7 Spectrogram of *Mutations* by Jean-Claude Risset. (DVD references 12 and 13)

evolution of a timbre that deviously emerges from a series of pitches (Dodge and Jerse 1997,108–9). Figure 1.7 is a spectrogram of the initial six seconds of *Mutations*. It reveals a sequence of discrete sonic events within the first second of the composition that fuse over time to create a singular timbre derived from its preceding events.

Analysis and synthesis, with the support of computer technology, advance our knowledge and understanding of timbre. Technology thrusts us into new modes of representation with increasingly sophisticated musical abstractions, which challenge not only human perception but also aesthetic sensibilities. Intellectual inquisitiveness coupled with the thrust to advance human creativity spur the motivation to understand these new modes of music making through analysis.

1.3. Overview of the Book

This book is but a window into the information age of music making through the careful analysis of eight representative compositions using various analytical methods. Chapter 2 by Norman Adams presents "Visualization of Musical Signals." Mr. Adams introduces the reader to the fundamental concepts of generating and interpreting images of sound such as time-domain and frequency domain representations, time-frequency analysis, and the spectrogram. Chapter 3 by Leigh Landy presents the "Intention/Reception Project." Readers are introduced to two electroacoustic compositions—*Prochaine Station* by Christian Calon and Claude Schryer and *Valley Flow* by Denis Smalley—that exist exclusively in a recorded medium. Mr. Landy explores the correlation between a composer's intent and the listener's perception using questionnaire and discussion methods. Chapter 4 by Mary Simoni presents a work for string trio and computer by Paul Lansky entitled *As If*. This composition in four movements combines violin, viola, and cello with a fixed tape part using both staff and graphic notation. Various representation methods are explored to derive meaning for the listener's perception of the work including spectrograms, time–domain representations, and set theory analysis. Chapter 5, an analysis of Alvin Lucier's *I am sitting in a room* written by Benjamin Broening, explores the relationship of signal processing techniques to the generation of musical form. Chapter 6 by Michael Clarke presents an interactive analysis of Jonathan Harvey's *Mortuos Plango, Vivos Voco*. Software developed by Mr. Clarke encourages a depth of understanding of the composition through guided interaction with sonic elements of the composition. Chapter 7 by Andrew May investigates Philippe Manoury's composition for flute and live electronics, titled *Jupiter*. Mr. May's analysis explores the orchestration of interactive behaviors in the composition by correlating aspects of its score, software, and sound. Chapter 8 by Mara Helmuth is an analysis of *Riverrun* by Barry Truax. The analysis of this composition for eight-channel sound system reveals carefully crafted synthesis techniques and the placement of sound objects in an octophonic sound stage. The final chapter, by Momilani Ramstrum is a cultural, theoretical, and musical analysis of Philippe Manoury's opera *K...* based on *The Trial* by Franz Kafka and staged at the Opéra Bastille in Paris. Ms. Ramstrum's analysis is a multipronged approach to the complex production of this formidable work.

Each of the works selected for inclusion in this book represents the breadth of creativity in the field of electroacoustic music—from music for stereophonic playback to multichannel, multimedia performance opera. The authors approach each work from a unique perspective, using a number of analytical methods designed to extend readers' appreciation of the work. Sound examples, images, documents, and movies that augment each analysis are included on the accompanying DVD. The breadth of electroacoustic genres and the multitude of perspectives supported by various analytical methods yield a depth of meaning to the understanding of electroacoustic music.

References

Apel, Willi. "Church Modes." In *The Harvard Dictionary of Music,*edited by 165–68. Cambridge, MA: Belknap Press/Harvard University Press, 1972,

Benedictines of Solesmes. *The Liber Usualis*. New York: Descless Company, 1961.

Boulanger, Richard, ed. *The Csound Book: Perspectives in Software Synthesis, Sound Design, Signal Processing, and Programming*. Cambridge, MA: MIT Press, 2000.

Brindle, Reginald Smith. *Serial Composition*. London: Oxford University Press, 1966.

Chowning, John. "The Synthesis of Complex Audio Spectra by Means of Frequency Modulation." *Journal of the Audio Engineering Society* 21 no. 7 (1973): 526–34.

Dodge, Charles, and Thomas A. Jerse. *Computer Music Synthesis, Composition and Performance*. New York: Schirmer Books, 1997, 108–9.

Forte, Allen. *The Structure of Atonal Music*. New Haven, CT: Yale University Press, 1977.

Grout, Donald J. *A History of Western Music*. New York: W.W. Norton, 1973, 82–83.

Kosmicki, Dorisanne. *Alleluia*. Rec. January 4, 2005.

Ma, Yo Yo. *Unaccompanied Cello Suites*. By J. S. Bach. CBS Records Masterworks.1983.

Mathews, Max V. *The Technology of Computer Music*. Cambridge, MA: MIT Press, 1969.

Moore, F. R. "An Introduction to the Mathematics of Digital Signal Processing." *Computer Music Journal* 2, no.2 (1978): 38–60.

Moorer, James A., and John Grey. "The Lexicon of Analyzed Tones: Part I, a Violin Tone." *Computer Music Journal* 1, no. 2 (1977a): 39–45.

———. "The Lexicon of Analyzed Tones: Part II, Clarinet and Oboe Tones." *Computer Music Journal* 1, no. 3 (1977b): 12–29.

———. "The Lexicon of Analyzed Tones: Part III, the Trumpet." *Computer Music Journal* 2, no. 2 (1978): 23–31.

Pressing, Jeff. "Black Atlantic Rhythm: Its Computational and Transcultural Foundations." *Music Perception* 19, no. 3 (2002): 285–310.

Risset, Jean-Claude. "Mutations." *Risset*. INA GRM INA C, 1003. 1987.

Rostropovich, Mstislav. CelloSuitenn by J. S. Bach. EMI Classics, 1995.

Sundberg, Johan. "Synthesis of Singing by Rule." In *Current Directions in Computer Music Research*, edited by Max V. Mathews and John R. Pierce, 45–56. Cambridge, MA: MIT Press, 1989.

Yamaha Corporation of America, Gary Davis, and Ralph Jones. *The Sound Reinforcement Handbook*. Milwaukee, WI: Hal Leonard Corporation, 1989, 19–21.

DVD References

Number	File Name	Description	Media Type
1	Alleluia.pdf	*Alleluia* from the *Liber Usualis*	600-dpi BW TIFF
2	Alleluia2.tif	Transcription of *Alleluia* from *Liber Usualis*	600-dpi BW TIFF
3	Alleluia.aif	*Alleluia* from *Liber Usualis* sung by a female cantor	Mono AIFF
4	Alleluia3.tif	Black and white spectrogram of sung *Alleluia*	600-dpi black and white TIFF
5	Alleluia4.tif	Color spectrogram of sung *Alleluia*	600-dpi color TIFF
6	Chowning.aif	*Alleluia* played by a synthetic bell	Mono AIFF
7	Chowning1.tif	Time-domain representation of "Alleluia" played by a synthetic bell	600-dpi color TIFF
8	Chowning2.tif	Black & white spectrogram of "Alleluia" played by a synthetic bell	600-dpi black and white TIFF
9	Chowning3.tif	Zoom of Black & white spectrogram of "Alleluia" played by a synthetic bell	600-dpi black and white TIFF
10	Chowning4.tif	Color spectrogram of "Alleluia" played by a synthetic bell	600-dpi color TIFF
11	Chowning5.tif	Zoom of Color spectrogram of "Alleluia" played by a synthetic bell	600-dpi color TIFF
12	Risset1.tif	Black and white spectrogram of beginning of "Mutations" by Jean-Claude Risset	600-dpi black and white TIFF
13	Risset2.tif	Color spectrogram of beginning of "Mutations" by Jean-Claude Risset	600-dpi color TIFF

Note

1. The author would like to thank James Borders for transcribing the neumes of the "Alleluia" found in the *Liber Usualis*. The author would also like to acknowledge the contribution of Dorisanne Kosmicki for her singing of the "Alleluia." Gratitude is owed to Norman Adams for developing the software that allows for the interactive modification of time-frequency images and creating the spectrograms in this chapter.

2

Visualization of Musical Signals[1]

NORMAN ADAMS

2.1. Introduction

This chapter provides a brief introduction to the field of time-frequency analysis and, in particular, the spectrogram, for the visualization of electro-acoustic music. The reader will be introduced to time-domain representations, frequency-domain representations, time-frequency analysis, and the spectrogram.

A visualization method that translates the aurally salient qualities of electroacoustic music into a static image is important to an understanding of electroacoustic music. Edward Tufte (1990) is one of a number of researchers who have addressed mapping dynamic events to a static two-dimensional visual representation. Visualizing sound (or music) is particularly difficult because the human auditory and visual systems are very different. For example, the human visual system has relatively fine spatial resolution but crude spectral resolution. Visually, humans can distinguish between two nearby points in space; however, the human visual system samples the optical spectrum in only three locations as represented by the three primary colors: red, blue, and green. Hence, different light spectra, so long as they have the same amount of red, blue, and green, appear the same to us. On the other hand, the human auditory system resolves the acoustic spectrum with fine precision but has crude spatial precision. Humans can often hear the difference between two sounds with similar spectra, but distinguishing between identical sounds from nearby points in space is difficult. There are, of course, many other factors that complicate the mapping from sound to image. The remainder of this section describes several approaches to visualizing sound and music.

The most common visualization of music is the score. A musical score is a symbolic, or discrete, representation—the score assumes that the music can be abstracted to a sequence of isolated events, or notes. The score is ill suited to visualizing electroacoustic music because it is often characterized by complex time-varying spectra that defy attempts to be abstracted to discrete events.

Numerous researchers have proposed alternative methods of visualizing music. Stephen Malinowski developed the "Music Animation Machine" (MAM) for real-time animation of simultaneous melodic lines. Sever Tipei has proposed a method for visualizing objects in virtual space that correspond to sound objects (see Kaper and Tipei 1998). Both of these visualization methods assume that the music is composed of discrete events. Jonathan Foote and Matthew Cooper (2001), Martin Wattenberg (2002), and others have explored a phenomenon known as "self-similarity" to reveal structural similarity within a sound (often a piece of music). Self-similarity is a measure of how similar two segments of a sound are. Self-similarity only reveals motivic or spectral similarity, rather than an objective representation of timbre.

The most common method of visualizing sound is based on spectral estimation, which models a signal as a collection of sinusoids. The simplest spectral estimator, the Fourier Transform, is described in section 2.3 below. There are numerous reasons to represent a signal as a collection of sinusoids; spectral estimation has found application in every branch of science and engineering from seismology to telecommunications to medicine. There is a rich literature devoted to the topic.[2] Furthermore, the human auditory system performs a type of spectral estimation (Moore 1997). The cochlea, the organ responsible for converting acoustic pressure waves into nerve impulses, is a frequency selective device. Spiral in shape and conical in bore, the outer end of the cochlea is sensitive to high frequencies, while the inner end is sensitive to low frequencies. Visualizing the frequency content of a sound is closely aligned with human auditory perception.

2.2. Time-Domain Representations

The two-dimensional time-domain representation of a sound portrays the fluctuation in acoustic pressure over time and is plotted with time as the horizontal axis and amplitude as the vertical axis. The left side of Figure 2.1 gives a time-domain representation of a square wave, and the right side of Figure 2.1 gives the time-domain representation of four sine waves. The signals in Figure 2.1 are periodic—they repeat exactly every t_0 seconds, where t_0 is the period of the signal. The frequency of the signal is given as the reciprocal

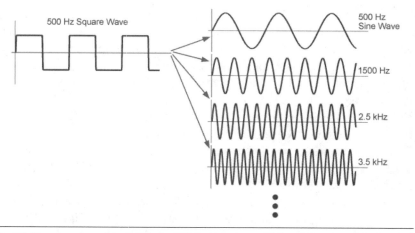

Fig. 2.1 Time-domain representation of a 500-Hz square wave (left) and its component sinusoids. (right)

of its period and is measured in Hertz (Hz). The 500 Hz square wave in Figure 2.1 has a period $t_0 = 1/500$ s. Using a time-domain representation for visualization is useful in revealing the fine detail of the waveform. However, the image does not correlate well to aural perceptions of the waveform. This discontinuity between visual perception of the image and aural perception of the sound is due to the time scale of acoustic fluctuations that humans are able to detect. Figure 2.1 shows approximately 2.7 periods of a 500 Hz square wave that corresponds to about 0.005 seconds—a very short time interval. To display a full second of the square wave, 500 periods of the waveform must be squeezed onto the page, yielding a solid image that loses the shape of the waveform. Hence, other representations must be considered.

2.3. Frequency-Domain Representations

Jean-Baptiste Fourier proved that any signal may be represented as a sum of sinusoids (Haykin and Van Veen 2002). For example, consider a square wave signal. The left side of Figure 2.1 displays a time-domain representation of a 500 Hz square wave (DVD reference 1). Since this signal is periodic, it is composed of uniformly spaced sine waves, or harmonics. The frequencies of the harmonics are given by integer multiples of the fundamental frequency, 500 Hz. The square wave is composed of only odd harmonics. The right side of Figure 2.1 displays the first four partials of the square wave: the first partial (fundamental) at 500 Hz, the second partial (third harmonic) at 1.5 kHz, the third partial (fifth harmonic) at 2.5 kHz, and the fourth partial at 3.5 kHz (seventh harmonic) (DVD reference 2).

A weight, or relative amplitude, is associated with each harmonic. The weights of the even harmonics (with frequencies of 1000 Hz, 2 kHz, 3 kHz, and so on) are equal to zero, since only the odd harmonics are present in a square wave. The weights of the odd harmonics are equal to the reciprocal of the harmonic number. The weight of the 500 Hz sine wave fundamental is 1, the weight of the 1.5 kHz sine wave is 1/3, and the weight of the 2.5 kHz sine wave is 1/5. An infinite number of sine waves are needed to perfectly represent the square wave. The human auditory system does not typically detect frequencies above 20 kHz; so, harmonics with frequencies greater than 20kHz are generally ignored. The series of weights (1, 0, 1/3, 0, 1/5, 0...) is referred to as the Fourier series expansion of a square wave.

One can verify that a square wave is constructed from a series of sinusoids by reconstructing the square wave one partial at a time. Figure 2.2 offers time-domain representations of six reconstructions. The left column shows reconstructions using one, two, and three partials, and the right column shows reconstructions using four, eight, and twelve partials. Notice that as more sine waves are added the waveform more closely resembles the square wave. These six reconstructions, followed by the original square wave, can be heard on the DVD (DVD reference 3). Notice that as more partials are added, rather than separate sine waves, a single tone with a timbre that is more closely related to the square wave is heard.

Fourier showed that any continuous signal may be represented as a sum of sinusoids, not only periodic signals. The continuous Fourier Transform (FT), or spectrum, of a signal $s(t)$ is defined as

$$S(\omega) = \tfrac{1}{\sqrt{2\pi}} \int e^{-j\omega\tau} s(\tau) d\tau$$

(see Haykin and Van Veen 2002) (1)

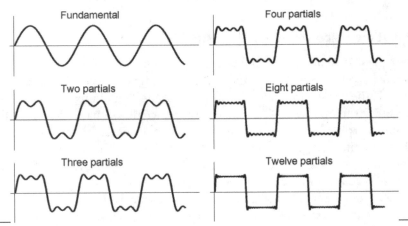

Fig. 2.2 Six square wave reconstructions.

The result of this equation, $S(\omega_0)$, gives both the amplitude and phase of the sinusoid with frequency ω_0, which is contained in $s(t)$. The amplitude indicates how much of the sinusoid is contained in $s(t)$, while the phase indicates the shift (from 0 to 2π, or equivalently from 0 to 1 period) of the sinusoid. $S(\omega_0)$ is computed by multiplying the signal $s(t)$ with a complex sinusoid, with frequency ω_0, and integrating (the $\int$ symbol) the result over all time. That is, $s(t)$ is correlated with $e^{-j\omega_0 t}$ to compute spectral component $S(\omega_0)$. The Fourier Transform maps the time-domain signal $s(t)$ to the frequency-domain signal $S(\omega)$.

Plotting the spectrum of an acoustic signal, such as a square wave, provides a powerful tool for visualizing music. Figure 2.3 shows amplitude (left) and phase, in radians (right), spectra for the square wave through the fifth harmonic computed using the Fast Fourier Transform (FFT). The amplitude spectrum verifies that the 500 Hz square wave is constructed of odd harmonics with frequencies of 500 Hz, 1.5 kHz, 2.5 kHz, and so on. The weights, or relative amplitudes, of the first three partials are 1, 1/3, and 1/5 respectively. Note that the amplitude spectrum outside of these frequencies is zero. This comblike spectrum is the result of the square wave being a periodic signal. The phase spectrum is more difficult to interpret. The phase of a zero-amplitude sinusoid is meaningless. However, at every odd harmonic, the phase is $\pi/2$, indicating that cosine waves are needed to construct this square wave. For most musical signals, the phase spectrum is not visually significant and, thus, is absent from most music visualizations.

The response of the human auditory system to amplitude is approximately proportional to the logarithm of amplitude (Moore 1997). The decibel (dB) is a logarithmic unit of measurement used to compare the amplitudes of two sounds. Amplitude is often plotted using a decibel scale, as shown in Figure 2.4. The left plot of Figure 2.4 displays the spectrum of the 500 Hz square wave on a decibel scale.

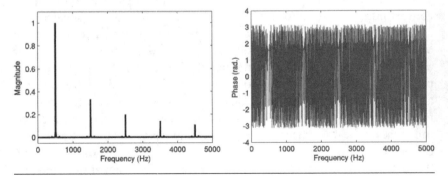

Fig. 2.3 Amplitude (left) and phase (right) spectra for 500 Hz square wave.

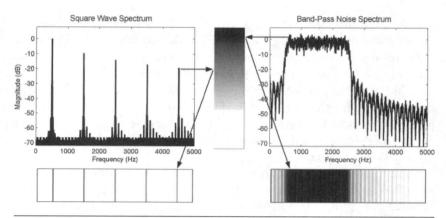

Fig.2.4 Decibel plots of the amplitude spectrum of a 500 Hz square wave (left) and bandpass noise, with cutoff thresholds 500 Hz and 2.5 kHz (right). Colormaps are shown under each plot.

Note that the reduction in amplitude or roll-off of the partials is much slower than the linear scale used in Figure 2.3. In addition to five harmonics, a collection of smaller peaks in the spectrum is now evident. These peaks are due to windowing, which is discussed in the next section.

Figure 2.4 also shows the dB spectrum of a bandpass noise signal (DVD reference 4). The bandpass noise was generated by filtering white noise. The noise is said to be bandpass if there is no acoustic energy outside of two cutoff frequencies (500 Hz and 2.5 kHz in Fig. 2.4). White noise is defined as a signal such that for all time t_A, the signal at time t_A is uncorrelated with the signal at any other time t_B. White noise produces a flat spectrum (Haykin and Van Veen 2002); so, bandpass filtering white noise yields a spectrum that is flat between the cutoff frequencies and close to zero elsewhere in the spectrum. Clearly, noise is not periodic; so, the spectrum does not demonstrate the comb structure of the square wave.

An alternative visualization of the spectrum employs a colormap to convert numeric values to colors. Rather than visualizing the spectrum as a contour by plotting numeric values on the vertical axis, a colormap can be used to "look down" on the contour from above as shown in the center and bottom of Figure 2.4. By contracting the conventional two-dimensional plot to one dimension, another dimension becomes available to represent a second independent variable. This dimension will be used to represent time in the next section. The precise choice of colormap has considerable influence on the final image; it is especially important that the bounds of the colormap control which numeric values are over- or underexposed. Note that this display visually emphasizes certain aspects of the signal that may not be acoustically or perceptually relevant. For example, in the bandpass noise example in Figure 2.4, the parallel lines in the bottom right panel represent the side-lobes of the noise. While these side-lobes are not obvious aurally, visually they draw the viewer's attention.

Compared to the time-domain representation, frequency-domain representations are better suited for visualizing acoustic signals. The spectrum of a sound is a fundamental component of the human perception of timbre. Direct use of the frequency-domain representations has a considerable drawback, however, it does not depict a time-varying timbre. The spectrum is defined over all time; the bounds of integration in (1) are ±∞. The human auditory system responds to changes in timbre over time; therefore, the frequency domain must be augmented to include time.

2.4. Time-Frequency Representations

To understand the need for time-frequency representations, we will consider an example (DVD reference 5). This example consists of three sounds played in a sequence: a 1 kHz sine wave, a burst of lowpass noise (with a sharp cutoff frequency at 1 kHz), and a burst of highpass noise (with a gradual cutoff frequency at 1 kHz). Listening to this example, it is aurally apparent which features of the sound are important. Figure 2.5 presents two possible visualizations of these three sounds played in sequence: a time-domain representation and a frequency-domain representation. It is visually evident in the time-domain representation that the example contains three bursts of acoustic energy, but the timbre of the bursts is not visible. From the frequency-domain plot, it is clear that the example contains a 1 kHz sine wave and some flat-spectrum noise, but the sequence of these sounds in time is not visible. The Short-Time Fourier Transform solves this problem by computing the spectrum from finite windows of the signal. By repeatedly estimating the spectrum for different windows of the signal, a visualization of the time-varying spectrum of a sound can be constructed.

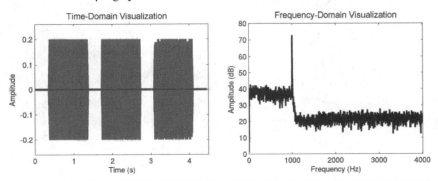

Fig. 2.5 Two visualizations of DVD reference 5.

The Short-Time Fourier Transform (STFT) of a signal $s(t)$ is defined as

$$S(\omega,t) = \frac{1}{\sqrt{2\pi}} \int e^{-j\omega\tau} s(\tau) w(\tau - t) d\tau \qquad (2)$$

where $w(\tau - t)$ is a window function (Cohen 1995). An example of several overlapping window functions is show in Figure 2.6. A window function, $w(t)$, is zero outside of some finite interval $[-A, A]$; peaks at the origin, $w(0) = 1$; and typically transitions smoothly from $t = 0$ to $t = \pm A$. Note that $S(\omega, t_0)$ is simply the Fourier Transform of $s(t)w(t-t_0)$. $S(\omega, t)$ is a complex quantity, but we often neglect the phase term and visualize only the logarithm of the amplitude spectrum. Such a display is known as a spectrogram. The computation of the spectrogram for the three sounds played in sequence is illustrated in Figure 2.6. The influence of the window function is obvious; the window steps along the time-domain signal at equal time intervals, estimating the amplitude spectrum at each step. In the resulting spectrogram, time indexes the horizontal axis (from 0 to 4.2 s) and frequency indexes the vertical axis (from 0 to 4 kHz). The colormap is shown to the right. The three sounds are clear in the time-frequency image in Figure 2. 6.

An important limitation of the spectrogram and STFT is the uncertainty principle (Cohen 1995). The uncertainty principle states that as the time resolution decreases, the frequency resolution increases and vice versa.

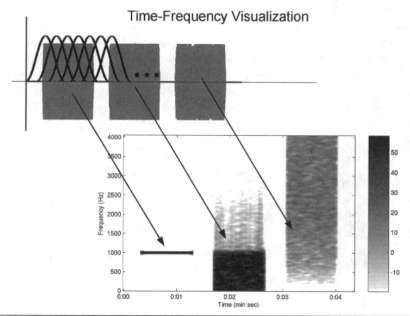

Fig. 2.6 Computation of spectrogram for DVD reference 5.

There is a tradeoff between time and frequency resolution. The time and frequency resolution are controlled by the window length $L = 2A + 1$; the time resolution is given by $L \cdot f_s$, and the frequency resolution is given by f_s/L, where f_s is the sampling frequency. Consider the following example (DVD reference 6). The first portion of the sound contains two sine waves, one with a frequency 471 Hz and the other at 529 Hz; then, there is a brief pause (about 0.05 seconds), followed by a single sine wave with a frequency 500 Hz. Three spectrograms of this sound are shown in Figure 2.7. For all three spectrograms, the frequency interval shown is from 300 Hz to 650 Hz. The three spectrograms were generated using three different window sizes: 1,536, 8,192, and 65,536 samples (with a sampling frequency of 44.1 kHz). All three use a step-size (the number of samples from the start of one window to the start of the next) of 1,024. For the shortest window length (1,536), the gap between the two events is clear, but the two sine waves in the first event are blurred. For the longest window length (65,536), the precise frequencies of all three sine waves are clear, but their start and end time are not. The correct choice of the window size (8,192) is able to resolve both the time and frequency information in this example. Unfortunately, determining the optimal window size for some signals is not always clear.

The STFT is only one of many possible time-frequency (TF) distributions. The Wigner distribution and modal distribution both mitigate the uncertainty principle, but at the expense of introducing cross-terms which don't exist for STFT distributions (Pielemeier and Wakefield 1996; also, Cohen 1995). The modal distribution in particular is useful for analyzing many musical signals, because it models the source as a collection of time-varying partials that are at least a chromatic half step apart. Other time-frequency distributions can be derived by applying additional parameters to the source, as is often done for speech analysis (Riley 1989). The choice of which distribution is best depends on the application. In general, the STFT and spectrogram are a reliable and easy-to-compute choice. It is important to remember that the forms seen in the final TF image do not necessarily correspond to psycho-acoustically important features (Scruggs and Wakefield 1992). Interpreting a spectrogram requires an understanding of signal processing and the psycho-acoustic concepts described above.

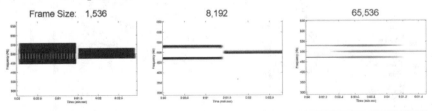

Fig. 2.7 Three spectrograms for DVD reference 6.

2.5. Spectrogram Examples

All of the spectrograms included in this section were generated using a MAT-LAB GUI developed by the author.[c] Consider the two spectrograms shown in Figure 2.7 (DVD reference 7). The first part of this audio example consists of a harmonic series that begins with a fundamental of 400 Hz and smoothly transitions up a perfect fifth to a fundamental of 600 Hz. The second part of the example consists of two claps—first a cupped-hand clap, followed by a flat-palm clap. Any sharp transient such as clicks, cracks, claps, and pops will appear as a thin vertical line in the spectrogram.

Note that low-frequency energy, around 600 Hz, of the cupped-hand clap is evident in the spectrogram. A color version of this spectrogram, and all other examples considered in this section, is available on the DVD (reference 8). For some spectrograms, the use of color is very helpful, but it also can be misleading, as the eye tends to aggregate similar colors into specific shapes. For example, a yellow ring could be visually more prominent than the red center it surrounds, even though the red portion is aurally more significant.

Typically the spectrogram is computed using the FFT, yielding uniformly spaced frequency bins. This spacing results in a TF image in which frequency increases linearly along the vertical axis, as shown in the left spectrogram of Figure 2.8. For musical signals, it is often useful to visualize the TF image such that frequency increases exponentially along the vertical axis (this is often referred to as log frequency; that is, frequency bins are spaced uniformly in log frequency). Hence, octave steps up are spaced uniformly along the vertical axis, rather than doubling in size with each step, as is the case with linear frequency. A log frequency spectrogram is shown in the right panel of Figure 2.8. Compare the harmonic series in the two spectrograms in Figure 2.8. In linear frequency, the harmonics are always uniformly spaced, but the spacing expands as the fundamental increases. In log frequency, the harmonics are not

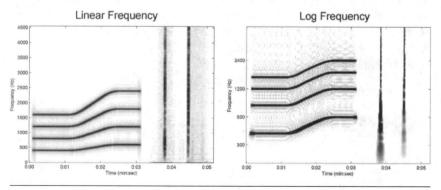

Fig. 2.8 Linear frequency (left) and log frequency (right) spectrograms for DVD reference 7.

uniformly spaced, but the spacing is constant as the fundamental increases. The log frequency spectrogram gives improved frequency resolution at low frequencies relative to high frequencies (hence, the time resolution gets worse at low frequencies; notice the horizontal smearing), which is often desirable for musical signals. Unfortunately, a log frequency spectrogram cannot be computed directly using the FFT. The Constant-Q transform, implemented with a variable-rate filter bank, is an efficient method for computing a log frequency spectrogram (Brown 1991).

The next example demonstrates how the auditory system clusters equally spaced sine waves into single pitches. Consider the spectrogram shown in Figure 2.9 (DVD references 9 and 10). At the beginning of the sound, there is a harmonic series with six partials and a fundamental of 400 Hz. After the series ascends a major third, the partials begin to diverge. The first individual sine wave that the listener hears is the second partial of the series; it ceases its downward descent before the others. When listening to the sound, the sine wave "appears" four seconds into the sound; yet, in fact, this is only when the listener's auditory system can no longer include it within the rest of the harmonic series. At 4.3 seconds, the fourth partial becomes distinct as it continues to descend in frequency after the other partials have stopped. The sound ends with six sine waves articulating two incomplete harmonic series with fundamentals of 200 Hz and 533 Hz.

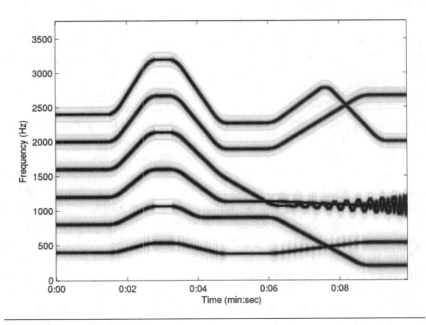

Fig. 2.9 Spectrogram for DVD reference 9.

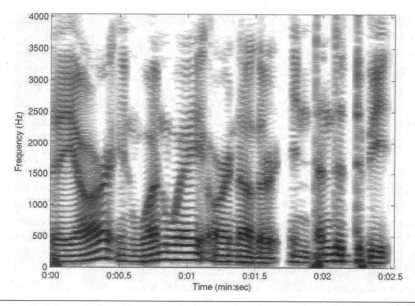

Fig. 2.10 Spectrogram for DVD reference 11.

Recorded acoustic signals rarely yield spectrograms as simple as those shown in Figures 2.8 and 2.9. Figure 2.10, with accompanying audio (DVD reference 11), provides a brief example of speech: the author saying, "They are in one or another intended to be…." Clearly, interpreting this spectrogram is more difficult than the previous examples. Changes in pitch due to inflection and intonation are visible in the spectrogram. Also evident are regions where the partials are much stronger. These regions are referred to as formants. Indeed, the formants are an important part of distinguishing between different vowels. Trained speech pathologists can often determine what was spoken simply by examining a spectrogram of the speech. The color version of this figure (DVD reference 12) uses a "VU" colormap, a useful analogy to the LED level meters on many audio devices.

Consider four harmonic series that have fundamental frequencies of 110 Hz, 220 Hz, 440 Hz, and 880 Hz. All four harmonic series correspond to the pitch class A. Indeed, human pitch perception is often modeled as circular using two numbers, one to indicate the octave and the other to indicate the pitch class within that octave (Shepard 1964). For harmonic analysis, we often wish to discard the octave distinction and only consider pitch class. This implies a wrapping of the frequency dimension such that octaves are mapped onto the same pitch class. The spectrogram can be wrapped in such a way, resulting in the chromagram (Wakefield 1999). Figure 2.11 gives a spectrogram and chromagram for a piano chord (DVD references 13 and 14) consisting of the pitches D#4, F4, G4, A#4, C5, F5, and G5. With seven

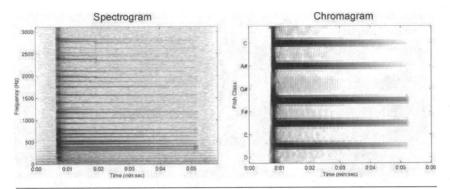

Fig. 2.11 Spectrogram and chromagram for DVD reference 13.

harmonic series, visually resolving which pitch classes are present is difficult. By wrapping all frequencies into one octave (and relabeling the vertical axis) the five pitch classes become apparent. Care must be taken in choosing the frequency range to wrap into one octave, because the upper harmonics do not all lie at octave frequencies. (For example, consider a fundamental of 110 Hz, which maps to pitch class A. 220 Hz also maps to A, but 330 Hz maps to E.) In this example, frequencies between 200 Hz and 1.2 kHz are wrapped to give the chromagram shown in Figure 2.11.

The last two examples are drawn from contemporary electroacoustic music. Figure 2.12 shows the spectrogram for a segment near the beginning

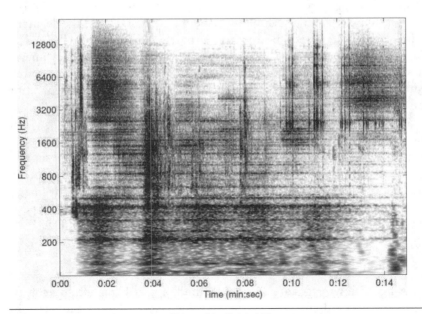

Fig. 2.12 Spectrogram for segment of "Arturo" by Elainie Lillios.

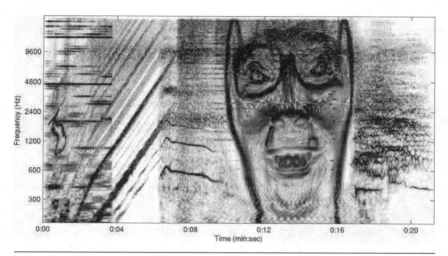

Fig. 2.13 Spectrogram for segment of "$\Delta M_i^{-1} = \ldots$" by Richard James.

of the piece "Arturo" by Elainie Lillios. A color version is included on the DVD (DVD reference 15). By listening to the segment while examining the TF image, the dominant elements of the sound are evident in the image. The segment begins with a brief portion of processed speech (around 400 Hz), followed by a swell of pitched, high frequency noise (around 5 kHz). The segment proceeds with a variety of pitched noises; the individual harmonics could be resolved by zooming in on the lower frequencies. A series of high frequency rattles can be seen about ten seconds into the segment. While Figure 2.12 reveals the dominant aspects of the sound, much detail of the sound is lost in the clutter of the image. Indeed, time-frequency images quickly become cluttered if more than one source is present. This clutter underscores how remarkable the human auditory system is at separating different sources into distinct auditory streams.

The final example is a segment from near the end of the piece "$\Delta M_i^{-1} = \ldots$" by the techno artist Richard James, who publishes under the pseudonym Aphex Twin (see DVD reference 16) for a color spectrogram. In this curious example, James's music results in the display of his own visage in the time-frequency image. While visually the face is the most recognizable feature in the image, it is also the least coherent sound; whereas, the less visually interesting parts of the spectrogram correspond to the coherent parts of the sound.

2.6. Conclusions and Summary

Time-frequency images are a useful method of visualizing electroacoustic music. The time-domain representation does not effectively portray timbre. The frequency-domain representation is an effective visualization of timbre but does note represent time-varying timbres. Spectrograms depict rich and evolving timbres that are characteristic of electroacoustic music. In generating time-frequency images, care must be taken in setting image parameters such as frame size and colormap to visually emphasize the important aspects of the sound. Time-frequency visualization is a useful tool that plays an important role in increasing understanding of electroacoustic music through analysis.

References

Adams, Norman. "Time-Frequency Music Visualizer." Available Online: <http://www-personal. umich.edu/~msimoni/analytical-methods/>

Brown, Judy. "Calculation of a Constant Q Spectral Transform." *Journal of the Acoustical Society of America* 89 (1991), 425–434. Available online: http://www.wellsley.edu/Physics/brown/jbrown. html.

Cohen, Leon. Time-Frequency Analysis. Upper Saddle River, NJ: Prentice-Hall, 1995.

Foote, Jonathan, and Matthew Cooper. "Visualizing Musical Structure and Rhythm via Self-Similarity." *Proceedings of the International Conference on Computer Music.* Havana, Cuba: September 2001.

Haykin, Simon, and Barry Van Veen. Signals & Systems. New York: John Wiley, 2002.

James, Richard (Aphex Twin), "$\Delta M_i^{-1} = \dots$" Windowlicker, Warp/Sire, 1999.

Kaper, Hans G., and Sever Tipei. "Manifold Compositions, Music Visualization, and Scientific Sonification in an Immersive Virtual-Reality Environment." Proceedings of 1998 International Computer Music Conference. Ann Arbor, Michigan: October 1998.

Lillios, Elainie. "Arturo." Rec. 1998. Music for SEAMUS v.10. EAM, 2001.

Malinowski, Stephen. The Music Animation Machine. Available online: <http://www.well.com/ user/smalin/mam.html>

Moore, Brian C. J. An Introduction to the Psychology of Hearing. Boston: Academic Press, 1997.

Pielemeier, William, and Gregory Wakefield. "A High-Resolution Time-Frequency Representation for Musical Instrument Signals." Journal of the Acoustical Society of America 99. no.4 (1996): 2382–2396.

Riley, Michael. Speech Time-Frequency Representations. Boston: Kluwer Academic, 1989.

Scruggs, Shelley, and Gregory Wakefield. "Time-Frequency Representations of Auditory Signatures." IEEE Digital Signal Processing Workshop. Sept. 1992.

Shepard, Roger. "Circularity in Judgments of Relative Pitch." Journal of the Acoustical Society of America 36 (1964): 2346–353.

Stoica, Petre, and Randolph Moses. Introduction to Spectral Estimation. Upper Saddle River, NJ: Prentice-Hall, 1997.

Tufte, Edward. Envisioning Information. Cheshire, CT: Graphics Press, 1990.

Wakefield, Gregory. "Mathematical Representation of Joint Time-Chroma Distributions." *Proceedings. SPIE, Advanced Signal Processing Algorithms, Architectures, and Implementations IX.* Nov. 1999.

Wattenberg, Martin. "Arc Diagrams: Visualizing Structure in Strings." Proceedings of the IEEE Symposium on Information Visualization (INFOVIS), Oct. 2002, 110–116. Available online: http://www.bewitched.com/research.html.

DVD References

Number	File Name	Description	Media Type
1	squareWave.wav	500 Hz square wave	mono WAV
2	squarePartials.wav	the 1st, 3rd, 5th, 7th, 15th, and 25th partials of the square wave, normalized	mono WAV
3	squareReconstruction.wav	square wave reconstruction using the partials listed above	mono WAV
4	bandpassNoise.wav	bandpass (0.5–2.5 kHz) noise	mono WAV
5	threeSounds.wav	three sounds played in sequence, a 1 kHz sine wave, LP noise, and HP noise	mono WAV
6	uncertainty.wav	two sine waves (471 Hz, 529 Hz), followed by one sine wave (500 Hz)	mono WAV
7	toneClap.wav	a harmonic sequence followed by two claps	mono WAV
8	toneClap.tif	color version of Figure 2.8	600-dpi color TIFF
9	sixPartials.wav	six diverging partials	mono WAV
10	sixPartials.tif	color version of Figure 2.9	600-dpi color TIFF
11	speech.wav	short segment of spoken word	mono WAV
12	speech.tif	color version of Figure 2.10	600-dpi color TIFF
13	pianoChord.wav	piano chord consisting of D#4, F4, G4, A#4, C5, F5, and G5	mono WAV
14	pianoChord.tif	color version of Figure 2.11	600-dpi color TIFF
15	Lillios.tif	color version of Figure 2.12	600-dpi color TIFF
16	James.tif	color version of Figure 2.13	600-dpi color TIFF

Notes

1. I would like to thank Mary Simoni for the invitation to author this chapter, as well as for her thoughtful comments on its scope and presentation. This work is part of a broader research project to explore time-frequency visualizations for the analysis of electroacoustic music. This research is funded by a CARAT/Rackham Interdisciplinary Fellowship at the University of Michigan. I would also like to thank Gregory Wakefield for his advice and research support.
2. This GUI is available from the URL: http://www.umich.edu/~msimoni/analytical-methods/

3

The Intention/Reception Project[1]

LEIGH LANDY

3.1. Introduction

The Intention/Reception Project involves introducing electroacoustic works to listening subjects and evaluating their listening experiences. Listening responses are monitored by means of repeated listening and the introduction of the composers' articulation of intent (by way of a composition's title, inspiration, elements that the composer intends to be communicated, and, eventually, elements of the compositional process). The intention/reception project not only opens up individual works to a number of listeners, it exposes entire repertoires of works to new audiences; the project is intended to help people find means to listen to, appreciate, and find meaning in electroacoustic works. In addition, the purpose of this research is to investigate the extent to which familiarity contributes to *access* and *appreciation* and the extent to which *intention and reception* meet in the very particular corpus of electroacoustic music (see Landy 2001; Landy and Weale 2003).

3.2. Project Background and Context

The project is rooted in the author's prior research concerning access and appreciation issues in contemporary art music and, in particular, electroacoustic music in the widest sense of the term. This investigation is based on the premise that certain forms of music deserve a larger audience than they currently have. In the case of much electroacoustic art music, that audience consists largely of electroacoustic music composers.

The author's research has given rise to a number of relevant observations, including the following (see Landy 1991, 1994):

1. There is a lack of support for new music in education particularly at elementary and secondary levels—as well as by the communications media. Without this support, finding a means of increasing access is challenging to say the least. Consequently, the music is relatively unavailable to the general public.

2. A significant number of composers have composed works of great complexity, particularly during the latter half of the twentieth century. The process by which a larger audience might acquire a taste for such works is normally a slow one. Because there are so few opportunities to learn to appreciate such works, the gap is perhaps a logical one.

3. The vast majority of published studies in contemporary music, especially electroacoustic music, involve high-level discussion. Furthermore, there appear to be very few basic publications of potential interest to or involving nonspecialists.

4. In electroacoustic music, as in vocal/instrumental music, inexperienced listeners enjoy being offered "something to hold onto" to help them cross the threshold of access and appreciation. Items such as homogeneity of sounds or textures, layering of sounds, or spatialization parameters have been found to make works accessible. In fact, it is fair to say that many types of music become more accessible after repeated listening, especially when listeners are offered something(s) to hold onto. Thus, there is no reason why the methodology of the intention/reception project shouldn't extend to other genres so long as intention data can be gained and play a central role in aiding appreciation.

The intention/reception project represents a step beyond the author's reception analysis based project, which led to the coining of the term *something to hold onto factor*. This assumes that both composers and listeners are interested in discovering meaning in electroacoustic compositions, at least those that include real-world sound references. Jean-Jacques Nattiez defines meaning: "An object of any kind takes on meaning for an individual apprehending that object, as soon as the individual places the object in relation to areas of his [or her] lived experience—that is, in relation to a collection of other objects that belong to his or her experience of the world" (Nattiez 1990, 9). Meaning need not be related to narrative but may include images or emotions that arise from moments in an electroacoustic work. The limitation of choosing works involving real-world sound references implies that shared experience may be linked to meaning, something that cannot be assumed of works that limit themselves to abstract sound references. Source recognition forms only part of the understanding of a work, and, in fact, may impede understanding. Nevertheless, real-world sound references also form part of the communality of experience, a necessity when looking for some things to hold onto. This notion is in distinct opposition to the Schaefferian concept of reduced listening (écoute réduite), which asks the listener or analyst to listen to sounds without regard to source or cause. Although reduced listening might seem to be emancipatory in nature, it is hardly useful in terms of supporting either access to or the communication of meaning.

Although a listener's acquired meaning from a work need not be static nor the same as any other listener's, including the composer's, the intention/reception project investigates whether elements of meaning are communicated from composer to listener and whether the composer's intention offers the listener another means of accessing a given composition.

The project is based on an ideal articulated by Lelio Camilleri and Denis Smalley: "We need to achieve an awareness of the strategies which listeners adopt and how they construct their meaning" (Camilleri and Smalley 1998, 5). They continue: "An important goal of analytical exploration is...to attempt to reconcile and relate the internal world of the work with the outside world of sonic and non-sonic experience" (Camilleri and Smalley 1998, 7). Clearly it is useful to identify the extent to which intention information from the composer can aid the listeners' experience.

3.3. The Analysis

This experiment is the second phase of a long-term multiphase dynamic project. The project is "dynamic," in that changes have occurred; for example, in permissible compositions and refinement of methodology.

3.3. 1. The Chosen Works

Two contrasting compositions were selected for this test. Each of the three composers—one work involved two composers—was offered a "composer intention questionnaire" (DVD reference 1) to complete. This questionnaire,[2] containing nineteen questions, was designed to solicit pertinent information concerning the compositional procedure, to trace the development of the work in terms of intention from the moment of inspiration through to its completion. The information acquired on these composer intention questionnaires was used during listening tests.

The chosen works are extremely dissimilar. *Prochaine Station* is a very short work that was realized quickly using material in its found state, so far as one can tell. It is a soundscape composition with very brief interlocking scenes. *Valley Flow*, a much longer, highly refined work is on the margin of compositions that the project has investigated thus far, as its source material is rarely overtly exposed. The composer, Denis Smalley, is very well known for the creation of morphologies of sounds and the development of these sound morphologies into structures, as well as for the design of analytical tools complementary to his work.

One hears immediately that the first piece involves underground train (metro/subway) travel. The research will determine whether the listener is able to identify the "subject area" of the Smalley piece without help. Still, both deal with the real world: Calon and Schryer offer their "narrative" quite directly, Smalley much more evocatively. This vast difference in approach serves as the criterion of choice.

Only "tape pieces" have been chosen here. Thus far the project has restricted itself to works on fixed media due to the manner in which tests have been administered. However, there is nothing standing in the way of, for example, interactive works being investigated, but this would best take place where live performance is possible. The choice was made due to circumstance, not limitation of method.

3.3.2. Listener Testing

The listener test volunteers were divided into two "user groups." (a) Inexperienced listeners: listeners who declared beforehand that they had no knowledge of electroacoustic music—in other words, the general public; and (b) experienced listeners who had a basic knowledge of electroacoustic music and who had heard and composed some electroacoustic music—in this case, undergraduate contemporary music students. Participants' lack of experience was assessed in the following manner: (a) they were asked if they had heard of or had ever knowingly listened to any electroacoustic music; (b) they were asked what types of music they listened to; (c) during the first listening session, they were asked whether they had previously listened to anything like what they had just heard; and (d) their questionnaire responses offered further pertinent information; for example, whether they used any relevant terminology that had not been introduced during testing. Ideally each level's user group consisted of approximately fifteen listening subjects. All volunteers signed a participants' ethics form stating that their information will remain anonymous. The ethics committees at De Montfort University, Leicester monitor all ethical procedures in the intention/reception project.

In addition, highly experienced listeners with a developed, in-depth knowledge of electroacoustic music, for example, postgraduate students and beyond, provided control data. This smaller group of highly experienced listeners demonstrated the degree to which "specialist" knowledge of electroacoustic music affects access and listening strategies.

Two types of questionnaires were created to record responses during the listening process. They offer a series of questions designed to solicit freely expressed thoughts, by not leading the listener in any interpretative direction. The "directed questionnaire" (DVD reference 2) was completed after the first listening. The "real-time questionnaire" (DVD reference 3) was completed during the three separate tests that occurred in a single listening session, involving playing a single composition three times in total.

Listening 1. The composition was played without providing the listeners with its title or program notes.

Listening 2. The same composition was played again, this time providing the listeners with its title or, if this was not helpful, one pertinent aspect of the composer's intention.

Listening 3. The composition was played again, this time providing the listeners with the composer's program notes and questionnaire responses.

These three rounds of listening are useful because they provide qualitative data concerning: (a) the extent to which the listener's access to the composition was possible without receiving any contextual data prior to listening to the piece; (b) what listening strategies were employed to make sense of the composition's content alone; (c) the extent to which the title and information concerning the composition's dramaturgy assisted the listener, and how these contextual elements informed the listening experience. *Dramaturgy*, a theatrical term, is the contextualization of a work or the interpretation of a performance. One important question here is: to what extent do the title and each composition's dramaturgy give listeners "something to hold on to" when engaging with a new electroacoustic work?

The real-time questionnaire allowed listeners to make notes as they experienced a composition, in order to capture their immediate responses without forcing them to dwell on a particular question; this would interrupt concentration and prevent continuous listening. The directed questionnaire (DVD reference 3) asked more focused questions and allowed the listeners to expand on their initial notes. These questions were intentionally left as open as possible. The listeners completed the questionnaire after the first listening—providing only important information about the initial experience—before any sort of context for the composition was offered. Both questionnaires are included on the accompanying DVD.

At the conclusion of all sessions, the group informally exchanged views. Notes were taken after every session and these informal discussions have proven invaluable. Particularly in inexperienced groups, new experiences were shared during such discussions and some views were altered, this, in turn, added to the intention/reception data acquired.

3.3.3. The Data Collected

Tests were carried out on two types of groups with no experience (N-E) in electroacoustic music: those of nonmusicians (N-E/N-M) and those involving music and music technology students in further education.[3] The music technology students were learning a more nuts and bolts approach to music technology tools than one focused on repertoire development. None of the students had ever heard a work like the two included in the tests. All were involved in popular music and ideally hoping to find careers in the music industry.

Twelve nonmusicians ranging in age from twenty to fifty-nine, the only group in which female members were in the majority (eight),[4] filled out forms for both compositions. Ten male students at Leicester College (N-E/1), mostly aged sixteen to twenty-two, although one student was fifty-eight years old, also participated in tests covering both compositions. In this category, five additional male students from the same institution of higher education, aged nineteen to twenty-three, sat in on the test for the Calon/Schreyer composition and three other male students, all aged sixteen, listened to the Smalley work (N-E/2). This is an exceptional case, so their results are listed separately in the tables below.

A group of nine students were also tested at another college in Hinckley. After a successful *Valley Flow* test, the group chatted together informally before the test was over, doing away with the atmosphere that had been sustained during the Smalley test. The access sections of the Calon/Schreyer questionnaires were filled in similarly, using the same expressions. Unfortunately, the return was not comparable with any other data and had to be disregarded.

The experienced group (Exp) consisted of thirteen final-year undergraduates at De Montfort University, Leicester. Twelve of these students were male; they were aged twenty-one to twenty-three, with one student twenty-seven, and one thirty-one-years-old. These students were studying music technology and most came from a background in popular music, although, by the final year many students' tastes have become more eclectic. The difference between the N-E and Exp students lies in the fact that electroacoustic music, both within art and popular music categories, forms an integral part of the Exp's course of study.

Finally, a control group of highly experienced (HExp) participants consisted of four postgraduate composers of electroacoustic music at Birmingham University. One student was twenty-nine and the others did not provide their ages. Only one member of this group was female; she was able to identify the composer while listening to *Valley Flow* for the first time, so her results form a small exception to the data acquired. No patterns were observed between the genders or based on age, except in the group of nonmusicians where older participants demonstrated less open-mindedness to adventure than younger ones. That said, no large-scale conclusions should be drawn here due to the modest sample sizes.

3.3.4. Prochaine Station—Christian Calon, Claude Schryer

Prochaine Station (Next Station) was commissioned to last about three minutes; it forms one of twenty-five, three-minute electroclips on the CD for which it was made. It is clearly a work made in the land where the word "soundscape" is best known, Canada.

3.3.4.1. The Work   One normally associates long time spans with soundscape composition, but this is an urban piece and logically reflects its city atmosphere through the high density of events, all clearly identifiable. As can be noted by the composers' remarks below, that next station is always the same one in the piece. As Christian Calon also describes below, the scenes are woven together, turning soundscape recordings into a soundscape composition. Claude Schryer makes it perfectly clear in his questionnaire that the work is intended to be accessible to the widest potential audience.

3.3.4.2. The Composers' Intentions   The easiest way to present the composers' intentions is to let them speak for themselves. The CD liner notes describe the composition in just three lines, simply mentioning that it is a Montreal piece and that it was realized in Schryer's home studio. The two composers answered their questionnaires independently. As some of the nineteen questions included in the questionnaire are not relevant to this piece, the following summary is restricted to the most relevant responses.

Sound Source(s)/Source Material
    Calon: Montreal subway, subway doors, voices, old Montreal horse carriage, steps, construction site, traffic, Chinatown voices and street music, radio, music, humor, hotdog stand with Claude Schryer's voice.
    Schryer: Soundscapes of Montreal over a three-day period.

What were your intentions concerning this particular composition?
    Calon: They consist mostly of impressions of the city, above and underground and glimpses of human experience on a normal day punctuated by unremarkable events. There is a sense of movement but always without movement. (The same station is always called.)

What methods are you using to communicate these intentions to the listener?
    Calon: Repetition and the use of short sequences (evocations) that open windows on the various "visions" weaving.
    Schryer: There are no [sound] manipulations, just field recording and editing. The soundscapes are musically rich and evocative on their own.

Is there a narrative discourse involved?

Calon: The piece is narrative in a nonlinear way.

Schryer:... in the sense of a story of Montreal being told by sound-scapes.

Where did the inspiration to create this particular composition come from?

Calon: It came from a walk through Montreal with friend and cocomposer Claude Schryer. It concerns a look at the sounds and spirit of the place we live in. It was not to become an acoustical document, but instead a poetic "ride" through the city. Another factor was the commission (electroclip) itself.

Is/are there something(s) in the composition that you want the listener to hold onto and why?

Calon: Yes, the alternation between subway doors/voices and the outside.

Schryer: [We would like listeners] to get a sense of what Montreal is like and our passion for the city.

At what point in the compositional process did you decide on a title for the piece?

Schryer: We decided near the end when we heard "prochaine station" being repeated in the piece.

How much do you rely on the title as a tool with which to express your compositional intentions and why?

Schryer: Not much in this piece—the title evokes the idea of traveling and of a multiple stop journey.

Do you rely on any other accompanying text in the form of program notes to outline your intentions prior to the listener's engagement with the composition and why?

Calon: No, but it is always a pleasure (as a listener) for an aftertaste to enrich and evaluate one's pleasure in the composer's textual propositions. They may bring in various unnoticed aspects of a work and unveil some of its hidden mysteries, unlock some chambers.

How important is it that the technical processes involved in the composition are recognized by the listener and why?

Calon: It is of no importance.

Under what listening conditions is your composition intended to be heard and why?

Calon: It probably works in most situations or places except the concert hall (or concert situation).

Schryer: Any, although the radio works well.

3.3.4.3. The Listeners' Experience   *Prochaine Station* was accessible to most listeners because all sounds in the work are recorded, untreated sounds. The use of recorded sounds, however, does not necessarily lead to greater appreciation of a composition; the risk of listeners rejecting a soundscape approach to composition as not being "music" must be taken into account. These assumptions were borne out by the acquired data. Most listeners quickly determined what the piece was about to a greater or lesser extent. One N-E/N-M listener, who clearly had not often been on an underground train, experienced a moon landing during the first listening; whereas, others experienced a cruise ship and a carnival setting. However, the same listener who perceived the moon landing also concluded that "a person can relate to everyday sounds." Another N-E/N-M listener felt that the piece was "not musical at all." In this case, access to sound organization did not translate easily into musical access. Nevertheless, in this group, the general view was of a piece that took the listener on a journey from point A to point B by way of a narrative discourse. Its short duration was also appreciated. With one exception, all of these listeners found the source material to be engaging. One listener stated that she enjoyed "hearing life from someone else's perspective." A predictable error concerning location was made (this happened at all levels), when a listener assumed the recordings took place in Paris, a city where many had traveled on the metro. In addition, one listener misunderstood "prochaine station" and thought "Panama City" was being called; this led him to think that the piece took place in Central America. Being provided with a title only confirmed first opinions in most cases; being provided with the composers' information aided in locating the piece, but not much more. Listeners found that repeated listening helped them to focus, to become more acquainted with sounds and how they were organized, and so to understand the work better. Unfortunately, many of the N-E/N-M tests took place either individually or in small groups. Therefore, no group discussion data were generated. As can be seen in Table 3.1, a sizeable majority found the work accessible.

The N-E groups demonstrated a fairly similar pattern. Perhaps because this group was generally younger, there was slightly less accuracy concerning what the piece might be about after the first listening. This might have been due to less travel experience. Still, the vast majority agreed with the journey notion, the sense of a narrative discourse, and the emotional content of the piece; although, those who "personalized" the experience sometimes added imaginative aspects to their scenarios. Perhaps because this group was overtly committed to popular music, much criticism of the composition came from its content and structure being different from familiar compositions. For example, complaints were made concerning the composition's lack of climax, melody, and rhythm. That said, a few listeners also complained about the presence of an accordion, something that they possibly associated with older people. One overtly confessed his distaste for music that the listener has to concentrate on. Yet, for every such remark several listeners stated that they were open to new listening experiences.

The French language played a role for both this group and the Exp group; some listeners were alienated by a language they could not understand; others were enticed by it. Oddly, one listener of African origin perceived an African language in the piece and another listener of South Asian origin perceived an Asian language. Most text material is in French, although some English from a radio can be heard from time to time, and is a clue to the work's location. During the first two listening rounds, few listeners noticed that the word *Montreal* is included within an English-language radio fragment. Most listeners attempted to imagine an audiovisual version of the piece, though few suggested that they would have preferred the work in audiovisual form.

Accuracy and sophistication of response were generally a bit higher within the group. One listener wrote that he kept arriving at the same train station. Another spoke of a work of "organized sound." Errors were also made. For example, one student discussed the prominence of synthesizer special effects. The following individuals' remarks represent a common ground among several listeners at this level: the piece was "quite gripping through individual association," it allowed one to focus on "emotions based on memories," and one was provided a "chance to pay attention to daily life [via] sounds which are beautiful."

During the postlistening session conversations, the participants seemed to like the idea of a movement without movement, in other words, the idea of the piece remaining in or near a single station. Many had a sense of the train's only arriving at a single point but did not trust their judgment. A few were interested in the gender of the person walking, assumed to be female, which led to discussions of a scenario similar to those they were acquainted with from film. During the discussion, a majority found that the composition became more engaging than they had originally thought. This engagement was partially due to the diverse experiences of their peers. Yet, they felt that the work did not involve much compositional virtuosity, that is, that it could have been made by anyone.

The Exp group reflected their greater knowledge of electroacoustic music by using significantly more appropriate terminology. For example, many identified the composition as a soundscape[5] composition, a cityscape, a soundwalk, or even ambient.[6] One listener associated the work with the soundscape movement in Canada. Moreover, these students also identified more technical aspects of the piece that interested them, such as engaging use of the stereo field. A few even echoed the composers' view that this work was not ideal for a concert situation; one listener called it a "hi-fi piece"—a piece meant to be heard on a CD player at home or during one's daily routine rather than in a concert performance.

Listening to soundscape recordings in no way stopped the Exp group from using their imaginations. Individuals claimed that this "immersive" work was based on the theme of "a day in the life." One found that the movement of the underground trains' doors led "to closed in and open sounds." Their complaints included the often present background noise. These remarks were an interesting commentary about real-world noise not being perceived as musical. The title was, again, of little help, and was more a tool in terms of confirming original impressions. However, the sharing of more information about the composers' intentions led one listener to state that the "radio [segments] made more sense" and another to confess his desire to know more about the city.

The Exp group conversation suggested that the simplicity of the work was effective; it provided for clear images; the lack of processing meant that "clutter" was avoided. Many had been more comfortable with the known, Paris, than they were with the unknown, Montreal. The group was quite split as to whether knowledge of French enhanced their appreciation, although the general consensus was that comprehension of the texts helped listeners to grasp the work's meaning. This view is rather salient given most students' general lack of desire to deal with meaning as fundamental to the music they are making themselves.

The resulting appreciation statistics from the Exp group were quite positive, although one provided contradictory answers to the access questions and another said he did not want to have any more to do with the work unless it was visualized.

The HExp small group played the role of determining how much a listener can perceive during these listening tests. One listener did take the trouble to create a scenario for the piece beyond the obvious one of moving about a city. Other listeners' responses were very technical and very accurate. They were not aided by the title because they had already determined what the piece was about. Surprisingly, there were no complaints about being provided with information about the composers' intentions, as was the case with a few *Valley Flow* listeners, for at this level many simply wanted to decipher a work on their own.

Their data included one graphic diffusion score of part of the work in response to the real-time questionnaire form; one listener queried whether a comb filter had been employed to separate a particular conversation. This group found repeated listening helped them to unpick the work's structure and to deal with formalization issues, aiding a more accurate interpretation. One listener knew the work of Yves Daoust, another Montreal-based composer of electroacoustic music, and so, was able to contextualize the piece. Another listener suggested that John Cage had inspired the composition, since it clearly avoided both a climax and a conclusion. Yet another complained that in a composition "collage isn't enough," stating that he would have preferred more acousmatic,[7] or less-identifiable, sounds. Expected remarks about the high quality of the recordings and studio-based mix were also included, one supporting the composers' subtlety—a nice compliment given how quickly this work was realized. The group's appreciation statistics are predictably positive.

3.3.4.4. Interpretation of Statistics and Closing Words   Directed questionnaires were completed after the first listening. Therefore, the statistics reflect participants' views without repeated listening. In all cases, discussions that took place after the three rounds of listening indicated that appreciation increased. The following are the four questions posed at the end of the listeners' directed questionnaire:

9. Did the composition make you want to keep listening or was it uninteresting? Why?
10. Now that you have heard the composition, would you choose to listen to a similar type of composition again in the future? (If yes, why? If no, why not?)
11. Now that you have heard the composition, would you choose to purchase a CD containing this type of composition? (If yes, why? If no, why not?)
12. Now that you have heard the composition, would you choose to attend a concert featuring these types of composition? (If yes, why? If no, why not?)

Some questions have turned out to be less useful than others. In particular, CD purchasing behavior varied from individual to individual. Some did not buy many CDs at all. Many only bought music they wanted to play in the background. Therefore, responses to question 11 had less to do with the compositions than with the individual's purchasing behavior. Therefore, this question was not considered in determining access. Similarly, concert attendance (question 12) varied by individual preference. Many young people go to clubs with live disk jockeys and video jockeys. Therefore, these responses provided a pattern that was not consistently useful to the goals of the project. Even so, a positive answer to this question was a clear indication of appreciation. In future trials these two questions will be revisited.

It was decided to set up a scheme as follows: A "no" answer to questions 9, 10, and 12 appears as a "no" in the statistics. One "yes" answer or any

Table 3.1 Access Statistics: *Prochaine Station*

	Yes	±	No	Yes%	± %	No%
N-E/N-M	9	1	2	75	8	17
N-E/1	5	1	4	50	10	40
N-E/2	4	0	1	80	0	20
N-E (1 + 2)	9	1	5	60	7	33
N-E (all)	18	2	7	67	7	26
Exp	11	1	1	84	8	8
Exp + N-E	29	3	8	73	7	20
HExp	4	0	0	100	0	0
HExp + Exp	15	1	1	88	6	6
HExp + Exp + N-E	33	3	8	75	7	18

Key: A "yes" answer signifies that the listener answered "yes" to two or three of the access questions (9, 10, and 12) listed above; a "±" answer signifies that the listener answered "yes" to only one of these questions or "possibly" to a combination of them; a "no" answer means that no question was answered in the affirmative.

combination of "possibly" answers—as this was an option—ended up in the "±" category. Finally, participants answering "yes" to at least two questions appear as a "yes."

The data demonstrate that two-thirds of all N-E participants replied "yes" in terms of access and just over a quarter replied "no." This contrasts with cultural attitudes toward electroacoustic music in general and soundscape composition specifically. Taking the experienced group into account, that "yes" total rises to over 70 percent and all groups to 75 percent. These might appear to be surprisingly high statistics when one considers that far less than 1 percent of CD sales and airtime are spent on this type of music. Before arriving at any conclusions, the investigation turns to a more sophisticated composition, *Valley Flow,* which will aid in determining whether these statistics are only relevant to this compositional approach to real-world sound organization.

3.3.5. *Valley Flow—Denis Smalley*

Where the Schryer/Calon work, *Prochaine Station,* is suggestive of sound-scape recordings through its woven structure, Denis Smalley's seventeen-minute work is more evocative in virtually all of its aspects.

3.3.5.1. The Work   As stated above, it is an unusual choice within the intention/reception project because Smalley's sound sources often remain unidentifiable, although, during an interview he let a few slip here and there, and a number of sources were, indeed, identified by listeners. *Valley Flow* consists of materials recorded and further manipulated at IRCAM in Paris; at Simon Fraser University in Burnaby, British Columbia; and at the Banff Centre for the Arts, Alberta. It was completed at Smalley's own studio in Norwich, UK. The notion of a narrative discourse is by no means foreign to this composer. His program note to the CD recording of this work states:

> The formal shaping and sounding content of *Valley Flow* were influenced by the dramatic vistas of the Bow Valley in the Canadian Rockies. The motion is stretched to create airy, floating and flying contours or broad panoramic sweeps, and contracted to create stronger physical motions, for example the flinging out of textural materials.
>
> Spatial perspectives are important in an environmentally inspired work. The listener, gazing through the stereo window, can adopt changing vantage points: at one moment looking out to the distant horizon, at another looking down from a height, at another dwarfed by the bulk of land masses, and at yet another swamped by the magnified details of organic activity. Landscape qualities are pervasive: water, fire and wood; the gritty, granular fracturing of stony noise-textures; and the wintry, glacial thinness of sustained lines. The force and volatility of nature are reflected in abrupt changes and turbulent textures.

On the basis of these program notes, one could conclude that this work is intended to be open to interpretation. Smalley is forthcoming concerning what he would like to evoke and how, stressing the salient characteristics of the piece as opposed to the specific sounds and their sources.

Due to the length of *Valley Flow* it was necessary to restrict the first two tests to listening to approximately the first third of the work. The composer accepted this proposal on the basis that the piece's material and its structuring principles are all exposed during that section of the piece and that the entire work would be listened to during the third test.

3.3.5.2. The Composer's Intentions   Denis Smalley was interviewed on the basis of the composer's intention questionnaire. Relevant points from the interview summary follow below:

Sound Source(s)/Source Material
Smalley is not interested in the identification of source materials in general. There are few sound sources in this piece. They consist of recordings of fire, rain, a Cameroon bean necklace that was exhibited on his office wall and wind chimes, which were sometimes lightly processed to gain a sustained

effect. They were also modified through the use of IRCAM's phase vocoder. Smalley noted his interest in fire's fragmented behavior and used a recording from Lucasfilm. Smalley's key areas of interest in this piece were morphologies, ranging from fragmented to sustained types, as well as pitches.

What were your intentions concerning this particular composition and what methods are you using to communicate these intentions to the listener?

First and foremost, the work reflects my own aesthetic, whether consciously or unconsciously. Therefore, for the frequent visitor, there is the identification of a signature, for the new one, an introduction. There is a broader semiotic imperative, but semiotics here is used in the more metaphorical sense as opposed to specific signifiers and signifieds. The morphology of the work is based on a spectromorphological[8] approach.

Is there a narrative discourse involved?

Yes, but not a specific one. The piece is teleological like all of my works. Its potential discourse is implied through my comments on the CD's program notes.

Where did the inspiration to create this particular composition come from?

As always, I start with my sounds, my source material. Still circumstances did contribute, for example, to the choice of the title, *Valley Flow*, which came to me during the early phases of my stay in Banff. The title, in turn, partially influenced the structuring and discourse of the work.

To what extent and how did your initial intention change as the compositional process progressed?

As the title arrived after commencing the piece, there was a certain influence in terms of structure and sonic contrasts, although some material was already prepared beforehand.

Is it important to you that your composition is listened to with your intentions in mind and why?

No, but I have no qualms about contributing this information after the fact. That said, the title does give quite a bit of a lead. The listener should be offered the choice whether to follow this information or not.

Is/are there something(s) in the composition that you want the listener to hold onto and why?

The work's title, the layering of sonic material, pitch, the work's sonic language.

Do you rely on any other accompanying text, in the form of program notes, to outline your intentions prior to the listener's engagement with the composition and why?

No, not necessarily. The CD text is identical to the concert program notes.

Who is your intended audience for this composition?
As wide as is feasible.

How is your compositional process influenced by the intended audience, if at all?
Only to the extent that I attempt to prejudge how other people may listen to the work.

How important is it that the technical processes involved in the composition are recognized by the listener and why?
It is not at all important. On the contrary, I am against technological listening. Technical processes do not advance the listening experience. The music should speak for itself.

Under what listening conditions is your composition intended to be heard and why?
Multiple: (a) Stereo (home) intimate surroundings although I am against headphone use—the space is wrong—or (b) a larger public environment with diffusion. My diffusion will be different from anyone else's with or without a diffusion score.[9]

If you intended for your composition to be diffused over a multichannel system, how did this intention affect your compositional techniques?
Techniques are not influenced as such, but this does form part of the aesthetic. The key here is the specific ability to represent musical gesture within a diffusion space. Intimacy may be lost (i.e., detail), but dramatic content is important here. I am interested in investigating the ambient [multichannel setup in a performance space] vs. focused [stereo] space. This choice leads to two different experiences of the same sound organization.

3.3.5.3. The Listeners' Experience   This work is one in which the composer is not chiefly interested in source recognition, so one might expect a much less consistent set of responses than proved to be the case. For example, in the N-E/N-M group one listener specifically stated that the new sounds used were engaging, while another found them "nonmusical" (without further explanation) and, thus, not engaging. Sources perceived ranged from those somewhat close to those used, such as water and wind sounds, to jet and train sounds, as well as those from a bathroom. Understandably, many believed most sounds to be unnatural in origin after their first listening experience. In addition, scenarios were quite varied, although many felt they were hearing a science fiction sound score. Others simply became slightly confused. The clearly programmatic title was found very useful by only half of the participants; some remained confused or obstinate at this point. All participants found repeated listening helpful. Two-thirds were aided by the intention information, whereas others were more pleased with their own original ideas about the work. For example, one listener wrote of "sounds not normally heard, like using a microscope or spying on the creatures without them knowing you are there." Many admitted, unsurprisingly, to having greater difficulty with this composition than with *Prochaine Station*.

Although the N-M groups from Leicester College demonstrated slightly greater accuracy in terms of sound sources, their mistaken choices took them equally far afield. Animal sounds, the scratching of glass, keyboard presets, special effects, and a theremin were perceived, as were the sound of a kettle, a gas oven being lit, and a recording of a stomach. However, wind chimes, bells, and "water stretching with patterns" were also heard. Participants imagined sounds of a jungle in space, the twinkling of stars, and cyber sounds. Therefore, the science fiction image held for many of these participants as well. Words like *paranoia, cold, eerie,* and *dark* were used regularly. Some linked the piece to the drug culture, the *Matrix* film series, or consumer computer game players. Their reactions ranged from one listener who did not consider the work to be music to two listeners who individually admitted to being "on the edge of my seat." Several listeners with basic backgrounds in music appreciated the composer's use of tension and release. Some were less attracted to the composition because of a perceived randomness or repetition; one found the work too long, even in this truncated form. The most intriguing response was from a listener who "enjoyed creating a story in my head" and felt that the piece might be better without a title.

Offering the title to these groups provided a slightly different pattern than that from the N-E/N-M group. Here, more participants claimed that they wanted to be guided by the title. However, a number of their descriptions of what the piece communicated continued to contain some of their original, mainly science-fiction associated ideas. Regardless, in some cases the title helped listeners to discover an enormous amount of detail during the second listening. One listener stated that the title offered clarity but allowed him the freedom to think of whatever sounds he pleased, in his case this included spiders. Another listener created a diagram of a flowing stream after learning the title. One listener who continued his sci-fi interpretation decided that the valley in question was on another planet.

After considering Smalley's remarks about the piece, most higher education participants felt more at ease with the work. Although there were comments about his "academic" language, interest in the work increased most for those who decided to hold onto the composer's ideas. A small group stayed with their sci-fi scenarios, as was their right. Two listeners felt that they had been provided with the intention information too late to change their minds.

One listener confessed that his "imagination must have been killed by the TV." While one listener complained that the intention information left no room for individual thought, others were able to make sense of the piece as more "physical" and felt that this information allowed for greater visualization. Repeated listening allowed participants to become more accustomed to the sounds and to appreciate the composer's use of different textures. Many stated that they hoped to hear the composition again but this time in an audiovisual version, something the composer would most likely never accept.

The group conversations proved very interesting. Listeners shared their thoughts about the surreal atmosphere of the work and its hallucinogenic aspects. Many wanted to hear the work in a dark room. A few, unaware of the composer's use of real-world sounds, wondered whether he was trying to artificially represent a natural environment. They were full of praise for the intention information. As the participants' ideas about their images and the narrative discourse of the piece led to so many new thoughts during the discussions, parts of *Valley Flow* were played a fourth time upon the students' request.

The Exp group demonstrated no less diversity, but involved greater accuracy than the first two groups. One participant spoke of "muddy granular sounds smelting" and others of underground caves and barren deserts. Another commented on the composition's lack of flow and implied structure; yet another complimented the flow of the composition. The balance in the movement from natural to unnatural sounds was cited as a strength of the composition by one member of this group. Another listener wondered whether the piece might be considered minimalist. Unlike the previous group, these listeners found the notion of randomness in *Valley Flow* to be a strong point. One listener spoke of the composer's focus on the morphology of his sounds—as accurate a remark as could be expected at this level.

The title was helpful in terms of focus for many in this group, for some to a very substantial extent. It led one listener to state that the title made the sounds become relevant, but then to one listener there were suddenly sounds that no longer fit. Similarly, intention information was enormously helpful to many of the group's members. One student admitted that his focusing on a dark location was a misinterpretation and should perhaps be replaced by a cold climate. Another felt much more focused but wondered why he had not heard any fire sounds. A third participant felt very comfortable with Smalley's notion of changing vantage points; a fourth listener claimed that everything had been put into perspective. One participant, who had been to the Canadian Rockies, said that he could now rely on his visual memories. All felt greater appreciation of the piece through repeated listening.

This group's conversation focused on the strong imagery gained from the piece, suggesting that it would make an excellent soundtrack. They were curious about when within the compositional process this intention information had evolved and decided that it was largely conceived beforehand, which was actually not the case. Many spoke of the virtuosity of the composition. The group decided that the intention information was highly informative, certainly able to influence the listening experience, and, therefore, that the piece had become not only clearer, but also more easily appreciated as a result of this information.

Finally the HExp group looked at the work from a professional's point of view. Here, more than elsewhere, there was a reticence to know more about the composer's point of view; one participant stated that intention information only represented one dimension of a composition's potential interpretation. One might conclude that this group, more than others, was open to more evocative or even abstract forms of composition. Hence, one listener wrote of the "shimmering behavior" of the sounds within a work that neither possessed many recognizable sources nor a specific narrative. He spoke of a "beautiful work" (a term not used elsewhere), one achieving "a good balance of sounds, masterfully controlled." Another participant referred to a fantasy landscape, but one that was more concerned with extramusical associations and structure than narrative. He spoke of the composition as dramatic, "built on many scenarios or shifts along a single one." The participant who realized she was listening to a Smalley work spoke of its sensitivity and enjoyed the spectromorphological evolution of each sound.

The title proved to be less important to this group than to others and the intention information was found important to the extent that it provided the listeners with the composer's perspective more than with something for them to hold on to. One found that possessing this information helped him to move from a fantasy to a more natural world, another emphasized a greater appreciation of the composition's spatial perspectives.

Valley Flow offered a greater challenge to the less experienced listener than *Prochaine Station*. The more advanced, in contrast, were intrigued by the greater sophistication of *Valley Flow*. What is most important to this project, however, is how the work fared in comparison with the soundscape composition and, more importantly, how accessible it was to the various listening groups.

3.3.5.4. Interpretation of Statistics and Closing Words　There is increasing scholarship concerning Smalley's theories and his electroacoustic output, particularly in recent years (e.g., Emmerson 1998; Hirst 2003; Lotis 2003). A clear focus is his spectromorphology theory, especially his articulate notions concerning gesture and texture, as well as those involving spatial behavior. When Smalley's clear intention information was introduced, many found access to this work heightened.

Table 3.2 Access statistics: *Valley Flow*

	Yes	±	No	Yes%	± %	No%
N-E/N-M	7	1	4	58	8	33**
N-E/1	7	2	1	70	20	10
N-E/2	3	0	0	100	0	0
N-E (1 + 2)	10	2	1	77	15	8
N-E (all)	17	3	5	68	12	20
Exp	10	2	1	77	15	8
Exp + N-E	27	5	6	71	13	16
HExp	4	0	0	100	0	0
HExp + Exp	14	2	1	82	12	6
HExp + Exp + N-E	31	5	6	74	12	14

Key: A "yes" answer signifies that the listener answered "yes" to two or three of the access questions (9, 10, and 12) listed above; a "±" answer signifies that the listener answered "yes" to only one of these questions or "possibly" to a combination of them; a "no" answer means that no question was answered in the affirmative. ** This line adds up to 99 percent due to all three entries rounding off downwards.

So how did these listeners react to the piece and how do these results compare with *Prochaine Station* in which all sound sources were identifiable? Table 3.2 summarizes the results. Please note that the N-E/2 group consisted of three participants this time.

The N-E/N-M group clearly found *Valley Flow* to be relatively more challenging. Still, a result of almost three-fifths is higher than many readers might expect. More significantly, the total N-E group result hovers just below the 70 percent mark, demonstrating a fairly significant interest from the musicians in the N-E category. This result is actually 1 percent higher than the "yes" result from *Prochaine Station*.

The Exp group saw a slight drop from 84 to 77 percent in the "yes" category; predictably, the HExp group demonstrated no change. As expected with the experienced group results, the totals throughout rise to just over 74 percent, less than 1 percent below *Prochaine Station's* 75 percent.

It was quite interesting to discover how high the final *Valley Flow* access results registered given the difficulties encountered concerning source identification. Consequently, a broader area of electroacoustic music should now be investigated, perhaps even including works for which composers have little to no intention information to share. It might also be interesting to have contemporary instrumental and vocal works undergo the same treatment.

Table 3.3 Access statistics: *Prochaine Station and Valley Flow*

	Yes	±	No	Yes%	± %	No%
N-E/N-M	16	2	6	67	8	25
N-E/1	12	3	5	60	15	25
N-E/2	7	0	1	88	0	12
N-E (1 + 2)	19	3	6	68	11	21
N–E (all)	35	5	12	67	10	23
Exp	21	3	2	81	11	8
Exp + N-E	56	8	14	72	10	18
HExp	8	0	0	100	0	0
HExp + Exp	29	3	2	85	9	6
HExp + Exp + N-E	64	8	14	74	9	16**

Key: A "yes" answer signifies that the listener answered "yes" to two or three of the access questions (9, 10, and 12) listed above; a "±" answer signifies that the listener answered "yes" to only one of these questions or "possibly" to a combination of them; a "no" answer means that no question was answered in the affirmative; ** this line adds up to 99 percent due to all three entries rounding off downwards.

The statistics in these two cases might not always end up as high as those from electroacoustic works with real-world sounds, but could suggest greater accessibility than is generally assumed.

For completeness, Table 3.3 presents the combined statistics from both works.

Of the fifty-two valid sets of questionnaires in the N-E group, two-thirds found the works accessible (as did the N-E/N-M group on its own). Of the twenty-six sets of questionnaires in the Exp group, 81 percent were positive and, of course, 100 percent of the eight results from the HExp group were as well. Of the total eighty-six valid sets of questionnaires, over 74 percent found the music accessible.

Many people, regardless of whether they make music or not, would place themselves in the N-E/N-M category. Our N-E/N-M group represents only three-eighths of our sample. Still, each line above represents a certain pattern of behavior, albeit with a reasonable margin of error. The pattern is nevertheless clear: the music this project covers is much more accessible than is usually assumed. Even if two-thirds of the evaluated positive responses can be related to curiosity only, the remaining percentage would still be quite substantial.

3.4. Conclusion and Where Does the Project Go from Here?

The research leading to the "something to hold onto factor" was, indeed, only a first step. That project assumed only that the music was available to the listener (Landy 1994). Certainly this postmodern society has supported the primacy of the ear and eye, but daily life demonstrates that there is more to art than the work itself—there are the means of presentation, the ideas the creator(s) wants to communicate, and what is communicated. Therefore, the first significant conclusion is that dramaturgy, that is, intention information, must be considered.

A second important conclusion is that music analysis can take both the composer and the listener (and, when relevant, the performer) into account, whether the listener be a highly seasoned professional musician or a non-musician. The ramifications of this treatment of electroacoustic music could be quite significant for tomorrow's pedagogy and community arts development. Furthermore, data acquired from this type of analysis potentially could influence composers, not to change their style, but instead to reflect those aspects of electroacoustic composition that are received by the listener. This is a twenty-first-century means of criticism and art development.

The third, and most important, conclusion from this project is that potential levels of access for a significant part of electroacoustic music are much higher than one might imagine. For those who believe that art is about life, what is more appropriate than involving sounds from the world in sound organization?

It is noteworthy that, whether independent of this research or not, the idea of gauging intention and reception is growing in popularity. For example, in March 2004, Bruno Bossis and colleagues hosted a day at the Observatoire Musical Français, University of Paris IV-Sorbonne titled, "Intention and Creation in Today's Art." They collected artists' intention data to assess the degree to which these artists are interested in the relationship between intention and reception.

The following are expected areas for future development of this research:

1. Expand the current project: Researchers will expand the quantity of data collected and broaden the demographics, and widen the repertoire to investigate how far accessibility may be broadened. Parallel to this, work with other composers will be undertaken to examine the potential influence of these results on their future work. Broadening the scope of the project to the web is also being considered.[10]

2. As an extension to the current project, one or more software development projects are being considered in order to offer affordable digital sound organization tools to new and less experienced users internation-

ally. The research group to which the project belongs is already affiliated with UNESCO's exciting Digi-arts project,[11] which investigates the pooling of resources in new digital media for developing cultures around the globe. Ideally the more analytical part of the project can be easily packaged with these creative tools to offer software that is adaptable to specific cultural contexts and, thus, support access.

3. Finally, there is a more philosophical task to be investigated: Where does this body of art fit? This is not a pedantic question concerning whether electroacoustic music is music or not. Instead, it is a question of whether sonic art, in its most inclusive sense, deserves to be seen as something that not only crosses existent boundaries of popular and art music but is, in fact, a diverse body of work of its own. If so, one might consider whether our normally accepted classification systems are really all that useful for this repertoire. François Delalande has contributed the term *paradigm of electroacoustic music* (Delalande 2001), which makes one wonder whether such a thing might exist. He focuses on works on fixed media, using the term *technological music* for what is known in the United States as computer music. There may be a paradigm of electroacoustic music that holds this repertoire together—a corpus ranging from the early works of musique concrète, *elektronische Musik,* and pop experiments including the Beatles' "Revolution Nine" to the wide world of electroacoustic musics made today that includes relevant areas of live electronics and interactivity. If this proves to be the case, yet more data will have been collected to combat the marginalization of much of this music.

References

Calon, C., and C. Schryer. *Prochaine Station.* Électro Clips: 25 electroacoustic snapshots. Empreintes DIGITALes IMED 9604, 1990.

Camilleri, L., and D. Smalley. "The Analysis of Electroacoustic Music: Introduction." *Journal of New Music Research* 27, no.1–2 (1998): 3–12.

Delalande, F. *Le Son des Musiques: Entre technologie et esthétique.* Paris: INA Buchet/Chastel, 2001.

Emmerson, S. "Acoustic/Electroacoustic: The Relationship with Instruments." *Journal of New Music Research* 27, no.1–2 (1998):146–164.

Hirst, D. "Developing Analysis Criteria Based on Denis Smalley's Timbre Theories." *Proceedings of the International Computer Music Conference* Singapore (2003): 427–434.

Landy, L. *What's the Matter with Today's Experimental Music: Organized Sound too Rarely Heard.* Chur, Switzerland: Harwood, 1991.

———. "The 'Something to Hold Onto Factor' in Electroacoustic Timbral Composition." *Contemporary Music Review* 10, no.2 (1994):49–60.

———. "Measuring Intention against Reception in Electroacoustic Music: A New Opportunity for Analysis." *Proceedings of the International Computer Music Conference* Havana (2001): 26–29.

——— and R. Weale. "Measuring Intention against Reception in Electroacoustic Music." *SAN Diffusion* (October 2003): 2–6.

Lotis, T. "The Creation and Projection of Ambiophonic and Geometrical Sonic Spaces with Reference to Denis Smalley's *Base Metals*." *Organised Sound* 8, no.3 (2003): 257–267.

Nattiez, J-J. *Music and Discourse: Toward a Semiology of Music*. Princeton, NJ: Princeton University Press, 1990.

Schafer, R. M. 1977. *The Soundscape: Our Sonic Environment and the Tuning of the World*. Rpt. of *The Tuning of the World*. Rochester, VT: Destiny Books, 1994.

Smalley, D. "The Listening Imagination: Listening in the Electroacoustic Era." In *Companion to Contemporary Musical Thought*. edited by J. Paynter, T. Howell, R. Orton, and P. Seymour, 514–54. London: Routledge, 1992.

———. "Spectromorphology: Explaining Sound-shapes." *Organised Sound* 2, no. 2 (1997):107–126.

———. "Spectro-Morphology and Structuring Processes." In *The Language of Electroacoustic Music*. edited by S. Emmerson, 61–93. Basingstoke, UK: Macmillan, 1986.

———. *Valley Flow*. *Denis Smalley: Impacts intérieurs*. Empreintes DIGITALes IMED-9209-CD, 1991–92.

Truax, B. 1984.*Acoustic Communication*. Rpt. Westport, CT: Ablex, 2001.

DVD References

Number	Name	Description	Media Type
1	Composer-Intention.pdf	Composer intention questionnaire	PDF (DVD ROM partition)
2	Directed.pdf	Directed questionnaire	PDF (DVD ROM partition)
3	Real-TimeListener.pdf	Listener questionnaire	PDF (DVD ROM partition)

Notes

1. The author would particularly like to thank Rob Weale, a current PhD student, not only for his important contributions to the Intention/Reception Project, a significant part of the methodology, as well as the questionnaires, but also for running the participant listening sessions, including the use of his questionnaires. His contributions form an important basis for this article. Rob Weale intends to publish his dissertation before this book appears. It is for this reason that the research presented here restricts itself to the two investigated works. The author would also like to thank Denis Smalley of City University, in London for allowing him an interview in lieu of filling out the composers' questionnaire. Thanks, too, to both Christian Calon and Claude Schryer in Montréal for their written responses.
2. The questionnaire can be found on the accompanying DVD.
3. In North American terms, these colleges cover the end of secondary/high school training as well as community college level. Higher education follows directly from either secondary or further education in Britain.
4. All N-E/N-M participants were acquaintances of Rob Weale (see note 1). Finding people eager to participate in the project at this level without remuneration is very difficult. Support could be found to offer some remuneration for participation, but it is unclear whether data gained in this way might be biased, as participation would then be more based on the completion of the form than interest in the project itself.
5. Soundscape composition is one in which the context, that is, the place where (most) sounds are drawn from, forms an integral part of the work. For an introduction to soundscape composition, see Schafer (1977/1994) and Truax (1984/2001).
6. Soundwalk—A walk when the participant plays greater attention than usual to the sonic environment. Soundwalks are sometimes educational, aiding more acute awareness of the environment; they sometimes are made to collect soundscape recordings. Cityscape—a soundscape that takes place in a (noisy) city; ambient music—associated with today's chill-out rooms, ambient music covers a diverse range of aesthetic approaches ranging from Satie's "Furniture Music" to muzak to new age music, and so on. Ambient music possesses a minimal character in general, one that allows for heightened awareness of detail.

7. A Pythagorian term, often used in conjunction with those adhering to a musique concrète approach, namely not being able to see the source of the sounds in an electroacoustic work.

8. Spectromorphology concerns the shaping of sonic spectra in time. This theoretical approach devised by Smalley goes hand in hand with spatiomorphology, a form of study of the spatial behavior of sound. (see Smalley, 1986, 1992, 1997)

9. Diffusion—sending sounds throughout a space by way of a multiple loudspeaker setup. A diffusion score is a form of graphic notation to help the person mixing a piece that is to be diffused during performance.

10. The web could prove to be useful as a bulletin board tool. It could eventually also be used for testing. The hesitation to do so currently has to do with maintaining control of the listener testing procedure and loss of the group discussions following the listening tests.

11. Digi-arts' home page at of the time of writing this chapter is: http://portal.unesco.org/culture/ev.php?URL_ID=1391&URL_DO=DO_TOPIC&URL_SECTION=201.

4

Paul Lansky's *As If*[1]

MARY SIMONI

4.1. Introduction

As If for string trio and synthesized tape was composed during 1981 and 1982 by Paul Lansky, who is currently a member of the composition faculty at Princeton University. The approximately twenty-two-minute composition is organized into four movements: "In Preparation" (4:48), "At a Distance" (5:36), "In Practice" (6:53), and "In Distinction" (4:16) (see Lansky 1982). The players read from the full score; the tape occupies a grand staff followed by separate staves for violin, viola, and 'cello. Both the score and tape part are available from the composer through Grimtim Music (see Lansky 2004). The recording used for this analysis is available from Centaur Records. All score excerpts included in this chapter appear with the permission of the composer.

4.2. Background

As If was commissioned by the Columbia-Princeton Electronic Music Center for the Speculum Musicae, an internationally recognized contemporary chamber ensemble formed in 1971. The premiere performance was held at the MacMillan Theater at Columbia University in 1983, soon after completion of the work. The tape part was synthesized on the IBM 3033 and 3081 computers at Princeton University and converted at Winham Laboratory—the music technology facilities of Princeton University at the time the composition was created.

Paul Lansky based the tape part in the first three movements on a recording of violinist Cyrus Stevens performing a previous composition. The recording was digitized using twelve-bit analog-to-digital converters available in the Winham Laboratory at the time and subsequently analyzed using linear predictive coding (LPC) with an eighteen-pole filter. Aspects of the LPC analysis were manipulated and resynthesized to create the tape part, closely retaining the identity of the violin but with innovative timbral twists. The tape part uses notes as well as graphic representation of the synthesized events that are generally metrically aligned with the string trio. The tape runs continuously during each movement and the performers are aided throughout by a click track except in the third movement, when the tape part is not metrical but marked rubato.

In the fourth movement, Lansky dramatically departs from the timbral characteristics of the violin in the tape part and moves to a processed sample from Coleman Hawkins playing a jazz tune entitled *Picasso*. The string trio follows suit to end the composition in a flashy virtuosic flare.

One of the principal compositional elements unifying *As If* is the composer's selection of pitches and how collections of these pitches, or sets, are presented both melodically and harmonically (see Perle 1996 and Rahn 1980). Rhythm serves as a unifying element as do the classes of timbres present on the tape. Since the tape is derived exclusively from performance on either the violin or the saxophone, the timbres are recognizable yet new to most listeners. Lansky elegantly exploits the timbral bond between the tape and string trio to craft remarkable juxtapositions: novelty with familiarity, and unity with variety.

4.3. The Analysis

Each of the four movements is analyzed in detail based on the principle compositional elements. Each analysis begins with an overview of the macroformal organization of the movement followed by a detailed discussion of the movement. The score, along with an exhaustive set theory analysis (see Simoni 1983), accompanies the fourth movement. The following convention is used:

- Sets in Prime Form are enclosed in brackets, for example [0,2,4,7]
- Sets in Normal Form are enclosed in curly brackets, for example {2,5,7,9}
- Sets in Score Order are represented by pitch class integers enclosed in greater/less than signs, for example <7,9,2,5>

4.3.1 The First Movement: "In Preparation"

Macroformal Organization

Section 1 (Introduction): mm 1–19
Section 2 (A): mm 26–45
Section 3 (B): mm 46–55
Section 4 (Coda): mm 56–63

As Lansky states in the performance notes, "The first movement, 'In Prepa-ration' is a study in tuning and intonation and is based on the open strings in perfectly tuned fifths." Figure 4.1 summarizes the pitches found in the first nineteen measures of the composition; a resynthesized violin successively presents seven perfect fifths beginning with G3 and D4 (Middle C = C4) as the members of the trio tune the open strings as double stops.

This alternation between the tape and string trio perfect fifths is quite witty as Lansky explicitly notates the practice of tuning; however, this time instead of tuning to the violin the members of the string trio tune to the tape. Figure 4.2 shows a spectrogram of a recording of the tape and string

Fig. 4.1 Pitch summary of mm. 1–19.

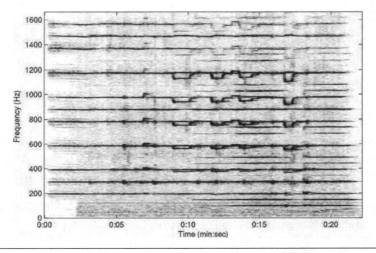

Fig. 4.2 Spectrogram of string trio tuning to the tape at mm. 1–6. (DVD reference 1)

trio clearly depicting descending and ascending fluctuations in frequency as the members of the string trio tune to the tape, which maintains a constant frequency.

Lansky describes the differences between "perfectly tuned fifths" and "tempered tuning" in significant arithmetic detail in the performance notes. A tuning anomaly is immediately evident as Lansky states that "...the violin's D string should be tuned to 294 Hz (A440)." Since pure fifths have a 3:2 frequency ratio, a pure fifth above a reference frequency of D4 = 294 Hz indicates that A4 has a frequency of 441 Hz (294 Hz × (3/2)). This 1 Hz discrepancy is further complicated by statements in the performance notes that "... the E string of the violin is 1/33 of a semitone sharper than in a tempered system and the C strings of the viola and 'cello 1/33 of a semitone flatter." Since there are 100 cents between adjacent equal-tempered half steps, 1/33 of a semitone sharp or flat is a difference of 3.03 cents (1/33 × 100 cents). Frequency ratios may be converted to the difference in cents using the formula:

$$\log_{10}(\text{frequency1/frequency2}) \times 1200/\log_{10} \tag{2}$$

Table 4.1 shows calculations comparing the tuning of the open strings based on reference frequencies of D4 = 294 Hz and A4 = 440 Hz (concert pitch). This table demonstrates that E5 is at most 5.76792 (rounded to 6) cents sharper than equal-tempered E5 given a reference frequency of D4 = 294 Hz. When the reference frequency is A4 = 440 Hz, E5 is 1.837 (rounded to 2) cents sharp. E5 is not 3 cents sharp relative to either reference frequency.

$$5.767 \text{ cents} = \log_{10}(661.5/659.3) \times 1200/\log_{10} \tag{2}$$
$$1.837 \text{ cents} = \log_{10}(660/659.3) \times 1200/\log_{10}$$

Table 4.1 Comparison in Cents Between Pure Tuning and Equal Temperament

Pitch	Given reference frequency: D4 = 294 Hz	Given reference frequency: A4 = 440 Hz	Equal temperament	Comparison in cents between reference frequency of D4 = 294 Hz and equal temperament	Comparison in cents between reference frequency of A4 = 440 Hz and equal temperament
C3	130.67 Hz	130.37 Hz	130.80 Hz	–2	–6
G3	196.00 Hz	195.56 Hz	196.00 Hz	0	–4
D4	294.00 Hz	293.33 Hz	293.70 Hz	2	–2
A4	441.00 Hz	440.00 Hz	440.00 Hz	4	0
E5	661.50 Hz	660.00 Hz	659.30 Hz	6	2

These minute discrepancies in tuning may be explored using spectrograms. For example, at measure 19 when the tape sounds the pure fifth A4–E5, the spectrogram in Figure 4.3 reveals A4 = 440 Hz. When the violin tunes to the same pitches performed as a double stop in m. 2, Figure 4.4 affirms a reference frequency of A4 = 440 Hz but with a wider variance from the reference frequency of the tape; this broadening of the frequency band is likely due to the blending of human and taped performance.

Regardless of these minute variances in tuning, the opening section (mm. 1–19) clearly establishes the significance of ascending perfect fifths. The open strings of the violin, viola, and 'cello are the pitches C, G, D, A, E. These pitches convert to pitch classes 0, 7, 2, 9, 4 that reduce to set 5–35 [0,1,3,5,8] (see Forte 1997).

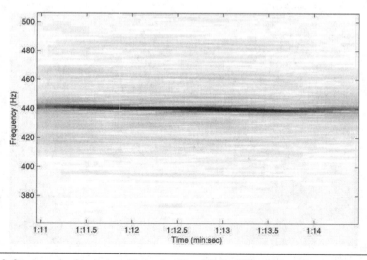

Fig. 4.3 Spectrogram of tape at m. 19 showing A4 = 440 Hz. (DVD reference 2)

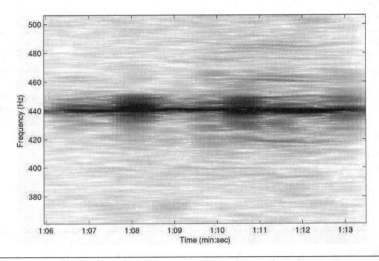

Fig. 4.4 Spectrogram of tape and string trio at m. 19 showing a broadening of the frequency band around A4 = 440 Hz. (DVD reference 3)

The second section (mm. 26–45) begins dramatically with a sforzando pronouncement of a B-flat in unison by the tape and string trio. The B-flat in the tape part (mm. 20–23) is gracefully followed by a subtle and elegant unfolding of the harmonic series as frequencies swell in prominence. Figure 4.5 portrays the spectral evolution of the harmonic series with a fundamental of B-flat (233 Hz). Meanwhile, the B-flat in the tape is quickly extended as the string trio continues with a melodic unfolding of a g-minor triad in unison (Figure 4.6).

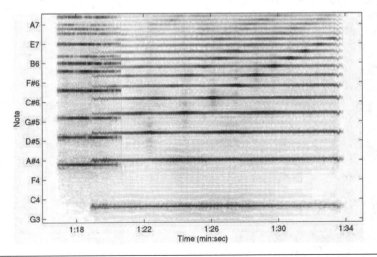

Fig. 4.5 Spectrogram of tape mm. 20–23. (DVD reference 4)

Fig. 4.6 String trio in unison mm. 20–24.

The succession of perfect fifths in the opening section and the juxtaposition of major and minor thirds performed by the string trio in mm. 20–24 gives rise to the extended tertian harmonies that unify the remainder of the first movement. Figure 4.7 is a notated summary of the series of 9th chords unfolding as perfect fifths that are a third apart. The string trio punctuates the perfect fifths that create the extended tertian harmonies by unmeasured sautillé using down bows and natural harmonics.

The succession of 9th chords in mm. 26–46 may be further compared using set theory analysis. The g9 chord that unfolds in mm. 26–29 consists of five pcs <7, 2, 9, 10, 5>. The set, when reduced to prime form, is set 5–27 [0, 1, 3, 5, 8]. Each 9th chord in mm. 26–45 may be reduced to set 5–27, unifying the variations in chord quality through set theory relationships and lending harmonic continuity to the section.

In the third section of the movement (mm. 46–55), the string trio becomes increasingly animated by rhythmic groupings that include sixteenth and thirty-second notes that contrast the sustained timbres of the tape. The string trio in mm. 20–24 foreshadows the rhythmic dichotomy of the third section of the first movement by its statement of the g-minor triad with both sustained and rapid rhythms. The string trio's pitches are primarily selected from those in the tape so that the rhythmic variety in the trio reinforces the harmony of the tape. For example in m. 52, the tape contains ascending perfect fifths—E-flat and B-flat; C, G, and D; and E and B—and those same pitches are present in the string trio. The sustained timbres of the tape in mm. 51–53 create set 5–27 arranged in ascending perfect fifths as notated in Figure 4.8 and summarized in Table 4.2.

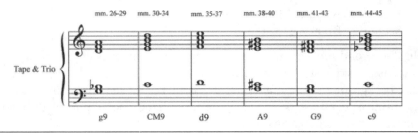

Fig. 4.7 Extended tertian harmonies mm. 26–45.

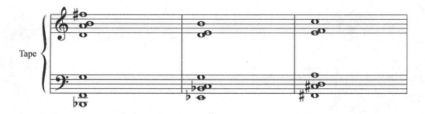

Fig. 4.8 Successive presentations of set 5–27 mm. 51–53.

Table 4.2 Successive Presentations of Set 5–27 mm. 52–54.

Measure	Pitch classes	Set
51	<10, 5, 7, 2, 9>	5–27
51	<7, 2, 9, 11, 6>	5–27
52	<3, 10, 0, 7, 2>	5–27
52	<0, 7, 2, 4, 11>	5–27
53	<6, 1, 2, 9, 4>	5–27
53	<2, 9, 4, 5, 0>	5–27

The final section (mm. 56–63) consists of separate tape and trio cadenzas. Measure 56 is a twenty-six-second tape cadenza with pitches again derived from successive perfect fifths: C and G, G and D, D and A, and B and F-sharp. The trio cadenza comprises the remaining seven measures which include appearances of set 5–27 in mm. 57 and 59 as well as double-stop perfect fifths again punctuated with sautillé and natural harmonics echoing section 2. The first movement recedes to silence with pianissimo sustained natural harmonics on E, B, and A played as double stops by each member of the string trio.

4.3.2 The Second Movement: "At a Distance"

Macroformal Organization

Section 1 (A): mm 1–37
Section 2 (B): mm. 38–71
Section 3 (A): mm. 71–112
Section 4 (B): mm 113–138

In the second movement, the tape reinforces the pitches of the string trio and, as Lansky states in the performance notes, "... should be thought of as a background rather than a counterpart." The movement begins with an eight-measure phrase as seen in Figure 4.9 with the tape supporting the pitch material of the trio playing in unison.

The pitch content of the initial phrase (mm. 1–8) as summarized in Figure 4.10 creates a diatonic scale that may be described as the Phrygian mode on

Figure 4.9 Second movement mm. 1–8 tape and string trio.

D. The same pitches are used in the second phrase (mm. 9–16) but the phrase begins on C. If we consider the tonal center of the second phrase to be its initial pitch, the resultant scale is Dorian mode on C (Figure 4.11).

These two phrases are unified not only by identical pitches but also by the recurrent rhythm of the first and second measures of the string trio, which emerges as an identifiable rhythmic motive in the first and third sections. Another significant feature of the first and second phrases are the small melodic intervals presented: the major second, minor third, major third, and perfect fourth. These small melodic intervals characterize most of the melodic intervals in the second movement. Table 4.3 presents a comparison of the melodic intervals used in the first and second phrases.

These opening sixteen measures are laden with droll humor. Lansky employs very traditional compositional resources, namely the diatonic scale, the eight-bar phrase, and traditional practices of motivic recognition and development to create a work that seems to have no tonal center or phrase structure. Perhaps the reason the movement is titled "At a Distance" is that

Fig. 4.10 Pitch summary of tape and string trio mm. 1–8, Phrygian mode on D.

Fig. 4.11 Pitch summary of tape and string trio mm. 9–16, Dorian mode on C.

Table 4.3 Comparison of the Melodic Intervals Used in the First Phrase (mm. 1–8) and the Second Phrase (mm. 9–16).

Phrase 1	Phrase 2
Down M2	Down M2
Up P4	Up P4
Down M2	Up M2
Down m2	Down m6
Down M2	Down M2
Up M2	Up P4
Down M3	Up M2
Up M2	Down P5
Up m3	Down M2 (viola and 'cello)
Up M2	Up P4
Down m3	Up M2
Down P4	Up m3
Down M2	Up M2
Same	Same
Up m3	Up M2

the listener is presented with traditional compositional elements dating to the medieval period of music history; yet, these compositional elements do not invoke a traditional response from the listener and, thus, are at a distance historically and perceptually.

The pitch content of the first and second phrase comes to an immediate halt at measure 17 with a subito piano on the pitch B by the tape and string trio, marking the beginning of a new phrase. This strategy of a pitched interruption is reminiscent of measure 20 in the first movement. The pitch content of the tape and string trio of the third phrase (mm. 17–26) of the second movement may be considered as b pure minor or the Aeolian mode: B, C-sharp, D, E, F-sharp, G, A, and B. At this point, we may become increasingly suspicious about the prominent use of the diatonic scale.

Another way of looking at the diatonic scales presented thus far goes beyond the liturgical modes of the medieval period to twentieth-century set theory. A set theory analysis of the Phrygian mode on D, the Dorian mode on C, and the Aeolian mode of B reveals that all of these scales, in fact, all of the liturgical modes, including major and pure minor scales, reduce to set 7–35.

The use of set 7–35 in the second movement builds a bridge back to the pitch content of the opening nineteen measures of the first movement. The tuning of the open strings of the string trio (C, G, D, A, E) form set 5–35. Notice that the set names of 7–35 and 5–35 both end in 35; these sets are the

Set 5-35   Set 7-35 or G-flat major

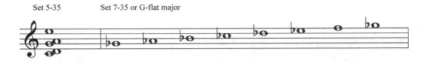

Fig. 4.12 Complementary sets 5–35 and 7–35.

complement of each other because the set number, 35, is the same and the sum of the cardinalities equal the modulus (5 + 7 = 12). Set 5-35 [0, 2, 4, 7, 9] and 7-35 [6, 8, 10, 11, 1, 3, 5] are complements of each other because the pitches not found in 5–35 are found in 7–35. Another way of looking at the relationship between the complementary sets 5–35 and 7–35 is that after the open strings of the 'cello, viola, and violin are tuned (C, D, G, A, E), the remaining pitches form a G-flat major scale (G-flat, A-flat, B-flat, C-flat, D-flat, E-flat, and F) as seen in Figure 4.12. The union of these two sets creates a set comprised of all twelve pitch classes, referred to as the universal set and synonymous with a chromatic scale.

During measures 26–37, a transition to a new section begins with a tape solo with pitches initially derived from 7–35 (m. 27) but quickly migrates into a succession of augmented triple octaves (mm. 29–31). These augmented triple octaves yield to clusters of sonorities that become increasingly complex at measure 31, emphasizing higher frequencies by measure 37, as seen in Figure 4.13.

The entrance of the string trio at measure 38 confirms the arrival of a new section characterized by short phrases punctuated by silence and glissandi performed by the string trio; many of the string trio's phrases loosely form

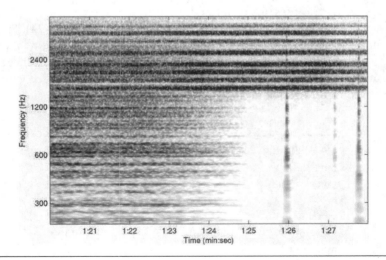

Fig. 4.13 Spectrogram of tape solo at m. 37. (DVD reference 5)

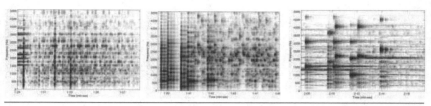

Fig. 4.14 Spectrogram of tape mm. 39–40, 43–44, and 56–58. (DVD references 6,7, and 8)

sequences. The tape has pitched struck sounds followed by rattling sounds as seen in Figure 4.14.

These short phrases extend in length and textural complexity until a tape solo begins at measure 63. The pitch content of the string trio and tape during measures 38–62 is summarized in Table 4.4.

The third section (mm. 71–112) serves as a recapitulation of the first section. With all of the humor of the early horn entrance at the recapitulation in the first movement of Beethoven's Third Symphony in E-flat ("The Eroica," op. 55), Lansky brings the string trio into the recapitulation one beat early (in measure 71). As in the opening phrase of the movement, all members of the string trio play the same pitches (mm. 71–80) but this time with registral displacement (Figure 4.15).

The pitches are drawn exclusively from set 7–35 over the next several phrases: mm. 71–80, mm. 81–85, mm. 87–91, mm. 92–102, and mm. 103–106. The tape in mm. 109–11 continues with a rattling sound unchallenged by any pitches in the tape or string trio. Figure 4.16 demonstrates the spectrum of these three measures.

The string trio presents material derived from the second section using glissandi to move between small melodic intervals (mm. 113–24). Subsequently, the string trio signals the end of the movement by a statement of set 5–35 that unfolds over measures 127–32 using exactly the same pitches as in the first section of the first movement (mm. 1–19) but here blended with the tape to sound a three-note cluster of major seconds that fade to silence.

Table 4.4 Summary of PC Sets in Section 2

Location	Pitch Classes	Set
mm. 38–40	<7, 9, 0, 2, 5>	5–35
mm. 43–44	<8, 10, 6, 3, 0, 5, 1>	7–35
m. 48	<2, 3, 5>	3–2
mm. 51–55	<6, 5, 10, 0, 3, 4>	6–Z41
mm. 56–58	<7, 5, 10, 0, 1, 3>	6–33
mm. 60–62	<1, 4, 6, 9, 11, 2>	6–32

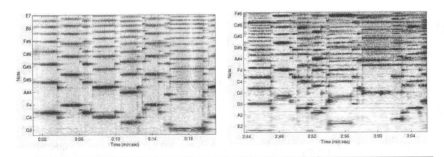

Fig. 4.15 Comparison of string trio mm. 2–8 with mm. 71–80. (DVD references 9 and 10)

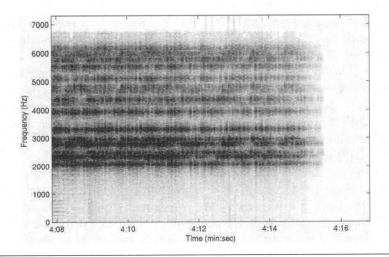

Fig. 4.16 Spectrogram of tape solo mm. 109–11. (DVD reference 11)

4.3.3. The Third Movement: "In Practice"
Macroformal Organization
 Section 1 (A): mm. 1–38
 Section 2 (B): mm 39–75
 Section 3 (A): mm 76–91
 Section 4 (Coda): mm 92–127

The third movement is a study in rhythmic precision between the tape and the trio. Lansky states in the performance notes, "While the tape part may seem to bend and sway a great deal, the string parts are to be played with as much rhythmic precision as possible." The composer requests that the performers

Fig. 4.17 Third movement opening tape solo.

delay or anticipate beats so that they coincide with the tape. Lansky draws attention to this aspect of the movement by declaring the approximate tempo as quarter note = 120 and notating rubato for the opening tape solo of the movement (Figure 4.17) indicating the rhythm of the tape is approximate.

The collection of pitches in the opening tape solo form set 5–35 and are presented melodically with adjacent intervals no larger than a perfect fourth. These nine pitches may be subdivided into three groups of three pitches—<7, 5, 10>, <0, 3, 5>, and <7, 10, 0>—each reducing to set 3–7. Set 3–7 is in a Kh set complex relation with 5–35, and both sets seem influential in the composer's selection of melodic and harmonic pitch constructs in this movement. The opening tape solo continues to wander pensively in an extremely high register mimicking string harmonics and lending an ethereal quality to its irregular phrases.

After the opening tape solo, the trio enters sempre forte con sordino reinforcing the melodic line and spectral character of the tape. The persistent rhythm of the trio (Figure 4.18) in note-against-note counterpoint repeats for eight consecutive measures, sometimes forming melodic sequences that lend continuity to the drifting tape melody. It is as if the string trio is trying to metrically anchor the tape while the performers heed its approximate rhythm. Several occurrences of set 3–7 presented melodically and harmonically unify this passage.

At measure 22, the tape solo continues for three distinct phrases, each metrically homogeneous, appearing in quintuple octaves, and punctuated by silence. These three phrases reveal spurious presentations of set 3–7 [0, 2, 5]. The first and second phrases of this tape solo share the same melodic contour, giving the aural impression of a melodic sequence.

A slight climax at measure 38, spanning several octaves, is marked with a salient accent that elides gracefully into the second section. This section (mm. 39–75) extends the use of sequence forming five antecedent and consequence phrases between the string trio and tape with both moving mostly in parallel

Fig. 4.18 Rhythm of the string trio measure 14 that repeats for 8 consecutive measures.

Fig. 4.19 Violin melody mm. 49–51.

motion. At measure 49, the violin capriciously introduces a melody (as shown in Figure 4.19) that is imitated by the 'cello and viola.

The violin melody presents multiple appearances of set 3–7 (<8, 6, 11>; <1, 11, 4>; <6, 9, 11>; and <1, 4, 6>) that are answered by set 3–7 in the 'cello and viola. Over the next several measures, successive presentations of set 5–35 in the violin and viola (mm. 57–58) build to a climax that evokes a sense of nobility between the trio and tape during mm. 59–60.

From measure 60 to 61 the listener is abruptly moved to something new; the tape cluster at measure 60 immediately slips downward in frequency creating the aural impression of a phrase modulation at 3:15 (Figure 4.20).

The thick texture of the tape immediately recedes at measure 61 with solo imitative melodic lines in the tape restating the significance of set 5–35; these extremely high frequencies of the tape melody occur over the receding, sustained clusters from the climax at m. 61. The second section draws to a close with the string trio presenting a virtuoso display of pizzicato and strummed chords immediately after the tape ends. The arco line of the viola emerges over measures 66–68 with another statement of set 3–7 <1, 3, 6> imitated by the other members of the trio.

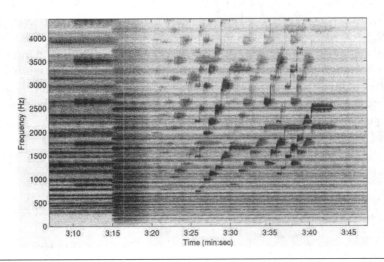

Fig. 4.20 Spectrogram of tape mm. 60–61. (DVD reference 12)

Table 4.5 Correspondence Between String Trio mm.
14–21 and Tape mm. 76–91

String Trio	Tape
m. 14	m. 76
m. 15	m. 78
m. 16	m. 80
m. 17	m. 83
m. 18	m. 85
m. 19	m. 87
m. 20	m. 90
m. 21	m. 91

The third section (mm. 76–91) recapitulates a portion of the first section beginning at measure 76, though with a marked change in rhythmic roles between the trio and the tape. The consistent rhythm of the trio in mm. 14–21 corresponds with eight successive statements in the tape as explained in Table 4.5. The pitch content, voicing, and melodic contour of these statements are remarkably similar, most notably the violin in comparison with the upper pitches of the tape. Just as the tape melody was in an extremely high register during mm. 14–20, the violin is likewise in its high register mm. 76–91 further accentuating the reversal of musical roles. This episode draws to a formidable climax between the trio and tape with the viola puncturing the sustained tones of the tape with an emphatic statement of set 5–35 while the violin and ʻcello join with statements of set 3–7 (mm. 90–91).

Measure 92 presents another significant turn of musical events as the trio engages in a Bartok-like solo, subito piano, and dolce con sordino. This whimsical melody of the violin melodically presents sets 5–35 and 7–35 in measures 92–93 and again in measures 94–96. A twenty-second tape solo reminiscent of the opening solo interrupts this melody that is, in turn, stubbornly interrupted by the string trio at m. 105. This interruption is marked by the same whimsical melody in the violin but this time with overlapping presentations of set 5–35 and 7–35 (Figure 4.21).

Fig. 4.21 Overlapping presentations of 5–35 and 7–35 mm. 105–108.

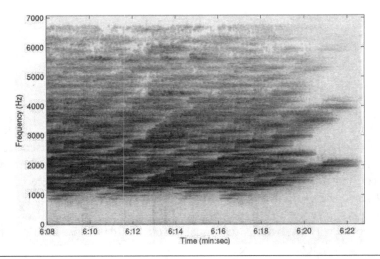

Fig. 4.22 Spectrogram of tape excerpt measures 109–125. (DVD reference 13)

The string trio at measure 108 draws to a curious close on the enharmonic equivalent of an A major triad; this is followed by a thirty-three-second tape solo, again very high in frequency, as seen in Figure 4.22.

The movement ends very quietly with the trio con sordino and sul ponticello. The violin melodically presents set 5–35 during the last two measures (Figure 4.23) accompanied by the viola and 'cello. They move mostly by half steps until the movement reaches a deceptively inconclusive finish, catapulting the listener into the virtuosity of the fourth movement.

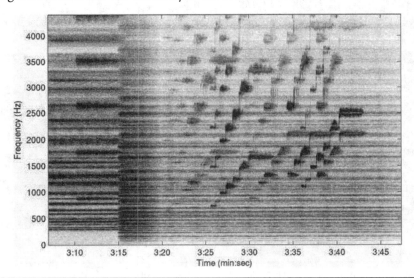

Fig. 4.23 String trio, final two measures of the third movement.

4.3.3 The Fourth Movement: "In Distinction"

Macroformal Organization

Section 1: mm 1–36
Section 2: mm 38–64
Section 3: mm 65–73

The fourth movement masterfully summarizes the principal musical elements of the entire work: timbre, pitch, and rhythm. Lansky describes this movement as a study in "… different kinds of musical conceptions [that] are counterpointed and counterposed." There are essentially three distinct timbres in the movement: a string ensemble on tape, a synthetic saxophone ensemble on tape, and the string trio. Each of these timbres is creatively juxtaposed with its own distinct musical role that develops throughout the movement, as if each timbre has its own personality.

As in the previous three movements, pitches are organized into sets. The association of these sets with one of the three timbres presents a narrative of, if not a commentary on, Paul Lansky's views on the genre of tape with live performers.

Figure 4.24, the full score of the fourth movement, offers one possible segmentation to facilitate the ensuing set theory analysis. Each segment

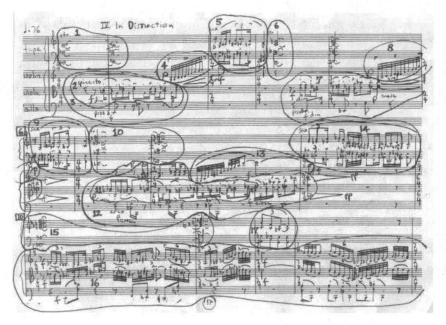

Fig. 4.24 Score of fourth movement with segmentation. (DVD references 14–18)

Fig. 4.24 Continued. (DVD references 14–18)

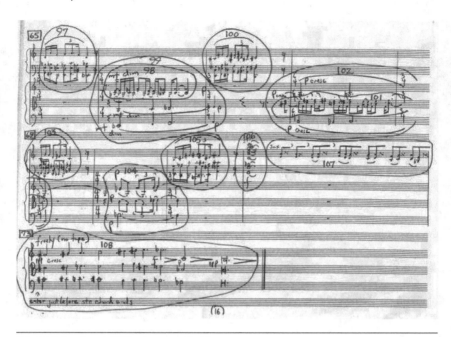

Fig. 4.24 Continued. (DVD references 14–18)

in the score has its own unique integer identifier that corresponds to the segment number in Table 4.6. Extended Forte numbers are used to identify sets of cardinality ten and eleven. The segmentation of the fourth movement honors underlying observations about the movement based on listening to the work several times. First, there is generally a distinction between the musical roles of the taped strings, taped saxophone, and string trio and for this reason, segments rarely combine these timbral entities. Second, consideration was given to the musical phrase; therefore, segments in the string trio do not begin or end in the middle of a bow stroke. Generally, but not always, segments begin and end during moments of temporal lull; in some cases, the rhythmic activity and abundance of notes form segments that coincide with measures.

The movement begins with the taped string sounding a chordal statement of set 5–27 (segment 1) reminiscent of the pervasive presence of this set in the first movement. During this sustained chord, the viola and 'cello present a syncopated and spiccato statement of set 9–7 (segment 3); the viola alone forms set 7–35 (segment 2). The presence of set 9–7 (pitch classes 0, 1, 2, 3, 4, 5, 7, 8, 10) foreshadows a pitch selection that juxtaposes diatonicism and chromaticism. The violin entrance dovetails the viola and 'cello with an arco ascending melodic presentation of set 5–35 (segment 4), recalling the pure

Table 4.6 PC Sets for Each Segment in the Fourth Movement (US = Universal Set)

Segment	Pitch Classes in segment	Prime Form	Forte number (extended)
1	0,2,3,7,10	0,2,3,7,10	5–27
2	0,2,3,5,7,9,10	0,1,3,5,6,8,10	7–35
3	0,2,3,4,5,6,7,9,10	0,1,2,3,4,5,7,8,10	9–7
4	0,2,4,7,9	0,2,4,7,9	5–35
5	0,1,2,3,4,5,6,7,8,9,10,11	0,1,2,3,4,5,6,7,8,9,10,11	US
6	0,2,3,5,8	0,2,3,5,8	5–25
7	0,2,3,5,7,9,10	0,1,3,5,6,8,10	7–35
8	0,2,4,5,6,7,9	0,2,3,4,5,7,9	7–23
9	0,1,2,3,4,5,6,7,8,9,10,11	0,1,2,3,4,5,6,7,8,9,10,11	US
10	0,1,3,5,8	0,1,3,5,8	5–27
11	0,2,3,5,7,8,10	0,1,3,5,6,8,10	7–35
12	0,1,2,3,4,5,7,8,9,10	0,1,2,3,4,5,7,8,9,10	10–5
13	0,2,4,5,6,7,9	0,2,4,5,6,7,9	7–23
14	0,1,2,3,4,5,6,7,8,9,10,11	0,1,2,3,4,5,6,7,8,9,10,11	US
15	1,3,5,6,8,10	0,2,4,5,7,9	6–32
16	0,1,2,3,4,5,6,7,8,9,10,11	0,1,2,3,4,5,6,7,8,9,10,11	US
17	0,2,5,6,7,8,9,10	0,1,2,3,4,5,7,9	8–11
18	0,1,2,3,4,6,8,9,10	0,1,2,3,4,6,8,9,10	9–8
19	0,2,4,5,7,9	0,2,4,5,7,9	6–32
20	0,2,3,4,5,7,9,10	0,1,2,3,5,7,8,10	8–23
21	0,1,2,3,4,5,6,7,8,9,10,11	0,1,2,3,4,5,6,7,8,9,10,11	US
22	0,1,2,3,4,5,6,8,9,11	0,1,2,3,4,5,6,7,9,10	10–3
23	0,1,3,6,7,8,10	0,1,2,4,6,7,9	7–29
24	0,1,3,4,5,6,7,8,10,11	0,1,2,3,4,5,7,8,9,10	10–5
25	4,6,7,9,10,11	0,1,2,4,5,7	6–Z11
26	1,2,4,5,6,7,8,9,10,11	0,1,2,3,4,5,6,7,9,10	10–3
27	0,1,3,4,5,6,7,8,10,11	0,1,2,3,4,5,7,8,9,10	10–5
28	1,2,4,5,6,8,9,10,11	0,1,2,3,5,6,7,9,10	9–11
29	2,5,6,7,8,10,11	0,1,2,3,5,6,9	7–16
30	0,1,2,3,5,6,7,8,10,11	0,1,2,3,4,5,7,8,9,10	10–5
31	0,1,2,5,6,7,9	0,1,2,5,6,7,9	7–20
32	0,2,3,4,5,6,7,8,9,10,11	0,1,2,3,4,5,6,7,8,9,10	11–1
33	1,2,4,6,7,10	0,1,3,5,6,9	6–Z28
34	1,2,4,6,7,9,10	0,1,3,4,6,8,9	7–32
35	0,1,2,3,4,5,8,10,11	0,1,2,3,4,5,6,7,9	9–2
36	0,2,3,4,5,6,7,8,9,10,11	0,1,2,3,4,5,6,7,8,9,10	11–1
37	0,1,2,3,4,5,6,8,9,10,11	0,1,2,3,4,5,6,7,8,9,10	11–1
38	0,1,2,3,4,5,6,7,8,9,10	0,1,2,3,4,5,6,7,8,9,10	11–1
39	2,5,7,10	0,3,5,8	4–26
40	0,2,3,5,7,9,10	0,1,3,5,6,8,10	7–35

(Continued)

Table 4.6 Continued

Segment	Pitch Classes in segment	Prime Form	Forte number (extended)
41	0,2,3,4,5,7,9,10	0,1,2,3,5,7,8,10	8–23
42	1,2,4,6,7,9,11	0,1,3,5,6,8,10	7–35
43	0,1,2,3,4,5,6,7,9,10,11	0,1,2,3,4,5,6,7,8,9,10	11–1
44	1,4,6,9	0,3,5,8	4–26
45	0,1,2,3,5,7,8,10	0,1,2,3,5,7,8,10	8–23
46	0,3,5,8	0,3,5,8	4–26
47	0,1,2,3,4,5,6,7,8,9,10,11	0,1,2,3,4,5,6,7,8,9,10,11	US
48	0,3,5,7	0,2,4,7	4–22
49	2,5,7,9	0,2,4,7	4–22
50	0,2,3,5,7,9	0,2,3,5,7,9	6–33
v51	0,5,8,10	0,2,4,7	4–22
52	0,2,7,10	0,2,4,7	4–22
53	0,2,5,7,8,10	0,2,3,5,7,9	6–33
54	0,1,2,3,4,5,7,8,9,10	0,1,2,3,4,5,7,8,9,10	10–5
55	2,5,7,9	0,2,4,7	4–22
56	4,7,9,11	0,2,4,7	4–22
57	2,4,5,7,9,11	0,2,3,5,7,9	6–33
58	0,1,2,3,4,5,6,7,8,9,10,11	0,1,2,3,4,5,6,7,8,9,10,11	US
59	1,6,9,11	0,2,4,7	4–22
60	1,3,8,11	0,2,4,7	4–22
61	1,3,6,8,9,11	0,2,3,5,7,9	6–33
62	0,1,5,7	0,1,5,7	4–16
63	2,3,7,9	0,1,5,7	4–16
64	0,1,2,3,5,7,9	0,1,2,3,5,7,9	7–24
65	0,1,2,3,4,5,6,7,8,9,10	0,1,2,3,4,5,6,7,8,9,10	11–1
66	0,1,2,3,4,5,6,7,8,9,10,11	0,1,2,3,4,5,6,7,8,9,10,11	US
67	0,2,3,7,10	0,1,3,5,8	5–35
68	0,3,5,7,9,10	0,2,3,5,7,9	6–33
69	1,3,5,6,10	0,1,3,5,8	5–27
70	0,2,3,5,7,10	0,2,4,5,7,9	6–32
72	0,1,2,3,4,5,6,7,8,9,10,11	0,1,2,3,4,5,6,7,8,9,10,11	US
73	0,1,2,3,4,5,7,8,9,10	0,1,2,3,4,5,7,8,9,10	10–5
74	0,1,2,3,4,5,6,7,8,9,10	0,1,2,3,4,5,6,7,8,9,10	11–1
75	0,1,3,4,5,7,8,10	0,1,3,4,5,7,8,10	8–26
76	0,1,2,3,5,6,7,10	0,1,2,4,5,6,7,9	8–14
77	0,2,5,7,9,10	0,2,4,5,7,9	6–32
78	0,1,2,3,4,5,7,8,9,10	0,1,2,3,4,5,7,8,9,10	10–5
79	0,2,3,5,7,10	0,2,4,5,7,9	6–32
80	0,2,5,7,9,10	0,2,4,5,7,9	6–32
81	0,1,2,3,5,7,9,10,11	0,1,2,3,4,5,6,8,10	9–6

(Continued)

Table 4.6 Continued

Segment	Pitch Classes in segment	Prime Form	Forte number (extended)
82	0,2,5,7,9,10	0,2,4,5,7,9	6–32
83	0,2,5,7,9,10	0,2,4,5,7,9	6–32
84	0,2,3,4,5,6,7,9,10	0,1,2,3,4,5,7,8,10	9–7
85	0,2,4,5,6,7,9	0,2,4,5,6,7,9	7–23
86	0,2,5,7,10	0,2,4,7,9	5–35
87	0,2,3,4,5,7,9,10	0,1,2,3,5,7,8,10	8–23
88	0,1,2,3,4,5,6,7,9,10,11	0,1,2,3,4,5,6,7,8,9,10	11–1
89	2,5,7,9,10	0,1,3,5,8	5–27
90	0,2,3,4,5,7,9,10	0,1,2,3,5,7,8,10	8–23
91	2,5,7,9,10	0,1,3,5,8	5–27
92	0,2,5,7,10	0,2,4,7,9	5–35
93	0,2,5,7,9,10	0,2,4,5,7,9	6–32
94	0,1,2,4,5,6,7,9,10	0,1,2,4,5,6,7,9,10	9–11
95	0,1,2,3,4,5,6,7,8,9,10	0,1,2,3,4,5,6,7,8,9,10	11–1
96	0,1,2,4,5,6,7,9,10,11	0,1,2,3,4,5,7,8,9,10	10–5
97	0,2,3,4,5,6,7,8,9,10,11	0,1,2,3,4,5,6,7,8,9,10	11–1
98	0,2,3,5,7,9,10	0,1,3,5,6,8,10	7–35
99	0,2,3,5,6,7,9,10	0,1,3,4,5,7,8,10	8–26
100	1,2,3,4,5,6,7,8,9,10,11	0,1,2,3,4,5,6,7,8,9,10	11–1
101	1,2,4,5,6,7,9,11	0,1,2,3,5,6,8,10	8–22
102	0,1,2,4,5,6,7,9,10,11	0,1,2,3,4,5,7,8,9,10	10–5
103	0,1,2,3,4,5,6,7,8,9,10,11	0,1,2,3,4,5,6,7,8,9,10,11	US
104	0,2,3,5,7,8	0,1,3,5,6,8	6–Z25
105	0,1,2,3,4,5,6,7,8,9,10,11	0,1,2,3,4,5,6,7,8,9,10,11	US
106	0,2,5,7,9,10	0,2,4,5,7,9	6–32
107	0,2,4,5,7,9,10,11	0,1,2,3,5,7,8,10	8–23
108	0,1,2,3,4,5,6,7,8,9,10,11	0,1,2,3,4,5,6,7,8,9,10,11	US

fifths that opened the first movement. In measure 3 (segment 5), the tape enters with a jazzy synthetic saxophone that bends and sways in intonation with notable vibrato at the close of the phrase (Figure 4.25). This bending of intonation of the saxophone mocks the trio that struggled to tune perfectly pure fifths at the beginning of the first movement. Although Lansky states in the performance notes that "... the notation of the synthetic saxophone part is only approximate," it is interesting that the part is fully notated on a grand staff. This initial phrase of the saxophone presents every possible pitch class—the universal set arranged as a succession of extended tertian sonorities. Clearly, the saxophone seizes the spotlight in its first phrase with brilliant pitch selection that retains the extended tertian sonorities reminiscent

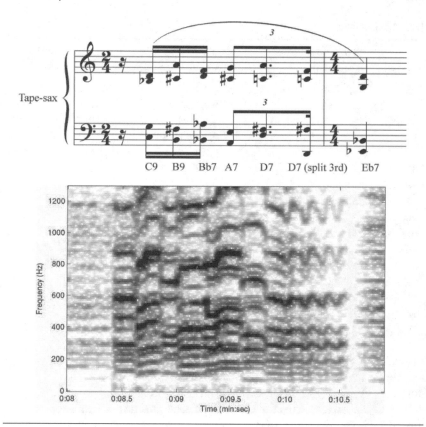

Fig. 4.25 Synthetic saxophone on tape m. 3–4, segment 5, and accompanying spectrogram. (DVD reference 19)

of the first movement while cogently introducing a jazz idiom employing the universal set. During the first four measures, the tape and trio succinctly present the principal musical elements; it is as if the two are engaged in a musically animated competition.

After the saxophone presents the universal set, the taped string ensemble immediately responds with set 5–25 (segment 6), as if to discipline the blatant flamboyance of the saxophone. The viola and cello immediately respond with set 7–35 (segment 7), harkening back to the diatonic melodies of the second movement. The violin follows its human colleagues as before, this time extending its pitch vocabulary by adding F and F-sharp. Immediately, the saxophone follows with another idiomatic jazz riff of extended tertian sonorities comprised of the universal set (segment 9). This succession of taped strings, trio, and taped saxophone, happens four times; each time the events are increasingly overlapped and temporally extended until eventually, by measure 12, the taped strings are pushed out of the music entirely. Finally, the string trio is able to muster the pitch resources for its own presentation of the universal set (segment 16), but it takes four measures for it to unfold (mm. 10–13). Clearly, Lansky is trying to tell us that the saxophone, albeit taped, has the advantage of musical prowess.

By measure 14, the taped saxophone and string trio are engaged in a frenzied debate, the rhythm of the string trio becoming increasingly complex. Finally, at measure 23, the taped saxophone and string trio rhythmically unite but only briefly when the bantering between the humans and tape resumes, during measures 25–31. At the end of measure 31, the string trio has had enough of the mockery of its taped counterpart and threatens to have the last word through a series of fortissimo scales. At measure 32, the string trio presents a succession of three-note sustained chords, piano, and dolce, through measure 36, as if summoning peace. The taped saxophone persistently tries to interrupt the string trio, but the trio does not yield. The taped saxophone's pitch resources have seemingly diminished during the sustained chords of the string trio since each of the saxophone phrases in measures 33, 34, and 35 (segments 36–38) is consistently one note short of the universal set; in measure 33 (set 33) the saxophone is missing C-sharp,

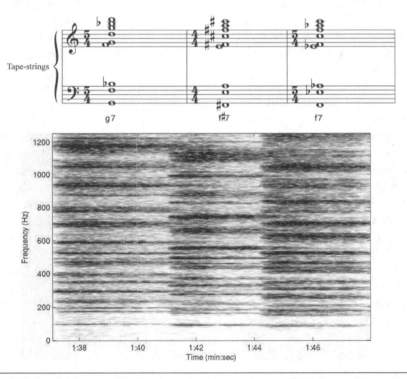

Fig. 4.26 Taped strings mm. 38–40 and accompanying spectrogram. (DVD reference 20)

Fig.4.27 Taped saxophone mm. 46–47. (segment 65).

in measure 34 (set 34) a G, and in measure 35 (set 35) a B. Finally, the string trio is granted a moment of peace but only for measure 37.

The second section begins with the return of the taped strings presenting three successive presentations of set 4–26, minor seventh chords, that slide down chromatically over measures 38–40 (segments 39, 44, 46) as seen in Figure 4.26 both in staff notation and as a spectrogram. The union of these segments is missing only pitch class 11 to be the universal set.

The string trio presents a rhythmically animated accompaniment to the sustained taped string chords. In the case of measure 39, the string trio presents set 7–35 (segment 42), a D major scale. The union of segments 42 and 45 yields the universal set. The taped saxophone follows the taped strings with four successive statements of set 6–33 (segments 50, 53, 57, 61), each statement comprised of two chords that each form set 4–22. Meanwhile, the string trio continues with its freely chromatic pitch vocabulary, piano and sotto voce, with statements of the universal sets in segments 47 and 58.

At measures 46 and 47 (segment 65), the taped saxophone repeats the rhythm from its initial statement in measures 3 and 4 but displaced rhythmically and extended, as seen in Figure 4.27. As in measures 3 and 4, seventh chords dominate the harmony but similar to measures 36–40, pitch class 11 is absent. Consequently, the segment is one short pitch class short of the universal set.

From measures 47–51, the taped saxophone summarizes several of the principal sets over all four movements: set 5–35 (segment 67), set 6–33 (segment 68), set 5–27 (segment 69), and set 6–32 (segment 70). These sets are presented as a series of two four-note chords that punctuate the string trio's statement of the universal set during mm. 47–50 (segment 66).

The strong evidence for organization of pitch material by sets is unified by the presence of such traditional compositional practices as motivic presentation and development. In measure 43 beats 1–4, the violin and viola present a melody in unison that is an unfolding of a g-minor triad with an added fourth comprising set 4–22 (Figure 4.28).

Fig. 4.28 Violin and viola in unison, measure 43, set 4–22.

These pitches reappear as a rhythmically altered melodic figure in the violin in measure 47 as set 5–35 (Figure 4.29) and measure 51 as set 7–35 (Figure 4.30).

The melodic statements in measures 56–61 in the violin build upon the melodic figures of measure 47 (Figure 4.28) and measure 51 (Figure 4.29) to create a playful motive that brings a dronelike consistency to these measures. This mischievous motive consists exclusively of the pitches G, A, Bb, C, D and F, leading to uncertainty if the pitch resources are drawn from G pure minor, G Dorian, or if they are simply presentations of set 6–33. At measures 61 and 62, the viola joins the violin in unison with the 'cello an octave below making one last emphatic statement derived from this motive.

During measures 65, 67, 69, and 71, the taped saxophone makes four statements that are rhythmically similar to its initial statement in measures 3 and 4 as well as measures 46 and 47. The first and highest pitch of each of these four statements descends chromatically, D—C-sharp—C—B, recalling the parallel descending chords in the taped strings in measures 38–40. The first two taped saxophone statements at measure 65 (segment 97) and measure 67 (segment 100) have all but one member of the universal set; segment 97 is missing pitch class 1 and segment 100 is missing pitch class 0. The last two taped saxophone statements at measure 69 (segment 103) and measure 71 (segment 105) are presentations of the universal set.

Fig. 4.29 Violin, measure 47, set 5–35.

Fig. 4.30 Violin, measure 51, set 7–35, segment 71.

Fig. 4.31 Taped saxophone, measure 72, segment 107.

The violin in measure 66 (segment 98) replays the same motive comprised of set 7–35 that was played by the viola in measure 1 and 2 (segment 2). At measure 67 and 68 (segment 101), the viola imitates the rhythmic motive and melodic contour of the violin at measure 66; the slow moving rhythms of the 'cello and its accomplice, either the viola or violin, suggest invertible counterpoint when comparing measures 66 and 67 with 67 through 69.

The taped strings enter for the last time at measure 72 with a presentation of set 6–32. The taped saxophone overlaps the sustained taped strings in measure 72 with sighing dyads of fourths and fifths that are processed using delay; that is, a copy of the original is played back at a prescribed time interval at a fraction of the amplitude. Figure 4.31 shows the notation of the taped saxophone in measure 72, Figure 4.32 shows its time-domain representation, and Figure 4.33 its spectrogram. Markers in Figure 4.32 indicate the initial dyad, its delay, and the occurrence of delay; the taped saxophone sound was excerpted, merged to one channel, and normalized to 100 percent so that variations in amplitude are easily discernable both visually and aurally. Examining the time at each marker reveals the time interval of delay: the first dyad, E-A, is delayed 700 milliseconds; the second dyad, E-A, is delayed twice at 700 milliseconds; the two dyads D-G/E-A are delayed once at 1500 milliseconds; the three dyads F-C/E-A/D-G are delayed twice at 1100 milliseconds; the two dyads B-F/C-G are delayed approximately 1400 milliseconds; and the last pair of dyads, D-A/Bb-E, are delayed six times at a rate of approximately 440 milliseconds. The change in delay time among

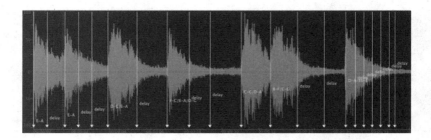

Fig. 4.32 Time-domain representation of saxophone m. 72 showing delay. (DVD reference 21)

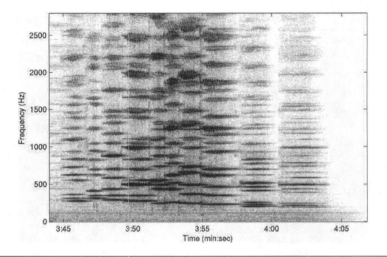

Fig. 4.33 Spectrogram of saxophone dyads measure 72. (DVD reference 22)

the dyads gives the aural impression of the taped saxophone performing in a cavernous, yet variable, acoustic space.

The piece concludes with the string trio performing alone, finally free from the metrical rigor of performing with the tape. Lansky chooses note-against-note counterpoint notably devoid of a time signature, as if the trio is simultaneously rebelling against the dictatorial determination of the tape and imploring a return to time-honored compositional techniques. The pitches of the string trio in measure 73 (segment 108) form the universal set (Figure 4.34). After all of the bantering back and forth between the three timbral sources of the movement, the string trio has the last word after all—as if Lansky has made his statement that the taped sources reinforce and add novelty to the music, but will never take the place of human performers and traditional compositional technique.

Fig. 4.34 String trio, measure 73, segment 108, the universal set.

Table 4.7 Statistical Summary of Pitch Class Sets Presented in the Fourth Movement

Set name	Number of occurrences	Percentage of occurrences
4–22	8	7
5–27	5	5
5–35	4	4
6–32	10	9
6–33	5	5
7–35	5	5
8–23	6	6
10–5	9	8
11–1	11	10
12–1	12	11

Table 4.7 is a statistical summary of the significant pitch class sets presented in the fourth movement based on the segmentation provided in Figure 4.24. Significant sets are defined as those sets that appear four or more times. The significant sets in order of cardinality are 4–22 (7%), 5–27 (5%), 5–35 (4%), 6–32 (9%), 6–33 (5%), 7–35 (5%), 8–23 (6%), 10–5 (8%), 11–1 (10%), and the universal set (11%).

Of these sets, some have ties to the previous three movements: The first movement uses set 5–35 and 5–27; the second movement uses sets 6–32 and 6–33; and the third movement pervasively uses set 3–7, which is a subset of 5–27, 5–35, 6–32, and 6–33.

Almost all of the sets with cardinalities of 4–8 are in a Kh set complex relation with each other—a set and its complement that contains or can be contained in another set of a different cardinality and its complement. The only exception is set 5–27, which is in a K relation with set 8–23—set 5–27 is a subset of set 8–23 but set 4–23 is not a subset of set 5–27. The strong correlation among the sets, as evidenced by the set complex relation, lends a high degree of uniformity to the pitch language of the composition. Table 4.8 summarizes the set complex relations between the significant sets of the fourth movement, many of which appeared in the previous three movements.

Of the sets listed in Table 4.8, sets 6–32 and 7–35 are particularly distinguished since they have interval vectors in which each interval class (ic) entry is unique: There are a unique number of occurrences of each harmonic interval m2, M2, m3, M3, P4, A4 and its inversion:

6–32 [1 4 3 2 5 0]
7–35 [2 5 4 3 6 1]

Table 4.8 Summary of Set Complex Relations in the Fourth Movement

	4–22 [0, 2, 4, 7]	4–23/8–23 [0, 2, 5, 7]/ [0, 1, 2, 3, 5, 7, 8, 10]
5–27 [0 1 3 5 8]	Kh	K (8–23)
5–35/7–35 [0, 2, 4, 7, 9]/ [0, 1, 3, 5, 6, 8, 10]	Kh	Kh
6–32 [0, 2, 4, 5, 7, 9]	Kh	Kh
6–33 [0, 2, 3, 5, 7, 9]	Kh	Kh

6–32 may be ordered as the first six notes of a major scale: set 7–35. Set 8–23 contains a major scale as evidenced in the Kh relationship between 7–35 and 4–23/8–23. Both sets 6–32 and 7–35 have the maximum number of interval class five (ic5): a perfect fourth or its complement, the perfect fifth. The high occurrence of ic5 in the interval vectors of 6–32 and 7–35 lends further evidence to the significance to the unifying ingredient of the perfect fifth—the opening interval of the first movement.

The remaining principle sets interval vectors are as follows:

4–22 [0 2 1 0 3 0]
5–27 [1 2 2 2 3 0]
5–35 [0 3 2 1 4 0]
6–33 [1 4 3 2 4 1]
8–23 [4 6 5 4 7 2]

The minor second (ic1) and tritone (ic6) comprise the smallest percentages of occurrences among the interval vectors—8.7 and 4.35 percent respectively. The greatest percentages of occurrences among the interval classes are the major second (ic2) at 24.64 percent and the perfect fourth (ic5) at 30.43 percent. The preference for major seconds and perfect fourths over minor seconds and tritones contributes to the high degree of consonance throughout the movement.

It is indisputable that the universal set is the ultimate nexus set: all sets map to the universal set. Lansky skillfully uses the universal set to establish the musical personality of the taped saxophone as early as measure 3 and affirm the musical superiority of the string trio in the last measure. Although these presentations of the universal set contain the same pitch resources, they undeniably link a twentieth-century jazz idiom with note-against-note counterpoint reminiscent of the sixteenth-century.

4.4. Summary and Conclusion

As If for string trio and tape presents a sweeping amalgamation of compositional techniques extended by the sonic resources of synthetic sounds. The compositional techniques that Lansky employs span centuries of Western classical music including note-against-note counterpoint, hints of invertible counterpoint, classical techniques of motivic development, Bartok-like phrases, relationships among collection of pitches as discovered by set theory analysis, and a humorous twist of jazz. Methods of synchronizing the string trio with tape include the regimented performance practice of performance with a click track as well as human performers receiving auditory cues from the tape; the latter method is suggestive of the suite of compositions *Synchronisms for performer and tape* by Mario Davidovsky. The four movements unify all of the performing forces—string trio and tape. Set theory and extended tertian harmonies are evident in the selection of pitches and analysis–resynthesis techniques influence the sonic characteristics of the tape. This work is a comprehensive study in compositional and performance practices that bridge tradition with innovation as if Lansky is thoughtfully illustrating the various paths to integrating electronic sounds with human performers.

References

Forte, Allen. *The Structure of Atonal Music.* New Haven, CT: Yale University Press, 1973.
Lansky, Paul. *As If (string trio and computer). The Virtuoso in the Computer Age 1.* Centaur Records, 1982.
———. E-mail to the author. July 28, 2004.
Perle, George. *Twelve-Tone Tonality.* Berkeley: University of California Press, 1996.
Rahn, John. *Basic Atonal Theory.* New York: Longman, 1980.
Simoni, Mary. "Computer-Assisted Analysis of Atonal Music: An Application Program Using Set Theory." Diss. Michigan State University, 1983.

DVD References

Number	File Name	Description	Media Type
1	Figure4,2_C.tif	Color spectrogram of string trio tuning to the tape mm. 1–6	600-dpi color TIFF
2	Figure 4.3_C.tif	Color spectrogram of tape at m. 19	600-dpi color TIFF
3	Figure 4.4_C.tif	Color spectrogram of tape and string trio at m. 19	600-dpi color TIFF

Number	File Name	Description	Media Type
4	Figure 4.5_C_ConsQ.tif	Color spectrogram using Constant Q of tape at mm. 20–23	600-dpi color TIFF
5	Figure 4.13-C-ConsQ.tif	Color spectrogram using Constant Q of tape solo at m. 37	600-dpi color TIFF
6	Figure 4.14_m39–40_C.tif	Color spectrogram of tape mm. 39–40	600-dpi color TIFF
7	Figure 4.14_m43–44_C.tif	Color spectrogram of tape mm. 43–44	600-dpi color TIFF
8	Figure 4.14_m56–58_C.tif	Color spectrogram of tape mm. 56–58	600-dpi color TIFF
9	Figure 4.15_m2–8_C.tif	Color Spectrogram of string trio mm. 2–8	600-dpi color TIFF
10	Figure 4.15_m71-80_C_ConsQ.tif	Color spectrogram using Constant Q of string trio mm. 71–80	600-dpi color TIFF
11	Figure 4.16_C.tif	Color spectrogram of tape solo mm. 109–11	600-dpi color TIFF
12	Figure 4.20_C_ConsQ.tif	Color spectrogram using ConstantQ of tape mm. 60–61	600-dpi color TIFF
13	Figure 4.22_C.tif	Color spectrogram of tape excerpt mm. 109–125	600-dpi color TIFF
14	Figure 4.24_Page01.tif	Page 1 of the score of the 4th movement with segmentation	600-dpi black and white TIFF
15	Figure 4.24_Page02.tif	Page 2 of the score of the 4th movement with segmentation	600-dpi black and white TIFF
16	Figure 4.24_Page03.tif	Page 3 of the score of the 4th movement with segmentation	600-dpi black and white TIFF
17	Figure 4.24_Page04.tif	Page 4 of the score of the 4th movement with segmentation	600-dpi black and white TIFF
18	Figure 4.24_Page05.tif	Page 5 of the score of the 4th movement with segmentation	600-dpi black and white TIFF
19	Figure 4.25_Sax_C_ConsQ.tif	Color spectrogram using Constant Q of synthetic saxophone tape mm. 3–4	600-dpi color TIFF
20	Figure 4.26_C.tif	Color spectrogram of taped strings mm. 38–40	600-dpi color TIFF
21	Figure 4.32.tif	Time-domain representation of saxophone m. 72 showing delay	600-dpi color TIFF
22	Figure 4.33_C.tif	Color spectrogram of saxophone dyads m. 72	600-dpi color TIFF

Notes

1. The author would like to express her gratitude to Paul Lansky for his review of this chapter and his mentorship to electroacoustic composers throughout his devoted career. Paul Lansky has served as a role model to many electroacoustic composers and this chapter is an expression of the author's appreciation. The author wishes to thank Marion Guck for her careful review of this chapter and her thoughtful comments about the presentation of the analysis. Gratitude is owed to Norman Adams for developing the software that allows for the interactive modification of time-frequency images and creating the spectrograms in this chapter.

5

Alvin Lucier's *I am sitting in a room*[1]

BENJAMIN BROENING

5.1. Introduction

Alvin Lucier's 1969 landmark piece *I am sitting in a room* is deceptively simple. The work, in its most widely known realization, opens with a recounting of the means of production (Lucier, Lovely Music). Lucier speaks:

> I am sitting in a room, different from the one you are in now.
>
> I am recording the sound of my speaking voice and I am going to play it back into the room again and again until the resonant frequencies of the room reinforce themselves so that any semblance of my speech, with perhaps the exception of rhythm, is destroyed.
>
> What you will hear, then, are the natural resonant frequencies of the room articulated by speech. I regard this activity not so much as a demonstration of a physical fact, but more as a way to smooth out any irregularities my speech might have.

As promised, the piece unfolds according to the description offered at its opening. The thirty-two iterations of the spoken text slowly transform from intelligible, if flawed, speech, into sustained and slowly changing pitches over the course of forty-five minutes. The "irregularities" of Lucier's speech (he stutters on the words *rhythm, not,* and *smooth* and hesitates very slightly over other words) are indeed smoothed out over the course of the piece as the resonant frequencies of the room interact with those frequencies present in the recording of his voice. As he plays each subsequent generation back into the room, only those frequencies common to both are reinforced while others are gradually attenuated, or as Lucier has said "those pitches that correspond to the resonance get amplified and those that don't go away" (Delio 1985, 268).

The score of the piece includes a list of necessary equipment, instructions for connecting the equipment, the text listed above, and instructions for realizing the work:

> Record your voice on the tape through the microphone attached to tape recorder #1.
>
> Rewind the tape to its beginning, transfer it to tape recorder #2, play it back into the room through the loudspeaker and record a second generation of the original recorded statement through the microphone attached to tape recorder #1.
>
> Rewind the second generation to its beginning and splice it onto the end of the original recorded statement on tape recorder #2.
>
> Play the second generation only back into the room through the loudspeaker and record the third generation of the original recorded statement through the microphone attached to tape recorder #1.
>
> Continue this process through many generations.
>
> All the generations spliced together in chronological order make a tape composition the length of which is determined by the length of the original statement and the number of generations recorded. (Lucier and Simon 1980, 30–31)

The instructions allow for different realizations of the piece. A text other than the one provided may be used, one or more speakers of different languages may be used, multiple rooms may be used, and the position of the microphone may be changed for every iteration of the text.

While the piece has been realized a number of times, two versions created by Alvin Lucier are most widely known. Lucier created a version using the text listed above for release on *Source Magazine* no. 7, Source Record 3 in 1970 that includes fifteen iterations of the text as it appears in the score and lasts about twenty-three minutes. Recently, Content Records rereleased this version of the piece, which has been out of print for a number of years.

In 1980, Lovely Music released a version Lucier created in a different space—his living room in Middletown, Connecticut—that includes thirty-two iterations of the text as it appears above and lasts approximately forty-five minutes (Lucier, Lovely Music). The piece was composed on a Nagra tape recorder with an Electro-Voice 635 dynamic microphone and played back on one channel of a Revox A77 tape recorder, Dynaco amplifier, and a KLH model Six loudspeaker.[2]

The room where the piece was made acted as a filter on the spoken text, absorbing some frequencies and reinforcing others. Exactly which frequencies are reinforced and which are attenuated is a function not only of the shape, size, and building materials of the room but also of its contents. Of the space at Brandeis University where he created an early unreleased version of the piece, Lucier has written that it was "a small, bright, somewhat antiseptic room.... It was filled with electronic equipment, and one wall consisted of several large glass windows. The resonant frequencies got reinforced after the fifth or sixth generation, resulting in harsh, strident sounds" (Lucier and Simons 1980, 37).

The space where he made the 1980 version, however, was "a softer, friendlier room with wall-to-wall carpet and drapes on the windows.... The carpets and drapes cut down on the production of the resonant frequencies so they took longer to achieve, but it gave us a more beautiful result" (Lucier and Simon 1980, 37). Each piece of equipment through which the signal travels (the microphone, amplifier, speaker, tape recorder) also colors the resultant sound. In addition, the relative position of loudspeaker and microphone affect the rate at which the acoustical signature of the room is imparted onto the recorded voice. Imagine, for example, if one realized the piece with a cardiod microphone placed inches from the loudspeaker. Due to the proximity to the speaker and the rejection pattern of the microphone, the amount of reflected sound affected by the characteristics of the room would be minimal. Such a realization would likely be far longer than the forty-five minutes of the Lovely Music version.

5.2. Background: Process, Reich, and Lucier

Lucier's score to *I am sitting in a room* bears a strong conceptual relationship, if not necessarily an auditory one, to some of the music of the early minimalist composers, especially that of Steve Reich. Over the span of a number of pieces Reich explored the idea of process music: given certain musical materials and a single idea of what to do with them, usually phasing in Reich's case, a piece is created.

Early in 1965, after hearing the work of Terry Riley, Reich began working with tape loops of a preacher he had recorded on the streets of San Francisco. Interested in the powerful effects of repetition but anxious to differentiate his work from Riley's repetitive materials, Reich's experiments led him to attempt to play two tape loops in unison. He found that the slight difference in tape speed between the two tape decks he was working with resulted in the loops slowly shifting out of phase with each other. Reich (2002) says, "As I listened to this gradual phase shifting process, I began to realize that it was an extraordinary form of musical structure.... It was a seamless, uninterrupted musical process" (20). The discovery was incorporated into several important tape pieces including *It's Gonna Rain,* in 1965, and *Come Out,* in 1966. Reich soon went on to apply the same technique to instrumental compositions; *Piano Phase* and *Violin Phase* were both completed in 1967.

Reich wrote "Music as a Gradual Process," a condensed expression of his musical values in the form of a series of short aphorisms, for the catalog of a 1968 exhibition at the Whitney Museum in New York. A selection of his statements is reprinted below:

> I am interested in perceptible processes. I want to be able to hear the process happening throughout the sounding music.

> To facilitate closely detailed listening a musical process should happen extremely gradually.

> What I am interested in is a compositional process and a sounding music that are one and the same thing.

> The distinctive thing about musical processes is that they determine all the note-to-note details and the overall form simultaneously. (Reich 2002, 34)

Lucier's thoughts about *I am sitting in a room* seem to reflect many of the same concerns. Around the time of the premiere someone indicated that they thought they could get the same result without taking all the intervening steps, Lucier objected. "He just didn't understand that what we found interesting was the gradual process itself," Lucier recalled (Lucier and Simon 1980, 34).

The ideas presented in *Music as a Gradual Process* characterize much of Reich's work but perhaps more accurately reflect the compositional practice of *I am sitting in a room.* Paul Epstein has pointed out that "few pieces by Reich or other composers actually present single unedited process" (1986, 494). Reich's pieces for voice on tape, for example contain several different phasing techniques. *Four Organs,* a relatively rare example in Reich's output of a piece largely defined by the articulation of a single process and Lucier's *I am sitting in a room* appeared on the same program at the Guggenheim Museum in New York in 1970. Reich has spoken highly of *I am sitting in a room,* and in at least one forum, Lucier has credited Reich, along with James Tenney, Robert Ashley, and himself with inventing "a new little form in music" that "came out of electronics, where you could get something started and it would just go by itself" (Lucier, 2001).

5.2.1. Compositional Process

Lucier composed the piece quickly. "*I am sitting in a room* was fast. I learned about the phenomenon, made some trial runs, and then did it. Just before I made the first recording, after I had set up the microphone and tape recorders, I sat down and wrote out the text" (Lucier 1995, 38). The finished text was shaped by two concerns. First, he wanted to avoid being either too "aesthetic or artistic" (Lucier, 2001) by using a poem, or too "composerly" by using instrumental sounds. Second, Lucier was motivated by a desire for clarity of expression. His solution to the problem was to use speech to explain the compositional process. In doing so he was self-consciously drawing on a genre of music in the 1960s "in which you told the audience what the structure of the piece was. You didn't try to hide it" (Lucier 2001).

Both reasons reflect his attitude to the compositional process. Lucier has repeatedly said that he is not interested in being "expressive" or "artistic" or "poetic." Rather, he is very interested in developing and finding way to present a single underlying fundamental concept in as clear a manner as possible and is very attentive to the means by which the fundamental concept is expressed.

For Lucier composition is a process of distillation, a stripping away of superfluous elements to reveal the central idea of a piece in an unadulterated form. "Often as I start making a work I imagine the need for more material than is necessary. . . . But as soon as I understand the basic principles behind the phenomena upon which the work is based, this need for complexity vanishes and the redundancies can be eliminated. The work may now exist in its purest form" (Lucier 1985, 466). Speaking on the same subject at another time he says "I bring it down to only one thing" (Smith and Smith 1995, 171).

The locus of most Lucier's compositional activity, then, is at the highest, most abstract level. The decision to make evident a particular acoustical phenomenon inaudible to many people is characteristic of much of his work. Lucier learned of Robert Bose's use of recursively cycling sound through a closed system to explore its frequency response. Having explored the effect on sound of resonant environments of different sizes in *Chambers* (Lucier and Simon 1980) and the articulation of space with echolocation in *Vespers*, Lucier's decision to use Bose's means of testing his speakers as means of exploring the sonic qualities of architectural space can be seen as part of a series of pieces that share similar concerns (Lucier 1985, 145). Subsequent compositional decisions, such as the choice to use text and the content of it, the care he takes with execution of process described in the score, and even, as he reports, with the presentation of the score, are based on the degree to which they transparently reveal the underlying concept of the piece. One might call these decisions "midlevel decisions." Lucier doesn't make "low-level" compositional decisions in this piece; that is, he does not make decisions about the quality of specific sounds at specific times. "I don't process sound all that much," he says "it doesn't interest me... I like acoustical space. I mean, if you use a band-pass filter, you'll have to decide where you're going to set the center frequency and I have no way of making decisions of that kind" (Smith and Smith 1995, 170). Other than adjusting the volume from iteration to iteration to avoid tape saturation, Lucier made no changes to the resulting sound. "I didn't do anything to make it more interesting. This is my basic idea, that you let one thing go without intruding on it" (Lucier, 2001).

This willingness to cede control of aural output to the process he has established is similar in some regard to several of Reich's phase pieces. Part I of *It's Gonna Rain,* for example, consists of a single, uninterrupted phasing cycle. Yet, elsewhere in that piece, and in most of his pieces, Reich either introduces other phase patterns or alters the technique in other ways.

In *It's Gonna Rain,* the phase pattern on the eponymous phrase that constitutes the main body of Part I is preceded by a single iteration of the passage of text from which the main phase pattern is taken. It is followed by a single statement of the phrase "after a while" which acts as a kind of cadential gesture. Reich is intimately involved with low-level decision making even in his phase pieces, notwithstanding his statements in *Music as a Gradual Process*. In contrast, Lucier, while he wrote the text used in the piece and practiced its delivery before committing it to tape, nevertheless adheres strictly to the process he set up in the piece's score. Of the distinction between his work and Reich's Lucier said, "He didn't just allow the process to go like I do" (2001).

While Lucier prepared the materials, defined the process, and "just let it go," he did not define any criteria for deciding when the piece should stop. Unlike Reich's phase patterns, which eventually cycle back onto themselves, there is nothing within the definition of the process that might suggest when it ends. The Source version ends after twenty-three minutes but a version presented at Oberlin, Ohio lasted twenty-four hours. That the Lovely Music version lasted forty-five minutes reflects its origins as two sides of an LP. Lucier notes, "I did it for 32 times because I was making an LP, 16 generations per side. But it doesn't need to be that way.... It's a little long, but that's the way it turned out" (2001).

5.3. Analysis

While *I am sitting in a room,* unlike most other pieces for electromagnetic tape or other fixed media, actually does have a score, the score is of relatively little use in describing the particular character of sonic events at specific times. This is a function not only of the descriptive nature of the score—it gives directions on how to realize the piece—but also on the degree of freedom Lucier affords those interested in realizing the score. The score does not stipulate which room or what text should be used, how the text should be read, exactly which equipment should be used, or its exact disposition. Nor does it indicate how long the piece should be.

To address some of the problems of writing about electroacoustic music, an increasing number of authors have turned to spectrograms,[3] two-dimensional graphic representations of frequency and amplitude as a function of time. Frequency is shown on the y-axis, time is shown on the x-axis, and amplitude is shown by color (in black and white images darker areas indicate higher amplitude).

Spectrograms are not without problems, however. While they can, perhaps, aid memory and analysis and enable the analyst to point to specific properties of sound over time, they do not necessarily correlate perfectly to perception. Most software implementations of spectrograms are based on the Fast Fourier Transform and consequently have poorer resolution at lower frequencies. Additionally, visual representations of sound do not compensate for the unequal perception of amplitude across the range of human hearing as represented by the Fletcher-Munson curve. A further complication is that spectrograms are perhaps less useful in black and white printed on a page than they are in color on a computer monitor. Many software packages for the creation of spectrograms allow the user to change important parameters including the size of the FFT analysis window, the frequency range to be shown, the time scale and the like. Despite these caveats, the spectrogram remains a valuable resource for the analysis of electroacoustic music.

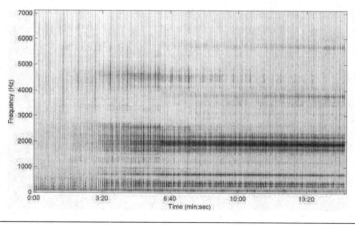

Fig. 5.1 Spectrogram of the first ten iterations. (DVD reference 1)

Figure 5.1 is a spectrogram of the first ten iterations of the text as it appears in the Source version of *I am sitting in a room*. Each iteration is approximately ninety seconds. The spectrogram obscures many details of Lucier's speech but very clearly indicates a gradual intensification of certain frequency bands over the course of the entire piece. The change in average amounts of spectral energy as shown in the spectrogram coincides with the boundaries of the iterations, as one would expect. The second iteration shows relatively little reinforcement of the frequencies present in the first. The third iteration, however, shows a marked increase of spectral energy and the emergence of what will become the principal frequencies of this version of the piece, corresponding to pitch classes B-flat and F.

While the use of pitch class language constitutes a certain amount of approximation, it is nonetheless useful in discussing this piece and is not foreign to Lucier's conception of the work. In the score and in conversations about the piece Lucier usually talks about frequency. He has, however, also talked about the resultant sounds in language reflecting traditional musical concerns: melody, pitch, interval. He has said of the piece, "Did you notice that tunes seem to start? Every room has its own melody, hiding in there until it is made audible" (Lucier and Simon 1980, 37).

The B-flat at around 116 Hz begins to emerge in the second iteration and is more clearly audible in the third, where it is joined by the F below at approximately 92 Hz. The two pitch classes are also heard in other octaves at the same time: B-flat's at approximately 466 Hz and 932 Hz, F's at approximately 369 and 698 Hz. As the piece progresses, these frequency bands are reinforced and augmented by the emergence of B-flats and Fs in higher registers, especially in the last few iterations, which are shown in Figure 5.2.

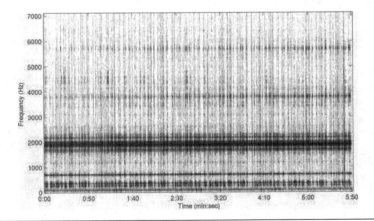

Fig. 5.2 Spectrogram of the last few iterations. (DVD reference 2)

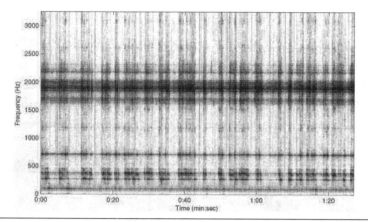

Figure 5.3 Spectrogram of the eighth iteration. (DVD reference 3)

There are, of course, other frequencies present. Perhaps the most prominent among them is the frequency band around 1900 Hz. Figure 5.3, shows that band as it appears in the eighth iteration. The most prominent frequency is at approximately 1900 Hz (a sharp B-flat), but there are many other closely spaced frequencies also at relatively high amplitudes between approximately 1800 and 1900 Hz, and others are intermittently prominent around 1850 Hz and between approximately 1910 and 1970 Hz.[4] This dissonant cluster remains prominent throughout the piece and perhaps prompted Lucier to characterize this version as "harsh and strident," as mentioned above. Figure 5.4 shows a spectrogram of the entire Lovely Music version using the same analysis settings as in Figure 5.1. The beginnings of each of the thirty-two iterations are indicated and are separated by approximately eighty

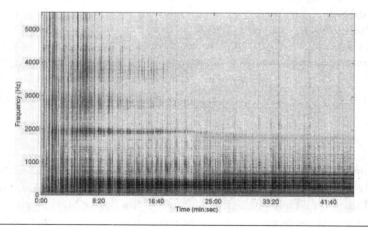

Figure 5.3 Spectrogram of the eighth iteration. (DVD reference 3)

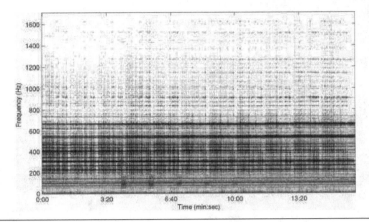

Fig. 5.5 Spectrogram of the last eleven iterations. (DVD reference 5)

seconds, about ten seconds shorter than the earlier version. At the beginning of the piece, the total time between iterations includes approximately eight seconds of silence. As the piece progresses the time between iterations remains constant, but the silence is gradually replaced by the sound of Lucier's voice resonating in the room.

The spectrogram reveals a spectral evolution different in many regards from that presented in the Figure 5.1. Rather than gradually reinforcing two pitch classes in several octaves and a cluster, as was the case with the Source version, a spectrogram of the Lovely Music version reveals a gradual attenuation of higher frequencies over the course of the piece, coupled with a gradual reinforcement of certain frequencies in the approximate range of 220 to 900 Hz, with most of the energy concentrated in the approximate range of 220 to 650 Hz. The most prominent frequency component is approximately 300 Hz, with significant energy at approximately 263, 225, 523, and 659 Hz. Figure 5.5 is a spectrogram of the last eleven iterations of the Lovely Music version and shows the process of attenuation and reinforcement. The dearth of spectral energy above approximately 466 Hz in the middle section of the piece and above approximately 667 Hz at the end accounts, perhaps, for Lucier's characterization of the room as "softer " and "friendlier."

5.3.1. "Rhythm"

In both the Source and the Lovely Music versions of the piece, Lucier stutters on the first syllable of the word *rhythm*. Figure 5.6 is a spectrogram of the word *rhythm* taken from the first iteration of the Lovely Music version with indications of the placement of the stuttered *r*'s and the complete word at the end. Here we encounter one of the problems of spectrograms: the tradeoff

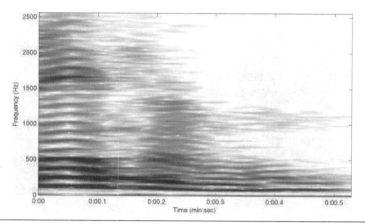

Fig. 5.6 Spectrogram of the word *rhythm*. (DVD reference 6)

between accuracy in the frequency domain versus that in the time domain. In order to show details of the rhythm, one has to set the analysis parameters in such a way that clarity of the representation of frequency is obscured. This is especially problematic with the lower frequencies, as the amount of change in frequency that correlates to a perceptible change in pitch is quite small. Thus, a coarse frequency analysis will tend to obscure perceptibly significant changes in low frequency content.

Despite these tradeoffs, the gaps when Lucier rearticulates the *r*'s are evident, as is the fact that there are clearly defined frequency bands. If we compare this to the spectrogram of the same word in the fifth iteration (Figure 5.7), using the same analysis parameters, we can still clearly see the

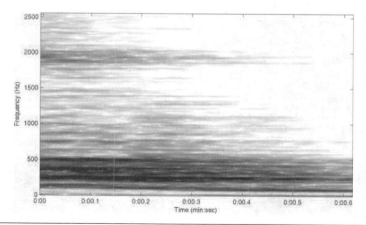

Fig. 5.7 Spectrogram of the word *rhythm* in the fifth iteration. (DVD reference 7)

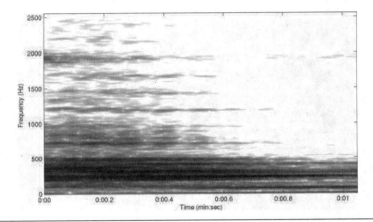

Fig. 5.8 Spectrogram of the word *rhythm* in the tenth iteration. (DVD reference 8)

principal breaks in the sound as Lucier struggles with the word; yet, many of the smaller hesitations have already been filled in. Even more dramatic changes are apparent in the frequency content of the sound of the word: the clearly articulated frequency bands in Figure 5.6 are now filled in, producing a thick band of sound. Looking at a spectrogram of the same word in the tenth iteration (Figure 5.8) shows both trends continuing. All but the most prominent of Lucier's hesitations are virtually erased, and those that remain are far less pronounced than in the fifth iteration. The closely spaced frequencies in the approximately 120 to 155 Hz range of the fifth iteration are even stronger here. At the same time, we begin to see the attenuation of higher frequencies.

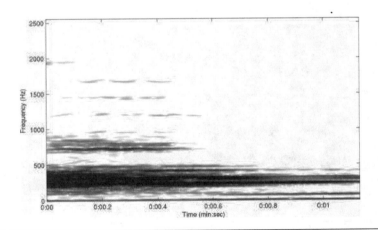

Fig. 5.9 Spectrogram of the fifteenth iteration. (DVD reference 9)

By the fifteenth iteration (Figure 5.9) even the most prominent break in the sound is almost filled in. The general rhythmic contour of the original is obscured except for the articulation of the complete word at the end. By the twentieth iteration, the many elongations, pauses, rearticulations, and the final successful utterance of the word *rhythm* that characterized Lucier's speech in the initial presentation of the text have been transformed into an audible rhythm of an amphibrach and a trochee. The final stressed–unstressed rhythm of the latter part reflects the rhythm of the end of the original iteration when Lucier was able to articulate the entire word *rhythm*, while the unstressed–stressed–unstressed rhythm of the earlier part represents an almost complete transformation—a successful elimination of the evidence of Lucier's speech impediment. In the remaining twelve iterations the undulating rhythms of the twentieth iteration are further smoothed; it becomes difficult to even distinguish when the word appears or to separate it from the words and phrases around it. The irregularities of Lucier's speech have been smoothed out.

5.3. 2. "Smooth"

Lucier also stumbles over the word *smooth* in the Source and Lovely Music versions. Figure 5.10 is a spectrogram of the word *smooth* from the first iteration of the Lovely Music version. Of particular note are the *s* sounds, the first two of which are elongated, that precede the full utterance of the word. The sibilance of the sound has a marked spectral profile easily distinguished on a spectrogram. Note the dramatic shift of the pattern of spectral energy when entire word appears. Also note the spaces between each of the *s*'s as well as the break between the final *s* and the "mooth" at the end of the spectrogram.

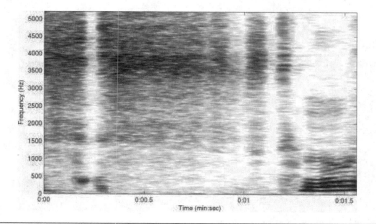

Fig. 5.10 Spectrogram of the word *smooth* from the first iteration. (DVD reference 10)

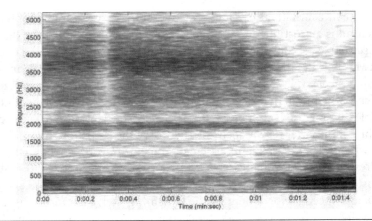

Fig. 5.11 Spectrogram of the word *smooth* in the fifth iteration. (DVD reference 11)

Figure 5.11 shows the same word at the fifth iteration. While most of the larger gaps are still evident, some of the smaller ones have been subsumed by the ringing of the resonating frequencies of the room. The large gap between the first two *s*'s has been completely filled in the lower frequency range, approximately 130 to 560 Hz; only partially filled in the approximately 1800 to 2000 Hz range; and hardly filled in anywhere else. The more clearly defined spectral bands at the end of the original excerpt show significant reinforcement. The tenth iteration shown in Figure 5.12 shows substantial, but not complete, attenuation of higher frequency components. The syncopations of the stuttered *s*'s remain clearly perceptible: while the rhythmic articulation

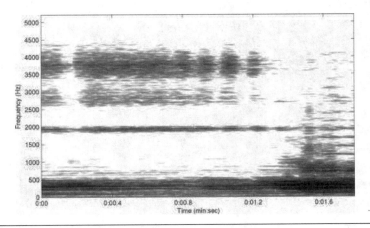

Fig. 5.12 Spectrogram of the tenth iteration. (DVD reference 12)

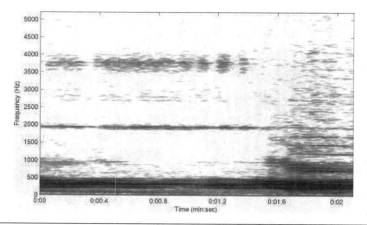

Fig. 5.13 Spectrogram of the fifteenth iteration. (DVD reference 13)

of lower frequencies is blurred, the rhythm of the sibilants around 1975 Hz and 3750 Hz are still perceptually prominent.

The spectral energy around 1975 and 3750 Hertz is particularly slow to dissipate and remains, weak but present, in the fifteenth iteration (Figure 5.13). The repeated *s*'s remain distinct, while the defining rhythmic articulation of the lower frequencies' components has long since been masked. The rate of transformation is slower for these higher frequencies. By the twentieth iteration the defining characteristics of the word as uttered in the first iteration are finally completely obscured. Important characteristics of the word remain intelligible later in the process than was the case with *rhythm*.

That the different words are affected by the process at different rates is, in a sense, predictable. Free vowels—the *u:* of "smooth"—and fricatives—the *s* of the same word—have significantly different spectral characteristics, as the spectrogram of the first *smooth* showed, and are apt to respond to the process outlined in the score differently in different acoustic environments. At the same time, however, it is the experience of this piece, either listening to it or thinking through the implications of what is described in the score, that leads us to that observation. That various vowel and consonant sounds will behave differently over the course of the piece, then, is predictable only in retrospect and is indicative of one of the strengths of the work. Other composers had led us to hear the musical qualities inherent in speech, but none had taught us to hear the music inherent in architectural space.

The thirty-two appearances of the word *smooth* are concatenated in sequential order in Figure 5.14. The spectrogram clearly shows the variable rate at which different frequency bands are attenuated or reinforced and

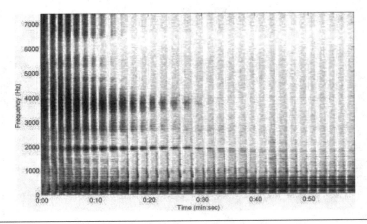

Fig. 5.14 Spectrogram of the thirty-two appearances of the word *smooth*. (DVD reference 14)

reflects the same changes in spectral characteristics over time, evidenced in the spectrogram of the entire piece as shown in Figure 5.1.

5.3.3. *Perception, Memory, and Intelligibility*

One of the striking characteristics of *I am sitting in a room* is the way that it plays with the interaction of perception, memory, and intelligibility. The stated goal of the piece, at least as expressed in the spoken text of the Source and Lovely Music versions, is to use the resonant frequencies of the chosen room to smooth out the irregularities of Lucier's speech patterns over time. Over the course of many iterations, the number of which are not specified in the score, the spoken text is gradually obscured by the resonating tones common to both his speech and the room. Determining the point at which the text finally becomes unintelligible, however, is more difficult than one might imagine. The point at which the text is obscured is, of course, different for every version of the piece: different rooms have different resonant frequencies and the spectral content of different readings of the text will be unique. The interaction of each room with the text that is played into it will determine the rate at which frequencies are reinforced. In addition, the point of unintelligibility, what Lucier has called "the climax" of the piece, is different for each listener, and perhaps different each time a listener experiences the piece. That this is true can be tied to the repetitive quality of the piece and the meaning of the text he recites.

In *American Minimal Music*, Wim Mertens has written, "In repetitive music perception is an integral and creative part of the musical process since the listener no longer perceives a finished work but actively participates in its construction.... So that goal-directed listening, based as it is on recollection and anticipation, is no longer suitable, and must be in favour of a random, aimless listening" (1983, 90). For all its merits, Merten's antiteleological understanding of minimal music is not well suited to a hearing of *I am sitting in a room*. The explicit self-awareness of Lucier's text—after all, he explains what he is doing, why he is doing it, and what he expects to happen—invites the listener to attend to the process that he describes. That the text articulates a goal—the destruction of intelligible speech—a means of attaining it, as well as directions to include the output of each iteration in sequential order suggest that progress toward the goal can be measured. Thus, as the piece unfolds the listener hears the text, processes its meaning, and then measures the current sound against her or his memory of the original and the iterations that have come before. It is precisely this ability to locate oneself in the course of the musical argument that undermines Mertens's assertion.

The musical argument of the work is the creation of a continuum between speech as having semantic meaning and speech as sound. Lucier explicitly articulates one way to create that continuum in his text. The act of repeating the text many times, however, can also lead the listener away from hearing the semantic meaning in speech and hearing it as pure sound. "Repetition objectifies a recorded word or phrase by announcing, in effect, that the delivery, intonation contour, and voice quality, is itself a unit—a 'building block' which can be repeated and divided—rather than simply a single instance of an infinitely flexible discourse" (Jones 1987, 146). A listener, then, might experience contradictory tendencies: the content of the text might encourage her or him to attend to the gradual transformation of sound as a manifestation of the text's meaning, while the high number of repetitions and relatively small incremental change in each iteration might lead the listener to ignore that meaning and listen inattentively. These contradictory impulses might account for the variable placement of the point at which the text becomes unintelligible. Each time one listens, the point at which the tendency to attend to the slow transformation gives way to the tendency toward inattention might differ for each listener.

Further complicating the matter, the listener may not be able to tell whether she or he can actually make out the words. By the time the piece progresses to the point at which it could be argued that the text is unintelligible, the listener has heard the entire text many times—in the Lovely Music version perhaps as many as nine or ten—and, thus, knows not only the words he or she expects to hear, but also the timing and rhythm of their delivery. If the listener has heard the piece before, she or he will, of course, know the text and its delivery even better. Knowing the text and the pacing of its delivery allows the listener to follow the progression of the text over the course of almost the entire piece, or the realizations of it under discussion here, but also to imagine that he or she is hearing the words that should be there even when the listener cannot actually make them out. As the process unfolds slowly, the small incremental differences and the tendency for the listener to mentally fill in the indistinct words obscure the exact point at which the text becomes unintelligible.

One might test the point at which the text becomes indecipherable by various means: perhaps by playing the iterations in reverse order to a group of people unfamiliar with the piece and asking them to transcribe the text. Such an exercise, however, would only reveal how a specific group of people responded to one realization of the piece; the results, of course, would not be generalizable to other versions of the work. Furthermore, one of the interesting things about the piece is not that the text is rendered unintelligible at this or that specific point but rather that the point at which this happens is variable. The piece is not only about sound in space, as is much of Lucier's work, but about the variable nature of perception. Some of the richness of the piece derives from the period of uncertainty when the listener is not quite sure if she or he is still hearing the comprehensible text or is projecting his or her memory of it onto the sound that is being heard.

Of the piece Lucier has written:

> The form of *I am sitting in a room*, for example, is a simple repetitive process of recycling pre-recorded speech into a room many times. And while the process does not change, the rate of speed of the modification of the speech does. It has its own shape, irrespective of and superimposed upon the regularity of the recording process. This shape changes, of course, from version to version, as different versions are explored. There is also the third variable in this work and that is the point at which the intelligible speech becomes unintelligible. It is a sort of lever with a sliding fulcrum which is re-positioned by each listener and may vary from performance to performance, even of the same recorded version. (1985, 460)

In a similar passage in *Chambers* he adds, "For the first few generations it moves at a seemingly constant pace, then, in one or two generations, the movement speeds up, then slows down again. It seems to operate on its own set of rules. It's very mysterious" (Lucier and Simons 1980, 39).

5.3.4. Continuum between Speech as Semantic Meaning and Speech as Sound

Both *It's Gonna Rain* and *I am sitting in a room* explore the continuum between speech as an indicator of meaning and speech as pure sound. While Lucier uses the resonant frequencies of a physical space to transform a sound over many iterations, Reich uses slowly shifting phase patterns. In both cases, the intelligibility of the spoken text gradually degrades as the pieces progress through their respective processes. *It's Gonna Rain* and *I am sitting in a room* travel along the continuum between speech and sound in a fairly linear manner as a result of the processes described above. The latter piece travels in only one direction: from "speech to music," as Lucier described it. The circular nature of phasing patterns allows Reich to move in both directions along the continuum. As the patterns diverge out of phase the text is increasingly obscured. As the patterns eventually move back into phase, the text becomes intelligible again. Also, as mentioned above, Reich brackets the main section of Part I of *It's Gonna Rain* with unprocessed, unphased excerpts of the source recording. In both cases, the transformation from speech to sound is effected by iterative processes.

Berio, in his 1958 piece *Thema (Omaggio a Joyce)* based on the eleventh chapter of Joyce's *Ulysses*, also explores a similar terrain, the space between speech, sound, and music. Reflecting Joyce's interest in syntactic and phonemic experimentation as well as the chapter's fugal structure, Berio consciously moved forward and backwards along the continuum between speech and sound in various places in the piece. He "was interested in developing new criteria of continuity between spoken language and music and in establishing continual metamorphoses of one onto the other" (Berio, *Thema* liner notes). Rather than defining a process and allowing it control the movement from speech to sound, as Reich and Lucier had done to different degrees, Berio instead engaged in what was defined above as "low level" compositional decision making. That is, given the manner and number of tape splices, he was intimately involved with decisions about the placing, character, and succession of sonic events. Like Lucier, however, Berio's decision to work with the continuum between speech and sound derived from "high level" decisions. Lucier used speech in an effort to most clearly and directly explore the phenomenon of resonant frequencies, while many decisions made by Berio, both of detail, such as onomatopoeic sound transformation, and large scale organization, such as the fugal elements in the piece, reflect his desire to produce a reading of Joyce's text consistent with the spirit of the text itself.

5.4. Conclusion

I am sitting in a room derives its strength from the transference of meaning into sound. The resultant sound of the piece is an embodiment of the meaning of the text that Lucier reads. Imagine, for example, if instead of the text that appears in the score, Lucier had chosen nonsense syllables or selections from the tax code. The aural result would be similar, but would miss several important features of the piece that define its character. First, the process

Table 5.1 Hierachy of possible realizations

Strong	Lucier reads text
↑	Someone else reads text
↓	Someone else reads different text
Weak	Nontext sound source

of transformation would not be made clear. Some listeners might intuit it, but most listeners would assume that some electronic transformation was taking place. Even after hearing the versions of the piece discussed here, Lucier reports that some listeners still think the sonic changes derive from degradation of the audio signal as it is played back from one tape deck into another, rather than into the room. Second, the connection between Lucier's stuttering as the measure of the transformative property of architectural space on acoustic signals and meaning of the text read would be lost, further obscuring the point of the piece. Third, the piece would lose its emotional resonance. While the acoustical phenomenon that the piece explores and the mechanistic process by which that phenomenon is made clear might seem objective or "scientific," the work as recorded is intensely personal. The piece directly derives from the idiosyncratic characteristics of Lucier's speech patterns and is a response to them.

That the work loses some of its principal strengths if the text, which is indicated as being optional in the score, is not used, has ontological implications. In spite of the directions in Lucier's score, the work can be said to exist in a hierarchy of possible realizations as listed in Table 5.1.

The strongest realizations are like those discussed in this chapter, in which Lucier himself reads the text. If another person reads the text, the clarity of the process is preserved but the emotional resonance of the listener's identification with Lucier's struggle with speech is lost. If another text is used, the central idea of moving from speech to music is preserved. If nontext sounds are used, many of the layers of meaning of the piece are lost. Other realizations are dependent on the "pure" version and act in relation to it, but don't have its strength or the clarity of expression.

Lucier addressed some of these concerns: "I also said in the finished score that other texts may be used. Perhaps that was a mistake because I don't want what goes into the space to be too poetic. I want it to be plain so that the space becomes audible without distractions" (Lucier and Simon 1980, 38).

References

Berio, Luciano. 1958. *Thema (Omaggio a Joyce)*. BMG Records, 1998.

Bernard, Jonathan. "Theory, Analysis, and the Problem of Minimal Music." In *Concert Music, Rock and Jazz since 1945*, edited by Marvin and Herrman. Rochester, NY: University of Rochester Press, 1985.

Cogan, Robert, and Pozzi Escot. *New Images of Musical Sound.* Cambridge, MA: Harvard University Press, 1984.

DeLio, Thomas. "Avant-Garde Issues in Seventies Music." *Art Forum* 18, no.1 (1979): 61–67.

———, ed. *Contiguous Lines: Issues and Ideas in the Music of the '60's and '70's.* Lanham, MD: University Press of America, 1985.

Epstein, Paul. "Pattern Structure and Process in Steve Reich's 'Piano Phase.'" *Musical Quarterly* 27, no. 4 (1986): 494–502.

Jones, David Evan. "Compositional Control of Phonetic/Nonphonetic Perception." *Perspectives of New Music* 25, no. 1–2 (1987): 138–55.

Licata, Thomas, ed. *Electroacoustic Music: Analytic Perspectives.* Westport, CT:

Lucier, Alvin. *I am sitting in a room.* (*Source Magazine* 7). Source Record 3, 1970. Released with: *Source: Music of the Avant Garde* 4, no.7 (1970).

———. "Tools of My Trade." In *Contiguous Lines,* edited by Thomas Delio. Lanham, MD: University Press of America, 1985.

———. *I am sitting in a room.* Lovely Music LCD 1013, 1990.

———. *Reflections: Interview, Scores, Writings.* Köln, MusikTexte, 1995.

———. Seminar at Ostrava Music Days, 2001. Available online: <http://www.ocnmh.cz/days2001_lectures_i.htm>

Lucier, Alvin, and Douglas Simon. *Chambers.* Middletown, CT: Wesleyan University Press, 1980.

Lucier, Alvin, and Loren Means. "An Interview with Alvin Lucier." *The Composer* 9.

Mertens, Wim. *American Minimal Music: La Monte Young, Terry Riley, Steve Reich, Philip Glass.* London: Kahn & Averill, 1983.

Potter, Keith. *Four Musical Minimalists.* Cambridge, UK: Cambridge University Press, 2000.

Reich, Steve. *Writings on Music 1965–2000.* Oxford: Oxford University Press, 2002.

Smith, Geoff, and Nicola Walker Smith. *New Voices; American Composers Talk about Their Music.* Portland, OR: Amadeus Press, 1995.

Strickland, Edward, ed. *American Composers: Dialogues on Contemporary Music.*

Zimmerman, Walter. *Desert Plants: Conversations with 23 American Musicians.*

DVD References

Number	File Name	Description	Media Type
1	Ex01_C.tif	Spectrogram of the first ten iterations	600-dpi BW & color TIFF
2	Ex02_C.tif	Spectrogram of the last few iterations	600-dpi BW & color TIFF
3	Ex03_C.tif	Spectrogram of the eighth iteration	600-dpi BW & color TIFF
4	Ex04_C.tif	Spectrogram of the entire Lovely Music version	600-dpi BW & color TIFF
5	Ex05_C.tif	Spectrogram of the last eleven iterations	600-dpi BW & color TIFF
6	Ex06_C.tif	Spectrogram of the word *rhythm*	600-dpi BW & color TIFF
7	Ex07_C.tif	Spectrogram of the word *rhythm* in the fifth iteration	600-dpi BW & color TIFF
8	Ex08_C.tif	Spectrogram of the word *rhythm* in the tenth iteration	600-dpi BW & color TIFF
9	Ex09_C.tif	Spectrogram of the fifteenth iteration	600-dpi BW & color TIFF
10	Ex10_C.tif	Spectrogram of the word *smooth* in the first iteration	600-dpi BW & color TIFF
11	Ex11_C.tif	Spectrogram of the word *smooth* in the fifth iteration	600-dpi BW & color TIFF
12	Ex12_C.tif	Spectrogram of the tenth iteration	600-dpi BW & color TIFF
13	Ex13_C.tif	Spectrogram of the fifteenth iteration	600-dpi BW & color TIFF
14	Ex14_C.tif	Spectrogram of the thirty-two appearances of the word *smooth*	600-dpi BW & color TIFF

Notes

1. The author wishes to thank Stephen Vitiello for his assistance in procuring materials about Alvin Lucier, Jacob Monaco for his assistance in realizing several versions of the piece, and Norman Adams for producing the spectrograms in this chapter.
2. See http://www.lovely.com/titles/cd1013.html.
3. Robert Cogan and Pozzi Escot first articulated the case for using sonograms in *New Images of Musical Sound* (1984).
4. It makes sense to talk about frequency in terms of Hertz here, because frequencies are so close together and lie between perceptually distinct pitches.

6
Jonathan Harvey's
Mortuos Plango, Vivos Voco[1]
MICHAEL CLARKE

6.1. Introduction

This chapter introduces an approach to the process of analyzing electroacoustic music through the use of interactive software developed by the author[2] (DVD reference 1) using Max/MSP (www.cycling74.com). This interactive software aids readers' exploration of the composition by allowing them to recall specific locations in the work—which can be retrieved from compact disc as they are discussed—and to juxtapose different passages from the work. Interactive examples of processing and synthesizing sounds are included to enhance understanding of the compositional process. The interactive aural analysis presents listeners with opportunities for continuing exploration of the composition. The software can be used in conjunction with any of the commercial CD recordings of Jonathan Harvey's *Mortuos Plango, Vivos Voco*.[3]

6.2. Background

Mortuos Plango, Vivos Voco was composed in 1980 at the Institut de Recherche et Coordination Acoustique/Musique (IRCAM) in Paris, France, with the technical assistance of Stanley Haynes. It was the first work that Harvey composed at IRCAM, although he had previously worked with electroacoustic media. The work was originally conceived as an octophonic (eight-channel) composition. Harvey asks that the loudspeakers for channels 1 to 4 be placed in a square at ground level and that those for channels 5 to 8 be staggered above them. The spatialization using eight channels helps to articulate the formal structure of the composition and differentiates complex textures. The composition is widely distributed in a stereo mix on compact disc.

The work uses sound sources associated with Winchester Cathedral. Jonathan Harvey has a particular connection with the cathedral where his son, Dominic, was a chorister. He has described hearing the choir sing, and at times this sound mingling with that of the cathedral bells. These two sounds, the voice of a chorister (his son) and a cathedral bell (the great tenor bell at Winchester), were recorded by Harvey and are the principal sound sources for the composition.

Inscribed on the tenor bell is the Latin text, "Horas Avolantes Numero, Mortuos Plango: Vivos ad Preces Voco," which can be translated as, "I count the fleeing hours, I lament the dead: the living I call to prayer." The vocal recordings include Dominic chanting this text, a collection of various isolated vowels and consonants abstracted from it, and a few short melodic phrases using the text from the bell with pitches derived from the spectrum of the bell.

Harvey is a deeply spiritual composer. He has described the interconnection of the spiritual and the aesthetic in his book *In Quest of Spirit* (1999). Such ideas are highly relevant to the shape and structure of *Mortuos Plango, Vivos Voco*. The choice of source material, the tolling cathedral bell, the text inscribed on the bell, and the distinctive sound of an English cathedral chorister, have spiritual connotations. Harvey himself has compared the evolution of the sound of a bell—its movement from outwardness to inwardness as the upper partials decay leaving the deep hum note—with the Eastern mantra "OM" (Harvey 1986, 181).

Hans Keller, one of Harvey's teachers, was a significant influence on his compositional development. "In context, Keller's view of a piece of music . . . is of unity within diversity: of constant 'latent' presence of a single basic idea, articulated in time as a succession of 'manifest' contrasts on the surface of the music" (Bent and Pople 559). Harvey, commenting on Keller's ideas, writes, "So music has to do with two things— with ambiguity. A drive to unity is there, but it must be by way of variety. Both must coexist, be held in vibrant tension—what Goethe called 'dynamic unity'" (Harvey 1999, 28). For Harvey, the more a work unites opposites the more spiritual it is. "The greater the conflicts it successfully unifies, the more spiritual the music" (Harvey, 1999, 52). The vibrant interaction of latent unity and surface variety—what Keller called the laws of "identity" and "contradiction" respectively—is particularly evident in *Mortuos Plango, Vivos Voco*.

Concern with the spiritual is also reflected in Harvey's use of timbre in *Mortuos Plango, Vivos Voco*. He writes:

...spectralism in its simplest form, as color-thinking, is a spiritual breakthrough.... Spectralism, like harmony, is in essence outside the world of linear time. In music, time is articulated by rhythm; in psychology, time is articulated by the process of chopping up and arranging experience into language, which separates us from the primary world and joins us to the linear symbolic order. But the fascination of spectral thinking is that it, too, can easily shift into the realm of linear time, into melodic thinking: there is a large borderland of ambiguity to exploit. (Harvey 1999, 39–40)

Spectralism (Anderson, 2001), plays a central role in *Mortuos Plango, Vivos Voco,* as in many of Harvey's other works, in shaping the formal structure of the work as well as in the transformation of timbres.

Other notable influences on Harvey are his teacher Milton Babbitt and Karlheinz Stockhausen, whose music he studied in depth (see Harvey, 1975). Although *Mortuos Plango, Vivos Voco* is not a serial work in the narrow sense, the rigorous application of pitch material derived from the analysis of the bell's spectrum to all aspects of the work's harmonic structure, and the linking of this to small- and large-scale rhythmic and durational structures, clearly resonate with the ideas of serialism. Harvey's planning of the work in eight sections, each with different predominant characteristics, is reminiscent of Stockhausen's charts for some of his "Moment Form" works. Each of eight sections is announced by a distinct bell strike articulating the "tonic" or focal pitch for that section. Although the outer sections of *Mortuos Plango, Vivos Voco* fulfill expositional and cadential roles, some of the central sections of the work might be considered interchangeable in theory if not in practice. The notion of interchangeability is perhaps supported by the fact that the order of two of the sections was switched during the compositional process.

Another link with techniques derived from serialism can be found in the way Harvey elaborates his pitch material, which resembles the multiplication techniques used by Boulez in working with motivic cells (see Boulez 1971; Bonnet 1988; Griffiths 1978, 41–42). However, in *Mortuos Plango, Vivos Voco,* the initial material is drawn from the partials of the bell, rather than a series based on the tempered chromatic scale.

Others have constructed aural analyses. Hans Keller (as mentioned above, a teacher of Jonathan Harvey), is noted for his "functional analysis." Eventually, he abandoned the use of words altogether in favor of music commenting on music. Keller (1985) decomposed compositions, by Mozart, for example, as a commentary on their structure and motivic content; he then had performers play the analysis interwoven with the original composition. Keller viewed the analyst's role as presenting the objective truth about a work and his analyses were closed and not interactive.

Pamela Alcorn, in her doctoral thesis on electroacoustic music in Britain uses tape recordings of extracts to make comparisons between and within pieces, including works by Harvey (see also Alcorn 1989). She references others who have taken somewhat similar approaches. However, the technology available at the time of her thesis precluded interactivity using a computer.

The CALMA project, in which the author was involved, is an example of an approach similar to that used here (Bowder, Clarke, and Saunders 2000). The CALMA software permits users to construct modules in which text and images can easily be combined with sound examples from compact disc.

An imaginative computer-based analysis of *Mortuos Plango, Vivos Voco* by Bruno Bossis (2000) combines text, illustrations, annotated sonograms, and audio examples in an attractive and approachable manner. For copyright reasons, it is currently only available for reference in the multimedia library of IRCAM, Paris; however, Bossis has also written an article based on his analysis (2004).

Other previous analyses of *Mortuos Plango, Vivos Voco* include Patricia Dirks's analysis (1998) using the software AnnaLies to examine the spectral content of specific events in the work. The analysis includes a score that uses symbols to represent different types of sounds. The score is clearly divided between sounds from a bell source and sounds from a vocal source. A short written commentary introduces the work and describes each section of the composition.

Anastasia Georgaki focuses on the role of the disembodied voice as a metaphor for the mystical in her analysis of *Mortuos Plango, Vivos Voco* (forthcoming). She has also written more generally about the role of the synthetic voice in electroacoustic music today (Georgaki 1999). Paul Griffiths discusses the work alongside an earlier composition by Jonathan Harvey, *Inner Light 3*, and the later *Bhakti* (Griffiths 1984). A detailed analysis by Jan Vandenheede (1992) gives an intricate account of the technical and compositional aspects of Harvey's later IRCAM tape work *Ritual Melodies*, which is interesting for comparison with the earlier work under consideration here.

The composer himself has written a concise summary of the techniques employed in *Mortuos Plango, Vivos Voco* (Harvey 1989).

6.3. The Analysis

The principal approach to this analysis is an interactive aural analysis. The reader has the opportunity to engage with the music by recalling, perceiving, and manipulating the sounds contained in the composition. Synthesis and sound processing are also used to illustrate some of the techniques used in the composition and the reader can experiment with modifying the parameters.

In this way, the interactive exercises give the reader the opportunity to gain some familiarity with the techniques used in the work, and develop further insight into the sounds themselves, and the compositional choices and their technical context. Graphs, charts, and musical notation are employed where useful, but much of the analysis is presented through sound. Trevor Wishart (1985) argues that Western music has become too dependent on notation to the point of distorting its evolution; it has become too constrained by the two-dimensional latticework of striated pitch and rhythm. Certainly, in the case of *Mortuos Plango, Vivos Voco*, where the "trace" (Nattiez 1990, 12) left by the composer is not a score but instead an audio recording, it seems appropriate that the analysis should avoid some of these constraints by featuring a significant aural component.

The indication "[SOUND LOCATION]," used throughout the remainder of this chapter, identifies audio excerpts that the reader may select using the software accompanying this publication in conjunction with one of the available CDs of the work.

6.3.1. The Sound Sources

Mortuos Plango, Vivos Voco is built out of two contrasting sounds: a bell and a voice. These sounds and the ways that they are transformed are central to the composition. Just as one would find it difficult to begin an analysis of a tonal piece without a basic understanding of tonal harmony and its potential and its implications, so is it important to understand these two contrasting sounds and the ways in which they may be manipulated before embarking on this analysis.

There are two main approaches taken by Harvey in this work. One is to manipulate the actual recordings of the source sounds—the tenor bell from Winchester and his son's voice. The other approach is to synthesize new sounds based on the analysis of the recordings.

The recorded sound was manipulated using the software Music V.[4] Using this program Harvey could play back the recorded sounds at different speeds, changing both the pitch and duration of the recording. Music V also allowed Harvey to reverse the direction of sound file playback. The sound file, or a portion of it, could also be read forwards and backwards continuously, in alternation. The technique is known as retro-scanning. Using this technique, the bell, which would normally just decay, could be made to decay and rise—both in amplitude and timbral richness—over and over again.

Bells generally have partials that are inharmonically related. These inharmonic ratios are different for each bell and, together with the way the partials evolve over time, they give a bell its distinctive character. In *Mortuos Plango,*

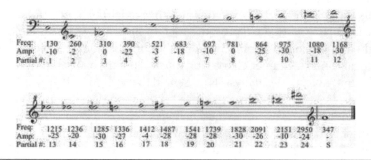

Fig. 6.1 Bell analysis data.

Vivos Voco, the partials of the bell form the basis of the pitch structure of the entire composition—from the large-scale formal organization down to the smallest detail. Harvey analyzed a recording of the Winchester Cathedral tenor bell at a point about 0.5" after the initial strike. This point was chosen so as to avoid the extreme complexity at the very beginning of the bell sound while still capturing its distinctive richness. The resultant frequency and amplitude data relating to the bell timbre at that particular instant were used to shape many aspects of the work. Figure 6.1 shows the first twenty-four partials of the bell with their relative amplitudes (in dB) and an additional F at 347 Hz. These twenty-four partials do not always fit into a twelve-tone equal-tempered scale, so microtonal adjustments are indicated approximately. The F at 347 Hz is a phenomenon known as a secondary strike tone and is common in large bells. A secondary strike tone is not physically present in the sound and does not show up in analyses of the timbre. The tone is a psychoacoustic effect resulting from the other elements of the sound. In this case, the bell contains several partials related to the harmonic series with a fundamental of 347Hz; therefore, the brain imagines the secondary strike tone at this frequency. So Harvey added the frequency to his analysis and used it in the structure of the composition.

The analysis data were obtained using the Fast Fourier Transform (FFT), a mathematical process that analyzes the spectrum of the sound. FFTs were used to derive frequency and amplitude data for each component of the sound and this data may be used to resynthesize an imitation of the original recording using additive synthesis. Working with synthesized simulations of the bell allowed Harvey to make more complex transformations than would have been possible simply by processing the recording directly. A common strategy employed in this work is to move from a recording of the bell (or voice) to a synthesized imitation, by smoothly cross-fading between the recording and the synthesized version, and then transforming the imitation.

INTERACTIVE EXERCISE 1 (3 software pages) provides the reader with the opportunity to explore this bell timbre. The reader may play a recording of the Winchester bell. Its timbral qualities may be explored by sweeping a filter through the sound as it is playing, emphasizing the different partials. Buttons on the screen allow the reader to transpose the bell. One of the things Harvey does in the work is to transpose the bell so that its fundamental becomes the frequency of one of the partials of the bell at its original pitch. As in the work, the transposition is made by playing the soundfile at different speeds so the sound changes speed and duration when it is transposed.

INTERACTIVE EXERCISE 2 encourages further exploration of the bell timbre through synthesis. This synthesis does not fully reproduce all aspects of the bell, but it does permit the reader to transform the sound more flexibly by changing the synthesis parameters. Sine waves are synthesized to correspond to each of the bell partials using the data for the frequency and amplitude of each obtained from the analysis of the Winchester Cathedral bell. The reader can change these frequencies and amplitudes, change the decay times of each partial, and, again, transpose the whole sound.

Unlike the bell, the human voice has harmonically related partials. The voice differs from the bell in a number of other ways. Once a bell is struck, it inevitably decays. The human voice, on the other hand, may be sustained and the sound altered over time. With a bell the pitch remains fixed, but with a human voice, vibrato adds slight fluctuations to the pitch. Even without vibrato there is always an element of random fluctuation, referred to as "jitter." The harmonic series generated by the vocal cords passes through the vocal tract, which resonates at certain frequencies depending on the shape of the vocal cavity, and increases the amplitude of certain harmonics. Changing the shape of the mouth allows us to adjust the frequencies of these resonances so as to produce different vowels.

As with the bell, additive synthesis was used to resynthesize a vocal timbre. However, another more sophisticated approach, very new at that time, was also used. The CHANT program, developed at IRCAM by Xavier Rodet (Rodet, Potard, and Barrière 1989), is based on the FOF synthesis algorithm, designed to re-create the formants that shape the spectrum of vocal and other sounds. CHANT can produce realistic imitations of vowel sounds, together with options for jitter and vibrato.[5]

INTERACTIVE EXERCISE 3 (2 software pages) gives the reader an opportunity to explore features of the human voice and its simulation by manipulating a synthesized imitation of vowel sounds. The manipulation is done using a more recent version of the same FOF algorithm used by Harvey. The reader may change the vowel sounds, adjust the amount of vibrato and jitter, and develop an understanding of how the synthesized voice may be manipulated.

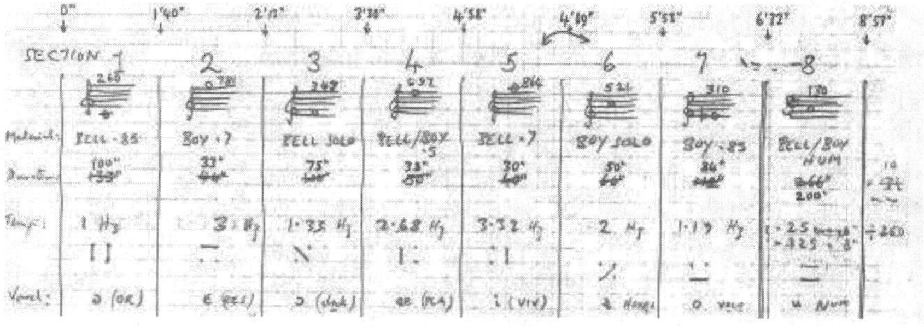

Fig. 6.2 Jonathan Harvey's sketch for the structure of *Mortuos Plango*.

6.3.2. Mortuos Plango, Vivos Voco—*Section by Section*

As already noted, each of the eight sections of the work is centered around a different frequency derived from the timbre of the bell. These frequencies are the lowest seven partials of the bell plus the secondary strike tone on F (347 Hz). The composer's sketch for the overall structure of the composition (Figure 6.2) shows the frequencies, the duration of each section, its start time, its predominant vowel sound and spatial positioning, the proportion of emphasis given to bell or boy in the section, and some additional annotations. The duration of each section is inversely proportional to its focal frequency, such that sections based on higher frequencies are shorter in duration. Tempi are also indicated in the sketch and these are also proportional to the frequency of each section. It should be noted that the sections are given here in their original order: sections 5 and 6 were later reversed as the arrows indicate.

6.3.2.1. Section 1 [SOUND LOCATION 1]   Section 1 is a highly structured and integrated exposition, forming an introduction to the sonic material for the entire work. It contains three different elements that enter successively. The first is a complex peal of bells. Second, there is vocal chanting; the chanting imitates the tolling of the bells. Finally, a synthetic bell enters based on the harmonic content of the Winchester tenor bell analyzed at a particular moment in its evolution, as described above. The overall shape of this section and its pitch structure are summarized in Figure 6.3.

Fig. 6.3 Section 1—Structural outline.

The octave of the bells is somewhat ambiguous because the second partial (an octave above the first) is stronger in amplitude than the lower octave. This tends to mean that the bell is perceived as being one octave higher than its lowest component. Therefore, Harvey and other commentators have generally described the structure in terms of this higher octave. That convention is followed throughout this analysis. When a bell pitch is identified in terms of its frequency, the frequency given is that of the second partial.

At the opening of the section, a complex texture is created by the tolling bell sounding at eleven different pitches corresponding to the first eleven partials of the bell at its original transposition (at 260 Hz) [SOUND LOCA-TION 2]. The timbre of the original bell is magnified (or multiplied, to use Boulez's term) by this transposition of the bell to the frequencies of its own partials. These transpositions are achieved by playing back the soundfile of the recorded bell at different speeds. As a result, the speed of each bell tolling is relative to its pitch; the bells on higher partials toll more quickly in direct proportion to their frequency as shown by Figure 6.4. Each tolling sequence has twenty-two strikes, with the exception of the lowest bell, which has a sequence of sixteen strikes but is still the longest in duration. Since the bells all start at approximately the same time (the start times are deliberately staggered to add greater richness to the texture), those bells articulating the higher partials finish much more quickly than those articulating lower partials. The higher bells gradually disappear from the texture, eventually leaving just the original, lowest bell (130 Hz). This unfolding of the bell texture mirrors the way in which the higher partials of a bell tend to decay more quickly, leaving the lower tones ringing.

However, this is not a simple pattern. First, the tolling itself is not regular. The period of time between successive bell strikes varies slightly. Furthermore, each tolling bell also slows down during its twenty-two-strike passage—the time interval between the final two strikes being almost twice that at the start of the passage. Since the higher bells are progressing through their patterns more quickly, they slow down sooner. In some cases, the higher bells begin to approach the speeds of lower bells that are still close to their initial speeds and have not yet begun to slow significantly. All of these factors contribute to a complex and rich texture in which there are many subtle harmonic and rhythmic relationships between the different bells. In the octophonic version, spatial distribution across all eight channels enhances this texture

| Period: | 3.2" | 1.6" | 1.4" | 1.08" | 0.8" | 0.623" | 0.61" | 0.54" | 0.48" | 0.42" | 0.39" |
| Partial #: | 1 | 2 | 3 | 4 | 5 | 6 | 7 | 8 | 9 | 10 | 11 |

Fig. 6.4 The eleven partials and their approximate periods of repetition at the opening.

significantly. Spatial separation enables the listener to hear more clearly the different components and their inter-relations.

INTERACTIVE EXERCISE 4 allows the reader to investigate the bell-tolling patterns. Synthetic bells are used in this exercise rather than the recorded bell but, just as in the work itself, bells are placed on each of the first eleven partials of the bell timbre, tolling at speeds relative to their frequency. The reader may control the staggering of the start times of different bells and experiment with the rallentando—the extent to which the tolling slows down during the passage. Bells may be muted so that different combinations of bells may be heard.

Overlapping with the tolling bells, the other main sound source for the work is introduced: the boy's voice [SOUND LOCATION 3]. The voice enters in the background at first, behind the tolling bells, chanting part of the text inscribed on the Winchester bell. (In the octophonic version of the composition, the voices are placed in the upper speakers.) Here, musical connections are being made between two apparent opposites—the bell and the boy. The chanting of the text on a single repeated pitch clearly echoes the tolling of the bell. As with the multiplication of the bell, so the voice is "multiplied" by a portion of the bell spectrum, chanting on different partials of the bell. The voice follows the same approach as the bells, although across a more limited range of pitches: the boy chants on C (260 Hz), E-flat (311 Hz), F (347 Hz), and C (523 Hz) and the speed of the chanting is proportional to the frequency. The lower C (260 Hz) chants at a rate of approximately once per second and the higher pitches are in proportion to this rate, so that the highest, the upper C, is twice per second. These rates are about twice those of bells' tolling at the same pitches at the start of the section.

The voices enter as the highest tolling bells, the highest "partials," are decaying, and the voices fill out the middle frequency range at this point. This emergence of the voices might be compared to the way the hum note emerges from a bell timbre. If so, again, the structure of this opening section is perhaps echoing the structure of the bell's timbre.

INTERACTIVE EXERCISE 5 allows the reader to play back the chanting voice at different speeds and with different offset start times. The reader can approximate this passage or try other alternatives.

With only the low fundamental C (130 Hz), C (260 Hz), and Eb (311 Hz) bells still tolling, the vocal chanting reenters as a single voice on C (260 Hz) [SOUND LOCATION 4]. Like the bell, the voice has narrowed its range, in this case sounding the focal pitch of the section. The chanting on C (260 Hz) is again at about once per second and, therefore, approximately four times faster than the low fundamental bell and three times faster than the C (260 Hz) bell, which is nearing the end of its pattern and, so, has slowed significantly at this point. Unlike most of the other sections of the work, which begin with an unambiguous statement of the key bell for that section, here the focal pitch (260 Hz) emerges during the course of the section. It is present from the start, but its significance is partially hidden by the proliferation of bell transpositions. It is at this point in the section, with the vocal chanting based around C (260 Hz), that the focal pitch becomes established. Rather like the bell timbre itself, with its ambiguity of octave placement, there is some uncertainty in this section about the priority of 130 Hz or 260 Hz. Once again the music mirrors the structure of the bell itself.

The bell tolling passage ends with just the low fundamental remaining (it never completes its full pattern and does not slow as much as the other bells do) at about 55" into the work. The final strikes of the fundamental bell overlap with the entry of a new element. It is a synthetic bell sound constructed of sine waves whose frequencies and amplitudes correspond to the analysis of the bell. However, a different overall amplitude envelope is applied to the sound. Unlike the original bell envelope, with its sudden sharp attack followed by an exponential decay, this envelope has a gradual attack, a sustained portion and then a decay. The composer's sketches (Figure 6.5) show this envelope.

The synthetic transformation of the bell introduces new principles into the work. One way to view the relationships between the sound materials in the work is on two axes: the one moving between bell and voice, and the other between "acoustic" and "synthetic" sounds. However, synthetic sounds are not so much an element in their own right but rather a means of transformation and of introducing ambiguity between bell and voice. This ambiguity is significant to Harvey's spiritual view of the nature of his music (as quoted above, see also: Harvey 1986, 178–79). Although the synthetic bell is made from spectral data relating to the Winchester bell, its envelope is closer to that of the voice. This synthetic bell is, therefore, a step toward creating a hybrid timbre.

The synthetic bell is used to play a short melodic passage that is repeated later in the section [SOUND LOCATION 5]. It comprises seven different

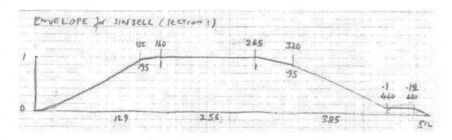

Fig. 6.5 Harvey's sketch for the synthetic bell envelope.

Fig. 6.6 Synthetic bell phrase.

pitches. An eighth pitch is added on the second occurrence of the melodic passage (this pitch appears on a different channel in the eight-channel version). The pitches correspond to the frequencies of partials of the original bell plus the secondary strike tone. In other words, the timbre of the bell is now being prolonged and articulated temporally (Figure 6.6).

In this melodic phrase, duration, and pitch are linked once again. The lengths of the different notes are inversely proportional to their frequency, so that the lower notes last much longer than the higher ones. Notes do not follow one another successively but overlap, each entering, as Harvey shows in his sketches, approximately halfway through the previous note. In other words, as the current note reaches it climax and begins to decay the next one starts to grow (Figure 6.7). So, although heard on one level as a melodic phrase, there is a sense in which each note seems to grow out of the last, and at times three or more of the notes are overlapping. (The exception here is the lowest and, therefore, by far the longest note, which only appears the second time around and begins just six seconds into the phrase, but only reaches its climax shortly after the penultimate note has climaxed.) Therefore, there is perhaps some ambiguity between whether this is a melodic phrase made

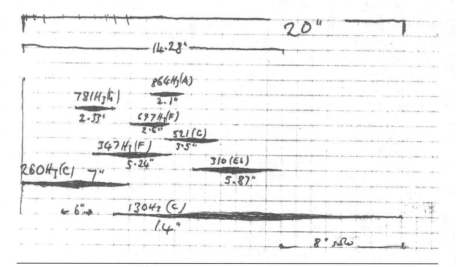

Fig. 6.7 Overlapping synthetic bell notes.

up of different independent notes or whether (since all the notes are from the same bell spectrum) the listener's ear is being guided through the bell spectrum, focusing in turn on different elements of a single unified whole. Such ambiguity would not be inappropriate; there is a sense in which the whole piece inhabits this same ambiguous territory. It is playing with the idea of unity and diversity. In terms of this particular moment in the work, it is on the cusp of where the timbre begins to unfold into a temporal structure. There is unlikely to be anything accidental about this ambiguity; it is key to the concept of the work.

This temporal unfolding of the timbre is also of larger scale significance in the work. The same sequence of eight pitches found in this phrase is also used as the pitch structure for the entire work. The pitches, in the order they appear here, are also the focal pitches for each of the eight sections of the work. In fact, that was the original plan; though, as previously mentioned, the order of the fifth and sixth sections was reversed late in the compositional process, they remain in the original order in this melodic phrase. The temporal extension of the timbre is used to organize the macroformal structure of the composition as well as to enunciate a melodic phrase.

INTERACTIVE EXERCISE 6 allows the reader to experiment with playing an approximation of the synthetic bell and the melody, and to explore the way the sound changes with different amplitude envelopes.

The end of the first occurrence of the synthetic bell melody overlaps with a further, more extended passage of vocal chanting [SOUND LOCATION 6]. It starts with chanting on a high F (697 Hz) at a fast speed followed by the C below (521 Hz) and then C (260 Hz). Then, rather in the reverse of the thinning out of the bell texture in the exposition, different voices are layered ranging from middle C (260 Hz) to the high F (697 Hz).

The vocal passage subsides as the synthetic bell reenters [SOUND LOCATION 7]. This time the final C (130 Hz) is added to the synthetic bell passage (on tracks 5 and 6 in the eight-channel version). The appearance of C (130 Hz) seems to provide some sense of closure to the sequence and to the section. However, this semblance of a cadence is immediately interrupted by a vocal phrase moving from C (520 Hz) to the F (347 Hz) below. This vocal phrase, in turn, is followed by a bell strike on G (781 Hz) that announces the start of the second section, a movement that is in some ways analogous to a sudden modulation away from the tonic in tonal music. The promise of closure is, therefore, undermined in favor of the larger-scale prolongation of the bell timbre [SOUND LOCATION 8].

6.3.2.2. Section 2 [SOUND LOCATION 9]   Section 2 comprises a main body in which vocal consonants alternate with sustained pitches and a transition to the following section. Figure 6.8 provides a summary. As in most of the

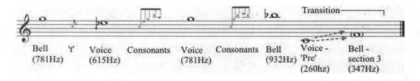

Fig. 6.8 Summary of section 2.

sections, a bell strike announces the focal pitch for the section. In this brief section the "resonance" of this bell on G (781 Hz) lasts almost throughout the entire section. The bell disappears only at the end of the transition to Section 3. Interest in this pedal tone is enlivened by the introduction of beating between two fractionally different transpositions of the sound. The composer's sketches refer to beating at 3 Hz [SOUND LOCATION 10].

Additional sustained pitches are added to the pedal tone. First, an E-flat (620 Hz) vocal in quality is immediately taken over by a more dissonant synthetic pulsing bell timbre [SOUND LOCATION 11]. The focal pitch of the section, G (781 Hz), is reinforced by another vocal entry [SOUND LOCATION 12] and is followed by a bell strike on B-flat (932 Hz). This bell has a "reversed resonance"—rather than decaying, its resonance grows both in amplitude and spectral richness [SOUND LOCATION 13]. The last pitch entry is a C (260 Hz), sung to the syllable "Pre" from "Preces" [SOUND LOCATION 14]. The significance of this final pitch in reuniting consonant and vowel is discussed below. The E-flat major harmony formed by these pitches is an inversion of the minor chord prominent in the bell timbre (C minor in the original bell transposition). It is later mirrored by a predominant minor harmony in Section 4.

Between the pitched entries are brief gestures built mainly out of vocal consonants isolated from their semantic context. Just as the bell began to be transformed in Section 1 through synthetic imitation, here the voice is destabilized as it begins a process of transformation. It is fragmented; vowels and consonants are dislocated. The final vocal F (347 Hz) of Section 1 articulated the Latin word *mort* from the text on the bell. The "t" is particularly strong, almost independent of the rest of the word [SOUND LOCATION 15]. There are three of these consonant gestures in between the entries of the sustained pitches. First, the consonant *t* appears once again, this time totally on its own without the rest of the word *mort* [SOUND LOCATION 16]. Second, a short rapid phrase of consonants on different pitches is spliced together (preceded by a brief synthetic bell sound) [SOUND LOCATION 17] and later another similar rapid phrase [SOUND LOCATION 18]. Unlike the vocal phrases in Section 1, none of these vocal fragments is intelligible semantically. Just as the bell has been pulled apart into its component partials so too has the voice been deconstructed, but temporally rather than harmonically.

Finally, as noted above, the syllable *Pre* [SOUND LOCATION 14] triggers a brief but complex transformation into the third section (see below). "*Pre*" might be seen as bringing together the play with consonants and the sustained pitches (it has the pitch C [260 Hz]) combining the two and reuniting consonant and vowel.

The transition between sections 2 and 3 has been analyzed in detail by Hans Tutschku in his DEA thesis. His analysis is supplemented here by frequency data from the composer's sketches for the piece. There are three stages to the transformation. First, there is the original vocal sound *Pre* [SOUND LOCATION 14]. This vocal sound cross-fades with sine waves on the most significant frequencies of the vocal sound. Next, these sine waves glissando toward the frequencies of selected partials of the bell on C (260 Hz), contracting in overall frequency range [SOUND LOCATION 19]. Finally, (overlapping with these glissandi) there is another, expanding set of glissandi with vibrato, leading into the bell strike for Section 3 [SOUND LOCATION 20]. Figure 6.9 uses a sonogram to show this transformation in outline, and Figure 6.10 shows its pitch structure in more detail, using semibreves to represent pivot notes.

The move from the recorded "Pre" to a synthesized imitation enables the sound to be transformed. The synthesized sine waves can glissando independently, each by different amounts, toward the partials of the bell. This

Fig. 6.9 Sonogram of transition between sections 2 and 3.

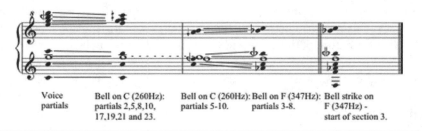

Fig. 6.10 Pitch structure of transition between sections 2 and 3.

would not have been easily possible with the technology available at the time by directly processing the recorded sound. The move from "real" voice to synthesized voice to bell is seamless. A superficially more abrupt shift follows, as the next glissando starts from a narrower range of frequencies. They are, however, still the frequencies of selected partials of the bell on C (260 Hz), and several frequencies remain in common—in particular G (781 Hz), the focal pitch of this section. In this final glissando, the sine waves of the C (260 Hz) bell move toward selected partials of a bell on F (347 Hz). F (697 Hz) is, however, common to both spectra and is sustained, serving as a pivot frequency. The partials from the F bell prepare for the start of Section 3 a few moments later, when the focal pitch of this new section is announced by a bell strike on F (347 Hz). The "modulation" in focal pitches from G (Section 2) to F (Section 3) is realized, on one level, through a movement from bells on G to C to F. Yet, these bell spectra are also linked by glissandi and shared pivot frequencies, first G (781 Hz) and then F (697 Hz). Throughout the work glissandi and pivot notes are used to move between and link different spectral regions. Therefore, spectral modulation performs a role somewhat similar to modulation between keys in tonal music.(Although Harvey sees significant differences between his approach to harmonic structure and traditional bass-oriented tonality, there are certain analogies.)

In his sketches Harvey notes alongside the data for the final set of glissandi, "Boy on each of these glissandi pitches." Whereas the first set of glissandi was based on sine tones, here each glissando is not a single frequency but a synthesized vowel sound. Therefore, each component glissando consists of a fundamental with numerous partials, all sliding in parallel motion. The introduction of the partials extends the overall spectrum and prepares the way for the broader spectrum of the bell that opens Section 3.

The sonogram in Figure 6.9 shows that each partial in the final vocal glissandi has vibrato (the lines waver). As noted earlier, vibrato is one of the features that distinguish the voice from the bell, making it more "human" and less mechanical. In this passage there is mixture of vibrato and nonvibrato. The original recorded "*Pre*" has vibrato but the synthesized voice that replaces it, and the glissandi that grow out of it do not. However, the second set of glissandi does have vibrato, but the bell that announces Section 3 is without vibrato. This transitional passage demonstrates a subtle interplay between the flexible nature of the voice and the rigid pitch of the bell.

INTERACTIVE EXERCISE 7 allows the reader to examine the pitch structure of this transitional passage aurally by playing each of the stages of the transformation separately and then combining them. This structural sketch may then be compared with the original.

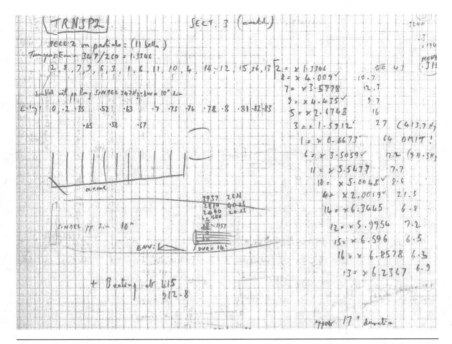

Fig. 6.11 The composer's sketch for the rapid arpeggio.

6.3.2.3. Section 3 [SOUND LOCATION 21]   Glissandi, introduced for the first time in the transition from Section 2, become the key feature of Section 3. The section is punctuated by bell gestures that precede each of three glissando passages. The bell strike announcing the focal pitch of this section, F (347 Hz), leads directly into the first glissandi [SOUND LOCATION 22]. The second bell gesture is a rapid arpeggio of bells [SOUND LOCATION 23]. Figure 6.11 shows the composer's sketches for this gesture, which, in the eight-channel version, is spilt between two channels. The sixteen bells, the original recording transposed onto each of the first sixteen partials of the bell at 347 Hz, are arpeggiated. Harvey's annotation of his sketch indicates that he eventually decided to omit the lowest of these.

INTERACTIVE EXERCISE 8 allows the reader to play a synthesized approximation of the sixteen bells in any order and at different speeds in order to explore the composition and the potential of this gesture.

The final bell gesture, introducing the final glissando, comprises just two notes: a flat C (251 Hz) and an E (662 Hz). In the sketches different frequencies are given, and the bells are described as the first and sixth partials of the bell timbre transposed to 337.7 Hz, the transposition that provided the termini for the end of the glissandi immediately preceding this gesture (see below). However, in practice, a different transposition seems to have been used, resulting in the first and sixth partials of a bell on 251 Hz—a flattened C [SOUND LOCATION 24].

The initial bell of the section leads directly into the first set of glissandi. There are eight successive compound glissandi in this set, all linked by a common pivot frequency (F 347 Hz), which is sustained and does not change pitch. It is no coincidence that this pivot frequency is that of the focal pitch of the section. In fact, each compound glissando comprises seven simultaneous sine wave glissandi, each sine wave moving independently (they glissando by different amounts and sometimes in different directions). The last glissando is the only exception; it comprises just six sine waves. The pitches that form the termini for these glissandi are drawn from the partials of the bell spectrum in different transpositions. Harvey's sketches for this section contain a chart (Figure 6.12) showing fifteen different transpositions of the bell spectrum

Fig. 6.12 Bell transpositions with common pivot frequency.

(not all are used). In all of these transpositions, F (347 Hz) features in the spectrum, in each case as a different partial, from partial 3 to 17: it acts as a pivot. Drawing on the original analysis data for the bell, Harvey's sketch also lists the correct amplitude (in dB) for the pivot F, appropriate to the partial number it occupies in each transposition (this appears just below the circled partial number). Therefore, the glissandi are not simply between frequencies but also between amplitudes [SOUND LOCATION 25].

Each compound glissando commences with frequencies of partials from one transposition and ends with those from another. Once a transposition has been selected, a group of its partials is chosen as termini for the glissandi. Different groups of partials are chosen as termini in each case (sometimes the same partial acts as the start or end of more than one glissando). This results in a more complex and far richer aural experience than if the same set of partials were chosen from each transposition (that would have resulted in parallel glissandi). For example, a group of partials from higher up the spectrum is likely to be narrower in overall range compared with one taken from lower in the spectrum. Figure 6.13 shows the process as annotated by Harvey in his sketches using partial numbers (horizontal lines link the partials acting as pivot, always 347 Hz, from which the transpositions can be derived). The first part of Figure 6.14 shows the same process outlined in terms of musical notation (upper and lower glissandi, and the pivot notes—shown as a semibreve).

Just three compound glissandi comprise the second set [SOUND LOCA-TION 26]. These glissandi follow the same basic principles just described, but this time the pivot frequency changes for each compound glissando. The pivot for the first compound glissando is F (347 Hz), for the second E-flat (620

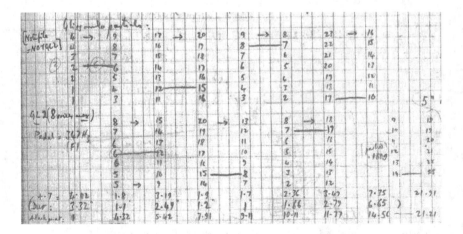

Fig. 6.13 Glissandi sketched by the composer.

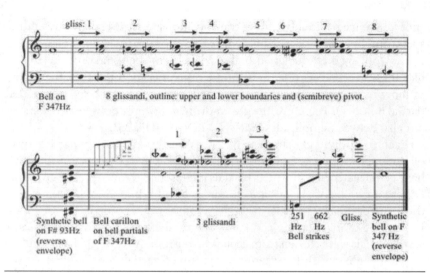

Fig. 6.14 Summary of section 3.

Hz), and for the third A (887 Hz). Each new pivot arises from the spectrum of the previous glissando, providing continuity. Nonetheless, the harmony of the section is becoming more mobile, as if to prepare for the modulation to a new focal pitch for the next section.

The third and final glissando passage comprises just a single compound glissando [SOUND LOCATION 27]. The pivot frequency is F (697 Hz), which, significantly, is also the focal pitch for the following section, Section 4. Whereas the first set of glissandi reinforced the focal frequency of Section 3 (F 347 Hz), the second and third glissando passages make the transition towards the new focal frequency (F 697 Hz), one octave above the focal pitch of Section 3. Figure 6.14 shows all the glissandi and the harmonic process for the whole section.

INTERACTIVE EXERCISE 9 (2 software pages) allows the reader to experiment with these glissandi. The reader may play each glissando separately or in sequence and modify the data to explore alternatives.

Section 3 is more "ethereal" than the previous sections; it is less grounded in the recorded sounds. The punctuating bells continue to provide a link with the physical world but for the most part the glissandi float free from realistic associations. Yet, these glissandi seem to grow naturally out of the more earthly material that precedes them because of the timbral relationships. The focal pitch F is strengthened by its presence in different contexts as the fundamental and in various other positions in the spectrum. Though, unlike a traditional tonic, it is not rooted to the bass of the texture.

6.3.2.4. Section 4 [SOUND LOCATION 28]   Section 4 begins with the new focal pitch, articulated by a bell on F (697 Hz) and elaborated by a vocal decoration around this F (a mordent with an upper auxiliary). The section is perhaps the most static in the work and consequently has a peaceful, meditative, almost luminous quality. Everything is based on a chord of B-flat minor. The pitches of a minor chord feature quite prominently amongst the partials of the bell. For example, partials 2, 3, 4, 5, and 8 form a C minor chord in the original transposition of the bell (see Figure 6.1). In this section these partials are transposed so that partial 4 becomes the F (697 Hz) focal pitch of the section and the chord a Bb minor chord. Long sustained sine waves on the pitches of this chord combine with sung vowels on different notes of the chord, which, in turn, fade gently in and out. There is a mixture of pure sine tones and the voice (with vibrato and harmonics) blending on the same pitches. It is as if the same object, the B-flat minor chord, is being viewed from different angles with an intense, loving contemplation. Further subtle variation in the timbre is provided by high bell partials that fade in and out. The sketches indicate that this variation was achieved by retroscanning a recording of the bell timbre. Since the higher partials of the bell are stronger toward the beginning of the sound, retroscanning results in these partials fading in and out as the file is scanned backwards and forwards.

INTERACTIVE EXERCISE 10 gives the reader the opportunity to experiment with retroscanning, adjusting the rate of oscillation, and the range of scanning.

Again, glissandi play a significant role in this section, here providing a symmetrical frame for the tranquil central portion of the section. The opening bell triggers a rapid glissando, which is then mirrored at the end of the section when, following an artificial bell strike, the glissando is reversed [SOUND LOCATION 29 and SOUND LOCATION 30]. The symmetry is clear: it is as if the listener enters an area of tranquility at the start of the section and leaves by the same route at the end. The harmonic structure reinforces this interpretation. The pivot frequency (F 697 Hz) of the opening glissando moves from partial 2 at the start of the glissando to partial 4 at the end. This same frequency then remains as partial 4 for the B-flat minor body of the section until the second glissando reverses the movement from F 697 Hz as partial 4 to partial 2. Figure 6.15 shows these glissandi and the pitches of the main body of the section. A distant, almost imperceptible glissando underlies the whole section transforming slowly over about 40″.

INTERACTIVE EXERCISE 11 allows the reader to play each of the glissandi separately and compare this structural sketch with the original.

6.3.2.5. Section 5[6] [SOUND LOCATION 31]   As noted earlier, this section and Section 6 were originally planned to be in the reverse order. The change

Decorated   Glissandi   Sustained   Reverse glissandi
focal pitch   pitches
F(697Hz)

Fig. 6.15 Summary of section 4.

was only made quite late in the compositional process for empirical reasons. The original numbering is often found in the sketches and some commentaries on the work confuse the ordering of these sections.

Section 5 starts with a hybrid voice/bell sound. Synthesized voices (with vibrato) are placed on the frequencies of significant partials of the bell in its transposition to the focal pitch of this section (C 521 Hz). The bell-like quality of the voices is further enhanced by giving them a sudden attack. A few high sine waves with abrupt attacks further add to the bell-like qualities. The hybrid nature of this initial sound underscores the increasing links between bell and voice as the work progresses [SOUND LOCATION 32].

There are two main features of this section: glissandi and vocal phrases. A sequence of four glissandi lasts throughout the whole section and, as in Section 3, glissandi underpin the structure of the entire section. The basic principles underlying these glissandi are the same as before, but this time the component glissandi are formed not from sine waves but instead from vocal sounds, using synthesized vowels (created with the CHANT program). So, instead of a number of single frequencies sliding in different directions, there are now several voices—each with overtones—making up the compound glissandi. The voice taking on the role of the sine wave partials of the bell is another example of the gap between bell and voice being bridged. Elsewhere in his sketches, Harvey refers to such placing of boys' voices on each partial of a bell as creating a "bell of boys." These vocal glissandi are spread across different channels of the eight-track tape adding spatial richness to the timbral transformations.

The four compound glissandi follow a gradual movement up into the higher partials of the bell timbre. For example, the first glissando uses partials 1 to 6 and the last uses partials 12 to 18. However, as can be seen in Figure 6.16, the pitch of the passage itself does not get higher. There is a constant pivot of C (512 Hz); the focal pitch of the section and the higher bell partials are transposed relative to this pivot. This may be compared with the transposition around the F (347 Hz) pivot in Section 3. Since the pivot remains constant, a contraction of range results (the higher partials being closer together in

Fig. 6.16 Section 5 glissandi (outline).

frequency). It is as if the sound is being concentrated and squeezed into the area around the pivot. Since this pitch is also the pitch around which the vocal phrases are focused (see below), this could be interpreted as the music focusing in on the voice and its call to prayer. As vocal sounds are being employed for the glissandi, there are, of course, other overtones sounding above the pitches shown.

INTERACTIVE EXERCISE 12 offers the reader a chance to re-create these glissandi and hear their structure more clearly, with their individual elements using sine waves rather than synthesized vocal timbres.

The other main feature of this section is the singing of the phrase "ad Preces"—"to prayer" [SOUND LOCATION 33]. This phrase stands out in the middle of the section, emerging from the vocal glissandi. Some have suggested it is the pivotal moment in the work, when the call to prayer is reached. The phrase focuses on C (512 Hz) as a tonal center (Figure 6.17). This pitch is both the centre of this section and, at a lower octave, of the whole work. The higher octave plus the context of the slowly gliding pitches of the glissandi give a sense of the sound floating, rather than the more traditional sense of being grounded by a tonic. Harvey has frequently talked about trying to create a music that is free from the tyranny of the bass line and traditional concepts of tonic (see Harvey, 1984).

6.3.2.6. Section 6 [SOUND LOCATION 34]   The focal pitch for this section, A (864 Hz), is the highest in the piece. Following the inverse relationship of pitch to duration, described previously, Section 6 is the shortest section. The focal pitch is followed immediately by a short glissando, but glissandi do not play the prominent role in this section that they did in the preceding sections. The A (864 Hz) focal pitch and the octave below (432 Hz) are sustained and varied by the retroscanning of vocal and bell sounds.

Over the retroscanning, eight high bell-like chords are played. Each is made from a selection of partials from the same bell transposition. Therefore,

Fig. 6.17 Section 5—vocal phrases.

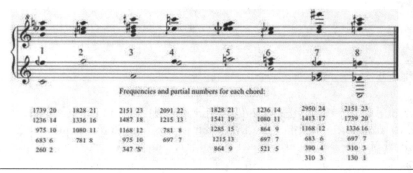

Fig. 6.18 Section 6—eight chords.

there is a sense in which these are not independent chords at all, but different fragments of the same spectrum. Figure 6.18 shows the chords in the original transposition (based on a bell at C 260Hz) so that the partials may be compared with the partials in Figure 6.1. Note that the lowest partials from each of the chords taken together form the same melodic pattern as found in Section 1 (Figure 6.6), which is also the basis of the entire structure. The individual partials appear on different tracks in the eight-channel version; generally they are sine waves with bell-like attacks. The whole sequence occurs not at 260 Hz but transposed to the focal pitch of the section, A (864 HZ). The sequence has a clear rhythmic articulation; yet, with its very high pitch, it is perceived as a decoration of the sustained tonic.

INTERACTIVE EXERCISE 13 gives the reader the opportunity to play this chord sequence as a whole or each chord individually in different transpositions.

A vocal timbre then emerges more clearly on the lower octave of the A pedal note (432 Hz) and becomes a repeated note, stuttering in stereo across different channels (there are two overlapping repeated-note patterns, each duplicated on two channels in the eight-track version (1 + 8, 3 + 6) [SOUND LOCATION 35]. This repetition leads into what Harvey calls in his sketches a "coloratura" passage. His sketches for this passage include a list of the available material including a range of recorded vowels and consonants, synthesized vowels on different pitches ranging upwards from middle C for two and a half octaves, as well as a small number of unpitched consonants. The rapid succession of sounds spreads across all eight channels. It is the combination that creates the virtuosic complexity, and the spatial movement increases the excitement as the sound darts around. During the passage there is a move from brief but recognizably vocal sounds to sounds with an artificial, electronic quality (they are in fact fragments of bell sounds) [SOUND LOCATION 36]. Tonally, the focal pitch evaporates, making way for a new focus.

6.3.2.7. Section 7 [SOUND LOCATION 37]   Section 7 begins with a gesture that grows out of a bell strike on the new focal pitch, Eb (310 Hz). The bell starts to decay but the reading of the soundfile does not progress smoothly to the end. Rather it retroscans backwards and forwards through the file while maintaining the same speed—the pitch, therefore, remaining unchanged—so that the overall amplitude and the upper partials recede and then reemerge. This retroscanning is heard, at first, as a relatively minor disturbance of the bell's decay. Then, briefly, it seems to be decaying normally, before returning toward the beginning of the bell sound. Finally, the forward and backward oscillations become more rapid toward the end of the gesture, together with rapid panning between channels. The retroscanning creates a gesture that draws attention to the upper bell partials, which also feature increasingly in other aspects of the final two sections [SOUND LOCATION 38].

An abrupt vocal entrance signals the beginning of the main body of Section 7 [SOUND LOCATION 39]. It is underpinned by another sound, which again involves retroscanning a sound file. In this case the sound file used is not a simple recording of the bell or voice but rather a recording of a transformation from bell to voice. The original process involved starting with the recording of the real bell, cross-fading imperceptibly into an equivalent synthesized bell sound and then manipulating the partials to transform the sound into that of a voice. This is done, as previously, by sliding the partials of the bell toward those of the voice in glissandi. Finally, there is a cross-fade from this synthesized voice into a recorded voice. The sound file resulting from this transformation process is subjected to retroscanning, resulting in a continual movement backwards and forwards between the timbres of bell and voice. In fact, there is a subtle spatial feature here too. Some channels have the pattern (over about 3") bell-voice-bell followed by a brief silence before it is repeated. Others have a similar pattern in reverse: voice-bell-voice-silence. Overall, the patterns dovetail creating a continuous transformation, but one in which there is movement backwards and forwards between channels as well as between bell and voice. Figure 6.19 shows this by superposing sonograms of a short passage from channels 2 and 4 of the eight-channel version. Once again, such small details, perhaps not even perceived consciously, are significant factors in making the experience of the work rich and rewarding even after many hearings. Perhaps the pattern also mirrors the morphology of bells swinging backwards and forwards—the sounds of bell and voice each approaching and then receding. This pattern continues, occasionally drifting away into the background, throughout the remainder of the section. Its regularity brings back a feature not heard since the opening: that of regular rhythmic repetition. The regularity and the ostinato-like effect of this process create the impression of an approaching cadence, the music becoming more

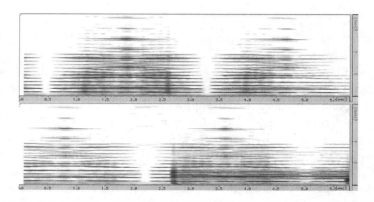

Fig. 6.19 Bell–voice oscillation—Channels 2 and 4 of the eight-channel version.

cyclical, drawing ideas together. These characteristics foreshadow aspects of the final section.

Over the bell–voice oscillation, the high "chords" (made from bell partials) used in the previous section return. This time, the eight chords are repeated four times with varied transpositions. The initial transposition is to the tonic of this section. There are four additional transpositions. (There are more transpositions than repetitions of the chord sequence because changes in transposition do not correspond to the start of the sequence; new transpositions occur midsequence.) These transpositions are to the frequencies of partials of the tonic bell of the section, the last being a very high transposition. Some of the chords are mixed with vocal sounds having some partials in common. The sequence of chords is also accompanied by a sequence of durations for each of these chords that also repeats, but not in synchrony with the chord pattern, creating an isomorphic structure. Although the overall interlocking pattern of chords, transpositions, and durations is complex, it is nonetheless a process that has a certain regularity, reinforcing the sense of relative stasis and "settling down" that is distinctive for this section. Figure 6.20 summarizes these patterns; the transpositions are shown as frequency ratios—a method employed by Harvey throughout his sketches. Just as a pedal note in tonal music often implies a dominant harmony leading to a tonic, so this section prepares for the final section, which is built on the fundamental frequency of the bell in its original transposition.

INTERACTIVE EXERCISE 14 allows the reader to play the bell's chords again, to hear the transpositions, and to experiment with these.

The transition into the final section is triggered by a vocal chord cutting across the processes of the section, followed by a reversed bell sound [SOUND LOCATION 40]. The vocal chord is built on the spectrum of the

Chord #:	1	2	3	4	5	6	7	8
Duration:	a	b	c	d	e	f	g	h
Transp:	310/260	- - - -	- - - -	- - - -	- - - - -	- - - - -	- - - -|	155/260

2	3	4	5	6	7	8	1
a	b	c	d	e	g	a	b
- - - - -	- - - -	- - - -|	370/260	- - - -	- - - -	- - - -	- - - -|

2	3	4	5	6	7	8	1
c	d	e	f	a	b	c	d
621/260	- - - -	- - - |	414/260	- - - -	- - - -	- - -|	1794/260

2	3	4	5	6
e	a	b	c	g
- - - - - - -	- - - -|	2346/260	- - - - - - -	- - - - - - -|

Durations: a = 2.5", b = .55", c = 1.85", d = .95", e = .3", f = 1.25", g = 1.9", h = 5.0"

Figure 6.20 Section 7—Chords, durations, and transpositions.

bell transposed to the E-flat focal pitch of this section and features an E-flat minor chord strongly. The amplitudes of the bell partials are inverted so that the upper harmonics are louder than the lower ones. It provides a dramatic upbeat to the entry of the tonic bell of the final section, which is also the tonic of the whole work.

INTERACTIVE EXERCISE 15 provides the reader with the opportunity to experiment with transforming a synthesized version of the bell. The reader can invert the normal amplitudes and also reverse the direction of the amplitude envelope of the bell.

6.3.2.8. Section 8 [SOUND LOCATION 41]　The final section is characterized by the continual tolling of the deep tonic bell on C (130 Hz). The opening of the section is marked by a strong vocal chord. The pitches of this chord are those of partials 5 to 11 from the low C (130 Hz) bell. When the vocal notes decay, their pitches can be heard echoed in the timbre of the tolling bell. The envelopes of the notes also reflect the bell timbre—the lower notes lasting longer. At first this chord repeats once every five bell strikes. Later, both the bell and the voices become slightly irregular, the bell's period lengthening and the voices' shortening result in a more complex interplay. This variation is another example of irregularity within a pattern adding to the richness of the music. A third element is the continuing repetition of the bell–voice oscillation from Section 7, which overlaps into the first 30" of this section. The oscillation continues, as in the previous section, repeating about every 3.2", slightly longer than the initial period of the deep bell (about 3.1"). The

Fig. 6.21 Schematic outline of section 8.

slight difference in the periods of these two patterns causes phasing. Subtle and varied patterns are created by the phasing relationships between the tolling bell, the repeated vocal chords, and the bell–voice oscillation. Figure 6.21 summarizes the structure of the section schematically.

Other details contribute to the richness of the sound. For example, some of the vocal chords are followed by distant vocal echoes. Furthermore, on their fourth, sixth, and eighth occurrences the vocal chords move to the upper speakers. On the last of these occasions a second chord echoes the original shortly after it [SOUND LOCATION 42]. The speeds of tolling are here the slowest in the piece (the vocal chords have a period of c. 15") reflecting the fact that the pitches are the lowest in the work.

Two factors help draw the composition to a close. First, from about 85" to 112" into the section, a long artificial bell sound is turned "inside out" [SOUND LOCATION 43]. The lower partials decay quickly and the upper partials continue to resonate, shifting the balance toward the high frequencies, which crescendo. This synthesized bell resembles a greatly slowed down version of the reversed-inverted bell at the end of the previous section. It is as if the solid core of the bell is receding into the distance, leaving only its aura. As this disappears, a second transformation becomes evident; aurally it almost seems as if the first has triggered the second. The tolling bell, which is now all that remains of the texture, is transformed—its envelope losing its sudden attack. The attack is replaced by a gentler envelope, gradually rising and falling in volume. The overall volume level then diminishes, reducing gradually to nothing [SOUND LOCATION 44].

6.3.3. The Large-Scale Structure of Mortuos Plango, Vivos Voco

Having studied the background to the work, its techniques, and the way in which each section of the work is shaped, it is now possible to make some observations on the larger scale structure. From what has gone before it will be clear that two aspects of the work—pitch and timbre—play particularly significant roles. That these are interrelated and that there is a certain ambiguity and artificiality about where the dividing line might be drawn, relate to Harvey's own comments concerning ambiguity quoted above (1999, 39–40). As has already become clear, the bell partials determine the pitch structure of the work. Harvey has compared this structure to the hierarchical structures in Schenkerian theory ("Mirror" 182). On one level, the whole composition is a prolongation of the original bell on C (260 Hz) by means of a "composing-out" (*Auskomponierung*) of its overtone structure. Each section elaborates one of the partials of this bell, that partial becoming a secondary tonic. This secondary tonic is then elaborated by further derivations, again based on exactly the same bell structure. Schenker's analytical approach was based on the idea of tonal movements as a goal-directed composing out, or horizontalization, of the tonic triad. In this piece there is also a movement through the bell partials used as local tonics or focal pitches for each section, toward the resolution on the lowest of these, C (130 Hz). However, Harvey's music is not as teleological as most tonal music, and there is a sense in which the whole work is an articulation within stasis—everything is enveloped by the bell timbre from beginning to end. It is from the bell timbre (at 260 Hz), expanded by multiplication onto its own partials, that the work emerges, and it is to a bell on the lowest partial of this 260 Hz bell (i.e., 130 Hz) that it returns (bell octave ambiguity is discussed above). Indeed, at the very end it is only the lowest partial of this 130 Hz bell that remains (i.e., 65 Hz), perhaps hinting at a recursive process in which the music continues its descent infinitely to a fundamental beyond human hearing and comprehension. It has already been suggested that the central sections, each of which contemplates a different aspect of the bell timbre, might, at least theoretically, be interchangeable as in Stockhausen's *Moment Form*. (Local transitions between sections preclude this in practice, although these have already been disrupted by the exchange of Sections 5 and 6.) The sections of this work might be considered not so much as progressing inexorably through time toward a final resolution, but rather as different perspectives on an object that is always present. The issue of whether this work is teleological or not is

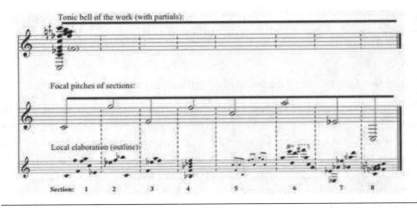

Fig. 6.22 Overall structure.

perhaps not a question of either–or; there is again an element of ambiguity that is of spiritual significance.

Figure 6.22 summarizes the pitch structure of the work and demonstrates its hierarchical nature. The upper stave shows the original bell timbre, the presence of which is felt throughout the whole work. The next stave shows the unfolding of this timbre to provide the focal pitches of successive sections. The final stave summarizes some of the more important pitch elaborations within each section—again these are derived in various ways from the original timbre, as previously described.

If the pitch structure provides the latent unity for the work, the timbral variations during the course of the work are its articulation in time. The starting point in terms of timbre is an opposition: between the bell and the voice. The former is inharmonic, fixed, decaying, without vibrato, and mechanical. The latter is harmonic, variable, can be sustained, always has jitter, may have vibrato, is human, and breathes. At the timbral level the work is about the unification of these opposites, and as such it is, by Harvey's definition quoted earlier, a spiritual work. These two elements are distinct from the beginning but immediately the barriers begin to erode. The boy imitates the frequencies and the tolling of the bell. The bell's envelope becomes gentler and sustained. Glissandi transform one timbre into the other, and bells are created out of choirs of boys. In the central sections, the sounds sometimes lose their grounding in "reality" and, so, the distinction between them is lost; they are unified by something that is higher, often literally—in terms of frequency. In the final section, the "bell of boys" is stated most explicitly and this choir of boys, together with the original bell itself and the pulsing oscillation between boy and bell, come together in a subtly varying tolling pattern. Finally the higher partials ascend and disappear, leaving just the deep hum tone resonating, the unifying foundation. The movement is complete.

The text inscribed on the bell is not merely incidental to the work; its meaning is woven into the fabric of the piece. Traditionally the three functions of the bell were to lament the dead ("mortuos"), to call the living to prayer ("vivos") and to keep the "fleeting hours" ("*horas*"—appropriately the great tenor bell at Winchester is also the bell used by the clock to strike the hours). On one level, the fixed, inert bell represents death and the lament of the dead. The living, breathing voice of the boy represents life, and his chanting is also a call to the living. Just as the bell strikes the hours at Winchester, so here it strikes the passing of the sections of the work. So all the three main functions of the bell are present in the work. Yet, again, the music dissolves boundaries—between the living and the dead, between finite time and eternity.

The final INTERACTIVE EXERCISE—PARADIGMATIC ANALYSIS— presents the whole work as a large-scale paradigmatic analysis. Buttons on the screen allow the reader to play different extracts from the work. Selecting these as in the order you would read a book (i.e., from left to right across the page, and from top to bottom) will present the whole piece in its original form. The extracts are positioned in columns according to their motivic/timbral similarity. (As will be evident from the complexity of earlier discussions this is inevitably oversimplified in some respects and does not take into account the ambiguity and the multidimensional relationships between many of the sounds.) So by playing extracts in the same column from top to bottom the reader can compare similar gestures/timbres and hear how they evolve over the course of the work.

6.4. Conclusions

Mortuos Plango, Vivos Voco combines complex computer music techniques and highly sophisticated musical design with a profound concern for the spiritual. It has survived the test of time and has probably been more widely appreciated by audiences, including those from more traditional musical backgrounds, than most other electroacoustic works. Despite its technical complexity, it does not sound mechanical and its poetic qualities are clearly evident. Its use of recognizable sources (bell and voice) may contribute to the accessibility of this work. The subtle blend of regular pattern and irregular variation, the gentle play with ambiguity, and the sophisticated interplay of unity and diversity are also all important aspects of the composition.

In a work as rich and complex as this, there can never be any final conclusions; a work of art is not a riddle to be solved. Perhaps, like a Buddhist koan, it is the unanswerable questions the piece asks rather than any solutions that are important: it points to the infinite. It is hoped that this analysis, and the interactive exercises, will have helped in the exploration of this work, revealed more dimensions to the questions it poses, and so will have enriched further listening to *Mortuos Plango, Vivos Voco*.

References

Alcorn, P. "Towards the Spiritual—The Electroacoustic Music of Jonathan Harvey." *Contact* 34 (1989) : 11–16.

———."Perspectives of Electroacoustic Music: A Critical Study of the Electroacoustic Music of Jonathan Harvey, Denis Smalley, and Trevor Wishart." Diss. University of Durham, 1992.

Anderson, J. "Spectral Music." In *The New Grove Dictionary of Music and Musicians*, edited by S. Sadie, vol. 24, 166–67. London: Macmillan Press, 2001.

Bent, I., and A. Pople. "Analysis." In *The New Grove Dictionary of Music and Musicians,* edited by S. Sadie, vol.1, 526–89. London: Macmillan Press, 2001.

Bonnet, A.. "Écriture et Perception: à propos de Messagesquisse de Pierre Boulez." *InHarmoniques* 3. Paris, IRCAM, 1988.

Bossis, B. *Mortuos Plango, Vivos Voco*. Paris: IRCAM Médiathèque (Multimedia Library), 2000. Available online: <http://www.ircam.fr>

———. "*Mortuos Plango, Vivos Voco* de Jonathan Harvey ou le miroir de la spiritualité." *Musurgia* 11, 1-2 (2004): 199–144. double issue (2004).

Boulez, P. *Boulez on Music Today*. London: Faber & Faber, 1971.

Bowder, J., M. Clarke, and J. Saunders. CALMA, 2000. Available online: <http://www.hud.ac.uk/mh/music/calma/calma.html>

Clarke, M. "FOF and FOG Synthesis in Csound." *The Csound Book*. Edited by R. Boulanger. Cambridge, MA: MIT Press, 2000, 293–306.

Clarke, M., and X. Rodet. "Real-time FOF and FOG Synthesis in MSP and Its Integration with PSOLA." *Proceedings of the International Computer Music Conference*. San Francisco, ICMA (2003): 287–90.

Dirks, P. L. "An Analysis of Jonathan Harvey's *Mortuos Plango, Vivos Voco*." 1998. Available online: <http://musique.freeservers.com/jharvey.html>

Georgaki, A. "À la recherche de la voix Protée: penser la voix de synthèse aujourd'hui." *Proceedings of the Journées d'Informatique Musicale*. Paris: Cemamu (1999): 97–108.

———. *Mortuos Plango-Vivos Voco (1980) de Jonathan Harvey: La Voix de Synthèse Comme Metaphore Du Metaphysique*. Barcelona: Musica e filosofia, forthcoming.

Griffiths, P. *Boulez*. Oxford Studies of Composers, vol. 16. London: Oxford University Press, 1978.

———. "Three works by Jonathan Harvey: The electronic mirror." *Contemporary Music Review* 1, no. 1(1984): 87–110.

Harvey, J. *The Music of Stockhausen*. London: Faber & Faber, 1975.

———. "Reflection after Composition." *Contemporary Music Review* 1, no.1 (1984): 83–86.

———. "The Mirror of Ambiguity." In *The Language of Electroacoustic Music*. Edited by Simon Emmerson, 175–190. Basingstoke, UK: Macmillan Press, 1986.

———. "*Mortuos Plango, Vivos Voco*: A Realization at IRCAM." *Computer Music Journal* (1981). Rpt. in *The Music Machine*. Edited by Curtis Roads, 91–94. Cambridge, MA: MIT Press, 1989.

———. *In Quest of Spirit*. Berkeley: University of California Press, 1999.

Keller, H. "Functional Analysis of Mozart's G minor Quintet." *Music Analysis* 4 (1985):73.

Nattiez, J-J. *Music and Discourse: Towards a Semiology of Music*. Princeton, NJ: Princeton University Press, 1990.

Ramstrum, M. *From Kafka to K...: A Multimedia Exploration of Manoury's Opera K....* Paris: IRCAM/Opera National de Paris, 2004.

Rodet, X., Y. Potard, and J.-B. Barrière (1989). "The CHANT Project: From the Synthesis of the Singing Voice to Synthesis in General." *Computer Music Journal*. Rpt. in *The Music Machine*, edited by Curtis Roads, 449–66. Cambridge, MA: MIT Press, 1984.

Tutschku, H. "L'application des paramètres compositionnels au traitement sonore." DEA Thesis. Université Paris-Sorbonne, 1999. Available online: <http://www.tutschku.com>

Vandenheede, J. "Jonathan Harvey's Ritual Melodies." *Interface* 21(1992):149–83.

Wishart, T. *On Sonic Art*. York: Imagineering Press, 1985.

DVD Reference

Index	File Name	Description	Media Type
1	HarveyOSX software	Macintosh OS X application and associated files for Interactive Analysis of "Mortuos Plango, Vivos Voco" by Jonathan Harvey.	Harvey_Analysis Max/MSP runtime application, MaxMSP Runtime 4.5, and soundfiles ("2. Horas avolantes (chant)" and "3. Bell tolling")

Notes

1. The author expresses his gratitude to Jonathan Harvey for being so generous with his time in advising on this work and in making his sketches and source sounds available. Also, thanks to Bruno Bossis in Paris and the author's colleagues at the University of Huddersfield, especially Steven Jan for his helpful discussions about the research.
2. The software can be found on the DVD accompanying this book and is intended to be used while reading this chapter. Updates to the software may be found at http://www.umich.edu/~msimoni/analytical-methods/
3. Mortuos Plango, Vivos Voco has appeared on several CDs including: Erato ECD88261 (1985), Erato 2292-45409-2, Sargasso SCD 28029 (1999), Unknown Public UPCD01, and Wergo WER2025-2 (1990).
4. Currently, Csound is perhaps the most widely used program of a similar nature. Though greatly enhanced since 1980, it is derived from the same family of programs as Music V.
5. For more recent developments related to CHANT and FOF synthesis see (Clarke 2000) and (Clarke and Rodet 2003).
6. Readers who use the eight-channel version of the work in conjunction with the data in this chapter should beware of possible minor discrepancies in frequency and timing between versions of the work. Hans Tutschku notes a difference throughout the work (twenty-five cents in pitch, two seconds in total duration). This discrepancy may be due to the fact that the computer files were originally assembled on analogue (sixteen track) machines for mixing and, at some point, a machine may have been running at a fractionally incorrect speed. The author's experience in comparing frequency data between the Wergo CD and a digital eight-channel tape (from IRCAM via the publishers Faber Music) is that they are largely identical apart from Sections 5 and 6 (as it happens the two sections that were reversed), which are very fractionally but perceptibly flat. The CD seems to correspond to the frequencies that would be expected.

7
Philippe Manoury's *Jupiter*[1]

ANDREW MAY

7.1. Introduction

Philippe Manoury's *Jupiter* for flute and computer broke new ground in using real-time pitch tracking and score following to correlate computer-generated sound with a live performer. Many novel approaches to real-time computer music were developed in the course of creating the work. *Jupiter* explores these resources, but more importantly, builds them into a work of orchestral scope. Its half-hour span develops a deeply interconnected network of musical relationships between flute and computer. The computer acts as conductor, musicians, and instruments in an invisible and disembodied but highly responsive digital orchestra, whose instruments and interactions with the flutist are carefully orchestrated. The conceptual distance between the flute line and the computer's sounds varies tremendously: sometimes the computer is very close to the flute in timbre, gesture, and temporal behavior; at other times it is very distant. Often different simultaneous layers within the computer part operate at different distances from the flute.

The disembodied orchestra presents particular challenges in analysis. The shifting relationships between flute and computer are not fully represented by the score, by the software that controls the computer part, or by the sonic result; all three elucidate the composer's intent and are necessary to understand this work. Each represents a different perspective on the music—the score speaks primarily to the performer, the software to the technologist, and the sonic result to the audience. The work itself is situated elusively between notation, software, performance, and sound. This analysis will correlate these divergent perspectives and address the essential issues of timbre, interaction, and form in *Jupiter*.

Manoury's orchestration of timbral, gestural, and temporal relationships reveals a clear and cogent formal design. Archetypal sounds, gestures, and interactive relationships are established in the first section of the work. They are developed and recapitulated in later sections, each distinct and clearly defined, but all implicated in a complex web of musical connections. In this form, the model of a classical concerto is invoked and radically extended. Manoury's notation renders his new electronic resources similarly "backward compatible" with musical expectation and tradition. In writing *Jupiter*, Manoury established an effective adaptation among technology, composition, and performance through the invention of new models of concerto, orchestra, and orchestration.

7.2. Background

Jupiter was the first work in Manoury's *Sonus ex Machina*, a cycle of interactive works for instruments and computer written between 1987 and 1991. The score to *Jupiter* lists the work as composed in 1987 and revised in 1992, though further revisions were made to the computer part at least through 1996 (see Puckette et al. 2003). This long process of design and revision, spanning many years and a variety of developing technologies, transformed the work substantially. The computer part was the result of an intensive collaboration at the Institut de Recherche et Coordination Acoustique/Musique (IRCAM) between Manoury and Miller Puckette, with assistance from Cort Lippe, Marc Battier, Olivier Koechlin, and Thierry Lancino (see Manoury 2002). According to Puckette, Tom Mays, Les Stuck, and Serge LeMouton made later additions and revisions (see also Puckette et al. 2003). Flutist Lawrence Beauregard instigated the *Jupiter* project (see Manoury 2002), but died before the work was completed; Manoury dedicated the work to Beauregard's memory. Puckette recalls that

> Beauregard...had developed a flute with fifteen switches on its keys to aid a computer in tracking its pitch quickly. (Beauregard did not live to see his invention used on stage.) Barry Vercoe invented a score following program to accompany Beauregard's flute. The combination of a flute pitch detector, with a piece of software allowing live electronic processing and synthesis to be controlled by an event stream from a live instrument, seems to have been Manoury's main inspiration in writing *Jupiter*. The directors of IRCAM probably saw Jupiter as an exploratory piece that would open up possibilities for other composers hoping to write interactive pieces, not least Pierre Boulez, who had

searched for many years for a way to add an electronic component to his *Explosante/Fixe.* (Puckette et al. 2003)

The 1987 version of *Jupiter* used Giuseppe DiGiugno's 4x synthesizer (see Favreau et al. 1986), Beauregard's MIDI flute, and the first version of Puckette's Max software—a text-based interface specifically designed to control the 4x (see Puckette 2002). The 1992 version of *Jupiter,* which no longer required Beauregard's MIDI flute, used Puckette's Max/FTS software (see Puckette 1991b). This software consisted of a graphical user interface (Max) that controlled signal-processing functions (FTS) running on the multi-processor IRCAM Signal Processing Workstation (see Lindemann et al. 1991). *Jupiter* has survived the evolution of technology remarkably well; versions reportedly exist for all three of the Max variants currently in circulation—Max/MSP, jMax, and PureData. This analysis will refer to the PureData (pd) version, to which Puckette and Manoury have made several improvements, and which they currently use in performance.

7.3. The Analysis

When analyzing a work of this scale, an overview of its structure provides a useful context. The *Jupiter* score makes this relatively simple: the piece is organized in thirteen distinct sections, identified in the score by Roman numerals; each of these is further divided into subsections, identified by letters. The large sections alternate focus between the solo flute and the computer. Puckette has described this form anecdotally as resulting from the nature of the 4x computer used in the 1987 version. Programs had to be successively loaded into the machine in real time; while the flutist played a solo, the technicians would load the next program. If this is so, Manoury made a virtue of necessity. The relationship to the alternation of solo and tutti sections in a traditional concerto provides a strong context for the form and reinforces the orchestral model of the computer's role.

The beginning time point, duration, and starting page for each section of Manoury's thirty-two-page handwritten score (at the time of this writing a printed score is in preparation) are given in Table 7.1, both for reference and to indicate the overall proportions of the work. Throughout this analysis,

Table 7.1 Overview of Section Form and Proportions

sect	I	II	III	IV	V	VI	VII	VIII	IX	X	XI	XII	XIII
start	0:00	3:16	4:58	7:44	9:42	13:02	16:07	16:57	19:15	20:50	21:44	23:07	26:27
dur	3:16	1:42	2:46	1:58	3:20	3:05	0:50	2:18	1:35	0:54	1:23	3:20	1:37
page	1	6	9	13	15	17	20	21	26	27	28	29	32

indications of time points and descriptions of sound will refer to Elizabeth McNutt's recording of *Jupiter*, with which the author became thoroughly conversant in the process of preparing it for release on CD.

An overview of the relationship between flute and computer is also relatively simple. This relationship is highly determinate: the parts are synchronized frequently at cues provided by particular notes in the flute line. The flutist reads from a score that includes the computer's part, as well as each numbered cue. The computer, too, reads from a score; each section of the work is represented to the computer by a pair of text files. One of these, the "follow" score, documents the flute's expected sequence of notes and relates it to a numbered sequence of cues. The other text file, the "qlist," correlates each cue with messages to software modules that determine the computer's responses. In this textual notation, the follow score corresponds to the flute part, and the qlist to the computer part. As the flutist reads the notated score in performance, the computer reads through the follow and qlist scores to find its way through the piece. The relationships between flutist and computer are constantly mediated by a combination of the computer's text scores and the flutist's notated score.

7.3.1. Technological Perspective: Instruments, Players, and Conductor

The *Jupiter* scores are parsed and put into action by a large and intricate patch written in the Max environment (see Puckette 1991a). This graphical document both creates and displays the flows of data, signals, and processes that produce the timbres and behaviors of the computer part. The patch is modular, consisting of numerous "subpatches" that are often nested inside one another. Each subpatch performs a specific function such as pitch tracking, score following, synthesis, or sample playback.

The *Jupiter* patch integrates the functions of orchestra, players, and conductor. The pitch tracker and score follower correlate the flutist's notes with the follow score and trigger messages from the qlist. The qlist messages instruct the various subpatches to generate the sounds and behaviors that make up the computer part. The messages are interpreted according to a syntax built into the design of each subpatch. Many subpatches can receive several different kinds of messages which trigger different behaviors. The instruments themselves are signal-processing functions buried within the patch; they receive data from a variety of other subpatches that mediate between the qlist's messages and the instruments. Thus, the score follower acts metaphorically as conductor; the players are the subpatches that interpret qlist messages and turn them into instructions to the instruments. Manoury describes the computer's role as "becoming more and more like a human being (a musician, in this case). In other words, the machine listens, waits for an event, and reacts when the said event occurs.... The machine accomplishes, in part, what a conductor playing with a soloist would" (2002, 2).

As the work was developed, patches and qlist messages were added, changed, and updated. The sound of the piece was gradually altered as the digital orchestra's instrumentation was expanded and "played" in new ways. This reorchestration also added sonic transitions between sections and subsections of the work, as well as accompaniments for the solo passages. New layers within the orchestration added subtle connections between different sections of the work, which can be traced through analysis of the qlists. The relationship between the *Jupiter* patch and those of other works in the *Sonus ex Machina* cycle was fluid; *Jupiter* both contributed to and borrowed from the other pieces. The digital orchestra grew to meet new musical needs, and the music was reorchestrated to embrace new opportunities.

7.3.1.1. The Digital Orchestra: Strategies of Timbre   As in a traditional orchestra, the digital instruments used in *Jupiter* can be divided into several distinct "choirs," each comprising several instrument types, of which there are several individual "players." The choirs consist of samplers, synthesizers, and signal processors. The resources included in each are outlined below.

Sampler (eight voices)
- flute tones
- flute tongue-rams
- tam-tam hits
- cross-synthesized timbre of tam-tam with piano chord

Synthesizers
- Twenty voices of additive synthesis (addsyn), with eight different waveforms available (each waveform is a sum of cosine waves, representing a particular combination of the first eight overtones)
- Twenty-eight voices of additive synthesis with spectral envelope applied to each partial ("chapo" synthesis)
- Eight voices of phase-aligned formant (paf) synthesis

Signal Processors
- Four voices of delay-based harmonization (harm)
- frequency shifter (fshift or freq-shift): single sideband modulator with separate frequency addition and subtraction outputs
- noise modulator ("noise"): an intricate network of comb filters and ring modulators
- infinite-hold reverberator ("rev∞" or "reverb∞")
- four-channel real-time spatializer (spat)
- phase modulator (fphase), applied to direct flute output only

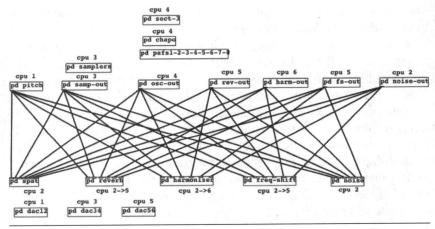

Fig. 7.1 "Grand-central" patch (used with permission).

These timbral resources are integrated in the "grand-central" patch shown in Figure 7.1, which permits flexible routing of nearly all signals. For those unfamiliar with PureData, a few explanations are needed. Each text box in this patcher window represents a subpatch with a distinct function; the "pd" prefix (similar to "patcher" in Max) is the PureData syntax identifying a subpatch. Signals are normally routed via "patch cables" that appear as lines between subpatches; outputs at the bottom of one text box are connected to inputs at the top of another.

Several subpatches in this example, however, send their outputs without patch cables. The four subpatches floating at the top of the window are among these; thus, the output of the "samplers" subpatch is sent from the "samp-out" subpatch in the top row of this signal routing matrix, and the outputs of the synthesizers in "pafs1-2-3-4-5-6-7-8," "chapo," and "sect-3" are added together and sent from "osc-out."

The rest of the top row of the matrix contains primarily subpatches that retrieve the outputs of the signal processors in the bottom row. Thus, "noise-out" provides the output of "noise," "fs-out" provides the output of "freq-shift," and so on. The exception is subpatch "pitch," which contains the pitch tracker and the "fphase" processor; its output is simply the direct flute sound.

Therefore, from left to right, the long top row of sound outputs comprises the direct flute sound; the sampler and synthesis outputs; and the outputs of reverberator, harmonizer, frequency shifter, and noise modulator. Each of these is sent to the inputs of the spatializer, reverberator, harmonizer, frequency shifter, and noise modulator in the row below. Each output module sends a signal to every processor's input except its own (for example, "noise-out" is not connected to "noise"). This does not prevent feedback;

the noise output could be sent to the frequency shifter, which could send its output back to the noise modulator, creating a feedback loop. Messages in the qlist must carefully choreograph the levels sent through each of these thirty-one connections to balance the orchestration and avoid unwanted sonic artifacts.

This extremely flexible mixing matrix imposes very few limitations. The synthesizers are always summed by the subpatch "osc-out" before being routed; the spatialization output is not routed in the matrix, but sent directly to speakers 1 to 4; and "fphase," hidden in the "pitch" subpatch, affects only the direct flute sound. Otherwise, any signal output can be mixed to any processing input. This provides an impressive range of hybrid timbres within the digital orchestra of *Jupiter*.

The numbered "cpu" notations in the patcher window refer to the earlier ISPW implementation, in which different signal-processing tasks were delegated to several hardware processors. The flow of audio between processors is still documented by these comments, although current versions run on a single central processing unit. In this way and others, the patch documents both function and history. The evolving orchestration of *Jupiter* is visible here and elsewhere in the patch. The synthesis modules in "grand-central" are shown in the order of their development. The paf synthesizer bank itself can be seen as a reorchestration of the work; the phase-aligned format technique (Puckette 1995) did not exist when the piece was first written, but it is used heavily in the current version. Likewise, within the "samplers" subpatch, a separate subpatch called "flute-samples" can be found. This handles the "addsamp" message (discussed below in 7.3.1.3), a feature that was added to Section III when the ISPW version of the work was written.

In the "grand-central" routing matrix, orchestration itself is reinvented. Sounds not only combine, but also interact and transform one another in the signal-processing "choir." This interaction between sounds in the digital orchestra parallels the interaction between performers and instruments in the traditional orchestra. Mixing and reprocessing provide a broad continuum of sonic identities that is parallel to, though vastly different from, the continuum of instrumental timbres and combinations in the orchestra. Manoury's control of mixing, layering, and reprocessing blurs the identities of sounds in the digital orchestra, much as in another era Berlioz, Debussy, and Ravel blurred the identities of instrumental sounds in their orchestral works.

7.3.1.2. The Digital Conductor: Relational Strategies and Tactics   The digital orchestra is conducted through the piece in real time by means of pitch tracking and score following, with every event ultimately triggered by a note in the flute line. In sharp contrast to the diversity and flexibility of the computer's sonic outputs, the computer's model of the flutist's behavior is very simple.

When the flutist plays a note, the pitch-tracking algorithm determines its pitch as quickly as possible. The score-following algorithm then correlates this pitch number with the pitch list in the follow score. Some pitch events will trigger cues, while others will simply be counted and registered by the score follower. If a new cue has been reached, the score follower sends out the messages in the qlist score corresponding to that cue.[2] Since cues can be flexibly assigned to notes, the computer's accompaniment can be more or less detailed and more or less correlated with the flute part, according to the needs of the music.

The pitch datum generated at the beginning of a note (henceforth the "note-incipit") is the computer's only connection to the flutist's behavior. All other data that could be used to control the computer such as amplitudes, durations, and rests, are ignored. Furthermore, within the linear progression of the computer's follow and qlist scores, backtracking in time is impossible. There is no provision for random access, or "skipping" to another cue in the score. The computer is only cognizant of note-incipits, and its sounds are frequently triggered in reaction to them. Cort Lippe has commented on the pitfalls of this model: "A common observation . . . is that real-time computer music has a static performer/machine relationship, one in which the computer always reacts to or transforms materials generated by a performer . . . a kind of 'call and response' relationship" (1996 116).

In *Jupiter*, several strategies are used to avoid a static relationship between flute and computer. The strategy of pitch-based score-following triggers systems that create varying degrees of temporal independence in the computer's behaviors, yielding a much more dynamic performative relationship than the note-incipit model of the flute's actions would suggest. The varying tactics of the computer's relationship to the flute are carried out within the qlist itself as well as within a host of specialized modules in the patch.

Each of the computer's instruments has not only a characteristic timbre, but also a characteristic relationship to the flute line. The fundamental tactics of relation may be divided into four basic categories: temporal extension (TX), rhythmic activation (RA), sonic extension (SX), and harmonic extension (HX), each defined below. All four are used in various ways from the start of the work to the end. Three further tactics of relation, introduced in particular sections of the work, will be discussed later; these are motoric coordination (MC), independent behaviors (IB), and spectral dynamics (SD).

Temporal Extension (TX): Notes growing out of the flute line are extended in time, generating a separate and slower rhythmic layer. This is often accomplished by the injection of flute sound into the infinite reverberator, which prolongs them until some later point in time (usually another cue from the flute).

Rhythmic Activation (RA): Sequences of notes in the computer part create an independent rhythmic behavior, usually faster than that of the flute line. This is characteristically accomplished using synthesized or sampled note events.

Sonic Extension (SX): The computer presents timbres that transform or present contrasts with the flute's sound. The phase and noise modulators, for example, do not affect time or harmony, but they provide extensions of timbre.

Harmonic Extension (HX): New pitches generated by the computer provide support or contrast to the flute line. This is typically accomplished using the harmonizer and frequency shifter modules (the latter affecting timbre as well).

The association between sound generation and relational tactics is strong but not absolute. Frequency shifting and harmonization are sometimes used as timbral extensions, synthesizer and sampler notes often extend the flute's notes in time or harmony, and shifting harmonizer settings are used in some sections to activate the rhythm. *Jupiter* combines all four relational tactics flexibly, and often simultaneously in different choirs of the digital orchestra.

7.3.1.3. Time in the Computer's Score: Message-Based Relationships Temporal data incorporated into messages are crucial to the tactics of relation in *Jupiter*. Most messages can include information about time—a span of time over which a level should fade up or down, for example. Similarly, note messages contain envelope data, usually including at least two stages of amplitude change over time. Depending on the complexity and duration of the behaviors invoked by these messages, they can produce a degree of temporal extension (TX); however, if a message is directly triggered by a flute note, and produces an event similar in duration to the triggering note, it usually will provide only sonic or harmonic extension (SX or HX) of the flute note. Several examples of messages in the *Jupiter* qlist that include time values are shown and interpreted in Table 7.2. The semicolon simply means, "send the following message."

Table 7.2 Time-Line Message Examples

; fto4 0, 117 500	set the send level from frequency shifter (f) to spatializer (4) at 0, then raise it to 117 over 500 milliseconds
; pitch3 5020 100	change the pitch of paf synthesis module 3 to 5020 MIDI-cents (MIDI note 50, tuned 20 cents sharp), over a portamento time of 100 milliseconds
; env1 −1, 150 5, 0 200, -2	apply an envelope to the amplitude of "paf" synthesizer module 1: "-1" begins and "-2" ends the envelope function, in which the level rises to 150 over 5 milliseconds, then drops to 0 over 200 milliseconds

```
;
addsyn 9 127 10 50 1000 8400 1.5 12. 4;
addsamp 8400 156 1000 90 90 150 110;
100 addsyn 10 127 10 50 1000 8000 1.5 12. 4;
addsamp 8000 156 1000 90 90 150 110;
100 addsyn 11 127 10 50 1000 7000 1.5 12. 4;
addsamp 7000 156 1000 90 90 150 110;
100 addsyn 12 127 10 50 1000 6900 1.5 12. 4;
addsamp 6900 156 1000 90 90 150 110;
100 addsyn 13 127 10 50 1000 6300 1.5 12. 4;
addsamp 6300 156 1000 90 90 150 110;
100 addsyn 14 127 10 50 1000 5200 1.5 12. 4;
addsamp 5200 156 1000 90 90 150 110;
addsyn 4 0 100 0 100;
addsyn 16 0 100 0 100;
addsyn 18 0 100 0 100;
addsyn 19 0 100 0 100;
addsyn 20 0 100 0 100
```

Fig. 7.2 Sequence within qlist (from subsection III-F, cue 66). (DVD reference 1)

Time delays within the qlist allow the computer to generate rhythmic activity (RA), increasing its temporal independence. An integer preceding a message causes the computer to wait that number of milliseconds before executing the message. This allows for a sequence to be programmed into the qlist itself, as shown in Figure 7.2.

The messages in Figure 7.2 are received by additive synthesizer ("addsyn") and sampler ("addsamp") modules in the patch. The sampler doubles the synthesizer, adding timbral depth to the beginning of each note before fading away. Six pairs of synthesizer and sampler note messages are sent at 100 millisecond intervals—one pair immediately, then five pairs in delayed succession. As the last note is played, five other notes already sounding in other synthesis modules are silenced.

Temporal data are also built into the definitions of "addsyn" and "addsamp" themselves. The first message in Figure 7.2, "addsyn 9 127 10 50 1000 8400 1.5 12. 4," means "make additive synthesis module 9 execute a two-stage envelope, rising to a level of 127 over 10 milliseconds, then decaying to a level of 50 over 1000 milliseconds, while playing a pitch of 8400 MIDI-cents (MIDI note 84 with a detune of 0 cents), with a vibrato of depth 1.5 Hz and speed 12 Hz; use the waveform in wave table 4 to generate the synthesized tone." After the envelope's decay stage, the note will continue to sound at a level of 50 until a later cue adds further envelope stages; as in the MIDI protocol, the "note off" is deferred to another message, creating temporal extension (TX) beyond the triggering note.

The "addsamp" message assumes a note of known duration, with no "note off" message needed. The message "addsamp 8400 156 1000 90 90 150 110" means: "trigger a flute sample note at a pitch of 8400 MIDI-cents, with a starting playback level of 156, lasting 1000 milliseconds before its release, reading from a point 90 milliseconds into the sample, and waiting 90 milliseconds after the note starts before decaying over 150 milliseconds to a sustain level of 110." The applied envelope is simple, since recorded samples contain their own intrinsic envelopes; using this message, the attack of a sampler note always lasts 5 milliseconds and the release 50 milliseconds.

The "addsynth" message can be truncated to include only envelope data; this is usually used to silence a note that was triggered earlier. Five such messages are given at the end of Figure 7.2; messages to additive synthesis modules 4, 16, 18, 19, and 20 fade their notes to silence over 100 milliseconds. Thus, as the last "note on" is sent, five other "note offs" are also sent.

Figure 7.2 demonstrates four relational tactics operating simultaneously. The computer plays short sequences in a different rhythm than the flute line (RA). Each note is orchestrated with a combination of synthesized and sampled timbres (SX). The sampler notes are short, while the synthesized notes extend temporally (TX) into flutelike drones at several pitch levels (HX) that shade and support the flute line.

7.3.1.4. Increasing Independence: Patch-Based Relationships

The four relational tactics described above are augmented by three other relationships that inhabit particular sections of the work—motoric coordination (MC), independent behaviors (IB), and sonic dynamics (SD). Each tactic increases the computer part's autonomy from the flute in a different manner, adding depth and variety to the relationship between flute and computer. All of these relationships rely on specialized modules within the patch to create complex behaviors without requiring constant triggering or mediation from messages in the qlist.

Figure 7.2 suggests one practical reason to use such modules: as sequences within the qlist grow longer, they become cumbersome. Subsection III-F, from which this example is excerpted, contains nearly 800 separate messages. To make longer sequences practical, the *Jupiter* patch includes eight simple sequence players, each invoked by a single message within the qlist. Sequence playback using sampled timbres characterizes Sections VIII and X of the piece; Section VIII uses tam-tam samples and Section X, downsampled flute tongue-ram samples.

Beyond the harmonic, rhythmic, and timbral expansion the sequenced samples provide, the use of extended sequences has significant consequences for the relationship between flutist and computer. Once a sequence begins, it cannot adjust to the flute; the computer takes absolute control of time. The flutist follows the computer based on the motoric rhythm established by the sequence. Thus, this relationship is described as motoric coordination (MC).

A flute solo in the middle of Section VIII continues the computer's motoric rhythm and leads directly into another sequence at the same tempo, emphasizing the flute line's subordination to the tempo of the computer's sequence.

Not all the sequencers in *Jupiter* are temporally inflexible. A bank of six interpolating ("interpol") sequence recorder/players generates a quite different relationship, in which the flutist's line predicts the computer's rhythms in a later section. Each interpol module records two short sequences of the flute's pitches and durations in real time during Section II. In Sections V and IX, interpolated playback of these recorded excerpts begins, using samples of either tam-tam hits (Section V) or cross-synthesis of piano and tam-tam (Section IX) as timbres. When triggered, an interpol module plays a sequence that gradually morphs from one of its recorded excerpts to the other via a series of interpolated versions.

The overall shape of each interpol sequence is clear, but the specific rhythms are hard to predict; the flute line can be correlated only roughly to the computer part. Accordingly, this relationship will be referred to as independent behavior (IB). Unlike the simple sequencers, the interpol playback engines can be affected by the flutist's playing; in subsection V-C, particular flute notes cue them to pause and later resume their activity. Much as the "addsyn" envelope messages in Figure 7.2 let the flutist cue the beginnings and endings of notes, here the flutist can cue the start and stop of sequences. This makes the large-scale trajectory of the computer's independent behavior somewhat similar to the earlier model of temporal extension.

In Sections VI and XII, the computer gains a very different kind of independence, created not by sequencing but by continuous transformation of timbre over time. This creates a unique relationship between flute and computer. Every other interactive relationship in the piece relies on the score follower to mediate between the flute's notes and the computer's responses. Here the flute's notes directly control the direction and rate of change of timbre over time. This is done through control of the spectral envelope of additive synthesis in the twenty-eight-oscillator chapo synthesizer. The flutist's note-incipits control the direction and speed of each oscillator's amplitude envelope independently, scaled according to the oscillator's frequency. As the spectral envelope opens, higher frequencies fade in; as it closes, only lower frequencies are audible.

The effect of these shifting spectral envelopes is both harmonic and timbral. However, this relationship goes far beyond the earlier models of harmonic and sonic extension. Instead of fixed behaviors triggered by each note, here the flute has a dynamic, real-time influence on a continuous process of timbral development of notes and chords. The computer's constantly changing sonic dynamics (SD) create a fluid connection between the flute's note-incipits and the computer's evolving timbres.

A remarkable range of technologies, described above, mediates the relationship between flute and computer. Additional subpatches invoked at a few particular cues expand this range even further. For example, in Section II, cues 77 to 78 feature iterated flute samples cycling at several different speeds. A small subpatch creates a beautiful and surprising texture through this simple technique.

The various relationships of temporal extension, rhythmic activation, sonic extension, harmonic extension, motoric coordination, independent behaviors, and sonic dynamics create an impression of varying distance between the flute and computer parts. Over time, the juxtaposition and layering of different distances between parts create a sense of perspective. Particular relationships between flute and computer are generally embodied in particular technological means, but these correlations are also fluid; special features invoked at particular cues also add nuance to the relational perspective of the piece. Even though it was the first interactive work of its kind, *Jupiter* largely avoids the "static performer/machine relationship" described by Lippe. Surprisingly few interactive works from later years have extended its basic relational strategy—a simple model of performance data giving rise to a complex interweaving of responses.

7.3.2. Performance Perspective: Score, Sound, and Expectation

The model of interaction between the flutist and the computer in *Jupiter* is a bit like an orchestra conductor with amazing agility in following the soloist. It is not necessarily a good conductor in other respects: it has no ability to count, follow tempo, or predict the soloist's timing. Once a cue is triggered, its results are inevitable. If the computer sets a tempo, it maintains it without regard for the flutist—an exceedingly autocratic style of conducting! Despite these caveats, the strategy is effective. Flutist Elizabeth McNutt states that the piece " … feels very much like a flute concerto in which the soloist is both performer and conductor.… It is lightning-fast in its response, and on the local level it provides excellent coordination between performer and machine" (2004 301).

The various processes instantiated within the digital orchestra can actually be much more independent from one another than in traditional orchestral writing. The computer part has elements of a musical mobile, like the open-form works of Earle Brown and others, in which "the composer typically notates musical elements or events which are assembled, ordered, and combined by the players or conductors during the performance" (Welsh 1995, 2). Table 7.3 analyzes cue 8, at the beginning of subsection VIII-D, and reveals a layering of three different relational strategies scheduled in real time.

The effect of these messages is threefold: to generate a sustained chord derived from the flute sound, to spatialize that chord in a rapid circular

Table 7.3 Messages in Subsection VIII-D, Cue 8 (DVD reference 2).

Message	Meaning
; dtoh 127;	send the direct flute signal to the harmonizer at full output
stoh 0 200;	fade the send level from samplers/synthesizers to harmonizer down to 0 over 200 milliseconds
hto2 104;	send the harmonizer output to the speakers at high output
tto2 120;	send the sampler output to the speakers at very high output
rto2 0;	do not send any reverberator output to the speakers
htor 127;	send the harmonizer output to the reverberator at full output
dtor 0;	do not send any direct flute signal to the reverberator
stor 0;	do not send any output from samplers/synthesizers to the speakers
rto4 127;	send the reverberator output to the spatializer at full output

Result: A new signal routing is set, sending
flute → harmonizer → reverberator → spatializer, and
(sampler + harmonizer + spatializer) → speakers

rgate 126;	open the reverberator's input gate nearly all the way
revfb 127;	set the reverberator feedback to maximum (reverb∞)
trans0 900;	transpose first harmonizer voice up 900 cents (flute A4 becomes F#5)
transl 800;	transpose second harmonizer voice up 800 cents (to F5)
trans2 -1100;	transpose third harmonizer voice down 1100 cents (to Bb3)
trans3 1100;	transpose fourth harmonizer voice up 1100 cents (to G#5)

Result: A chord is built up in the harmonizer, and injected into the reverberator,
to be sustained through infinite reverberation (reverb∞)

spaton 1;	start the spatializer's circular movement function
spatinc 130;	set the increment, or speed of movement, of the spatializer quite high
radius 127;	set the spatializer's radius of movement to maximum

Result: The spatializer spins the sound rapidly around the four-speaker array, creating the
effect of a rhythmic pulsation applied to the sustained harmonizer chord

ost4-start bang;	start sequence number 4; this fast, motoric series of 32nd notes played as tam-tam samples will continue through the next thirteen cues (its tempo is slightly different than that of the spatializer's pulse)

Result: All three layers are now instantiated; the reverberator's input gate is open,
but will be closed by the next cue, "freezing" the reverb∞ sound

300 rgate 0;	following a 300 millisecond delay, close the reverberator's input gate

movement around the room, and to play a rapid motoric sequence in tam-tam sounds. The three sonic layers of harmonization, spatialization, and sequence have increasing degrees of timbral distance and temporal autonomy from the flute. An auditory perspective of multiple distances between flute and computer is achieved.

This layered perspective sets the terms of the interactive relationship. The flutist listens to the sequence to follow the computer. At the same time, flute notes trigger the sequence, and, subsequently, all the other layers of sound and response. Thus, the computer follows the flutist even as the flutist follows the computer. The flutist is at the center of a network of sonic and temporal relationships; it is up to the flutist to mediate time, dynamic, and timbre through her playing.

The flutist's task of mediating time is particularly challenging in this example, because the conceptual distances between parts are heightened by spatial movement. The sequence is rotated through the four-speaker array, with each successive note sounding from a different speaker. This complicates the task of following the computer's rhythm; the flutist must count precisely in tempo and listen carefully for the moving tam-tam sounds. Additionally, the pulsation created in the harmonized chords by the spatializer's rapid movement interferes slightly with the rhythm and spatial movement of the sequence. Unlike a conductor and orchestra, the computer's process of accompaniment is hidden from the flutist; its results are manifested only in sound, and the sound is not always easy to follow. The written score is the flutist's only guide through this difficult terrain.

7.3.2.1. The Jupiter Score: Communication and Mediation   The primary functions of the notated score of *Jupiter* are to communicate the flute part to the performer and to mediate between the flutist and the digital orchestra. The score is also the center of a more complex mediation between the perspectives of composer, technologist, and performer. The score documents not just the events of the piece, but the relationships that are most significant in each section. It is a subtly nuanced communication from composer to performer, elucidating a complex web of connections.

The flute soloist is the central figure in performance, and the lyrical, imaginative flute line is the source of much of *Jupiter*'s vitality. Nevertheless, the majority of space in the score is taken up by the computer part. The flutist reads from the full score, with the flute part at the bottom of the score and the computer part shown above. This inverts the traditional placement of solo music above accompaniment, and disguises the central role of the flute. A tension is immediately established between the roles of flute and computer.

The flute part is traditionally notated, for the most part. The most obvious exception is that meters and bar lines are not consistently used. When meters are present, they are written below the score where they do not interfere with the flute line. This subordinate placement of meter emphasizes the rhapsodic, lyrical aspect of the work—the flutist is generally free to adjust tempo and rubato. This is reinforced by frequent indications of tempo fluctuations, notated with words and with arrows slanting up and down. Toward the end of Section VII, these arrows become beams slanting up and down to indicate accelerando and rallentando. The notation takes pains to point out the interpretive opportunities provided by the score follower.

The correlation of the computer part to the flute part is clearly shown throughout the score. A vertical line and a circled cue number highlight each flute note that cues the computer. This can be seen in all the notation examples below except Figure 7.4, where double bars before the cue substitute for vertical lines. This focus on cues is striking, given that the flutist does not ideally have to follow the computer's cues at all; rather, the computer should respond to the flute at each cue. However, in practice the notation of cues is necessary for the flutist. To skip one of the cue notes could result in the absence or temporal displacement of the cued event. The notation also details the computer's response at each cue, allowing the flutist to observe any uncorrected score-following errors. This is crucial in performance: if the computer jumps ahead, the computer operator cannot make the computer backtrack. Instead the flutist must adjust by jumping forward to the cue the computer has reached. The notation of cues also facilitates communication between flutist and technologist in rehearsal.

Manoury uses a variety of notations, giving successive pages very different appearances. The computer part is particularly varied, ranging from traditional pitches and rhythms, notated on as many as four staves, to entirely graphic notations. The type of notation Manoury uses in each section creates a "notational look," to use Morton Feldman's term (1985), that strongly evokes the computer's sound and relationship to the flutist. Traditional markings of dynamics and articulations augment the notation in many sections, even where nontraditional notations are employed. The computer part also includes technical indications of various kinds that describe the actions and interactions of the computer—modes of signal processing, frequency shifter settings, signal routings, and so forth.

A few unusual notations are used frequently; however, most of these are easily reconciled with common practice. For example, a horizontal line extending to the right of a note head is often used to indicate duration in the computer part and some sections of the flute part. This correlates strongly with the traditional notation of a tie. Exceptions occur when the computer's sounds or the relationship between flute and computer cannot be expressed by traditional notation. The "backward compatibility" of the score helps mediate between the perspective of a traditionally trained flutist and the new ideas proposed in this work.

7.3.2.2. *Degrees of Freedom and Their Notational Looks*   The flutist's degree of temporal freedom varies through the course of the work, corresponding

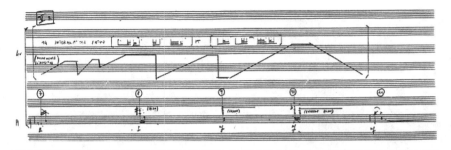

Fig. 7.3 Graphic notation of the computer part (subsection V-B, cues 7–11) (reference used with permission). (DVD reference 3)

to changes in the interactive relationship between flutist and computer. This is made clear by the changing notational look of the score. Figure 7.3 shows one of the most striking notations in *Jupiter*, introduced in Section V and later echoed in Section IX. The computer part is given in graphic notation, showing pitch contour over time. A description of the interpolated rhythmic patterns augments the graphic notation. The flute's sporadic notes are given in time-space notation below. The flutist must follow the overall pitch shape of the computer's interpolated sequences based on the graphic notation and place notes and patterns accordingly. These, in turn, will cue other layers of activity in the computer.

The notation in Figure 7.3 exemplifies two important features of Manoury's notation. First, where certain dimensions of the music are hard to follow by ear (in this case, rhythm and pattern), others that are relatively easy to follow (in this case, the general contour of pitch and register) form the basis of the notation. This tendency is similarly clear in the examples of notation given below, especially Figures 7.5 and 7.6. In Figure 7.5, the temporal relationship between the computer's gestures is unpredictable; therefore, the gestures themselves are notated precisely. In Figure 7.6, the precise pitches are hard to hear; therefore, the meters and pitch contours are shown. The second tendency is that wherever an independent process (in this case, the interpolation engine) accompanies the flute instead of accompaniment that closely follows the flute line, other modes of interaction are also implemented; the flute's notes modify characteristics of the computer sound such as reverberation, harmonization, and spatial modulation, for example. This will be demonstrated below, particularly in 7.3.3.2.

In Figure 7.4, the flute part fluctuates between traditional and time-space rhythmic notation; the computer part, in contrast, is completely blank. This is typical of Sections VI and XII, where the flutist's notes not only trigger chords, but also open and close the chapo synthesizer's spectral envelopes (as described in 7.3.1.4). The blank computer part in these sections emphasizes the flutist's freedom to shape time according to the sonic dynamics of the

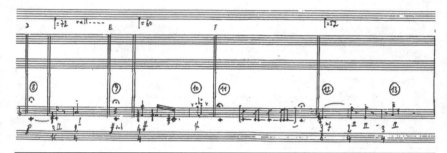

Fig. 7.4 Blank (cues only) notation of spectral enveloping (subsections VI-DEF, cues 8–13) (reference used with permission). (DVD reference 4)

computer's sound. The flutist is encouraged to listen to the computer's part rather than looking at it. The flutist can adjust the dynamic extremes of the spectral envelope by manipulating tempo and phrasing, letting envelope stages continue for a longer or shorter time. The notational look of empty space conveys the flutist's freedom to shape time and timbre in this relationship with the computer. In the published score, graphic notation (rising and falling lines) will show the trajectory of the spectral envelope, but will continue to leave these issues of pacing open to the flutist.

In contrast to the blank notation of Figure 7.4, the notation from subsection III-F in Figure 7.5 is almost indecipherably dense. Here the sequence

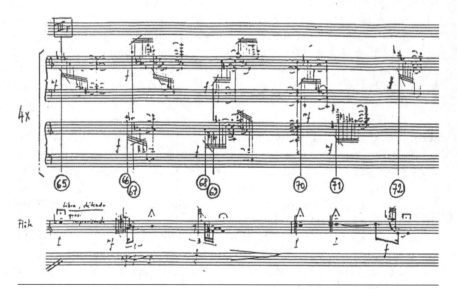

Fig. 7.5 Dense notation of sequenced notes (subsection III-F, cues 65–72; cf. Figure 7.2) (reference used with permission). (DVD reference 1)

examined in Figure 7.2 can be seen in context at cue 66, where it will overlap with another sequence triggered at cue 67. The flutist is unlikely to read each note of the computer part in Figure 7.5, but can easily scan the gestures and correlate them with the sounds emanating from the speakers, verifying that cues have been triggered and adjusting dynamics to balance with the computer's sound. The flutist's complete freedom to shape time is underscored by the marking "libre, détendu, quasi improvisando."

The notation tactics visible in Figure 7.5 also point to the flutist's temporal freedom. Several types of fermata encourage a flexible range of pauses. Precise rhythmic figures alternate with grace note rhythms. The computer's sequences, though precisely timed, are notated as grace notes tied to floating note heads. This is reminiscent of piano scores in which the pianist uses the pedal to sustain an unmeasured flurry of notes; the flutist is not encouraged to count along. Later in this section, where the grace note flurries thin to individually cued notes, horizontal lines indicate the extension of notes through time from one flute cue to another. In both notations, it is evident that the computer will wait for the flutist's next cue.

In contrast, the sequence playback in Section VIII is completely inflexible. Figure 7.6 shows the notation of subsection VIII-D, cues 8–10 (described above in Table 7.3). Rhythms, patterns, and meters in the sequence are the primary notational elements. Meters are written between the computer part and the flute part; their position above the flute line indicates the primacy of metric time in this section. The flutist counts the meters and follows the contours of the computer's motoric 32nd notes to place each flute note correctly. Precise pitches are not given; they would be hard to hear and would not add useful information. As the flutist plays, the notes of the flute line trigger spatialized chords, as previously observed. The flutist will not follow

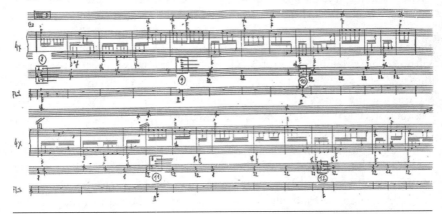

Fig. 7.6 Notation of sequenced samples, harmonizer chords (subsection VIII-D, cues 8–10). (DVD reference 2)

these, but simply verify that they took place. The primacy of the sequence is reflected in its position at the top of the score. In addition, the proximity of the chords to their triggering notes shows their dependent role and keeps them out of the way of the primary line. In fact, the meter changes are much more visible than the music in this staff! Relationships between parts are made evident graphically, through their relative positions in the score.

As Section VIII continues, the notation becomes less rigid. The computer's pitch contour becomes more vague and generalized, and the regular rhythm becomes increasingly irregular. This is shown through the time-space notation of the computer part, combined with verbal comments such as "de plus en plus irrégulier." The flutist switches from following patterns and meters to following dynamics, rhythmic densities, and degrees of irregularity. The relationship between flute and computer becomes more approximate. This creates a transition into Section IX, where graphic notations reminiscent of those in Section V are used, and the flutist has greater freedom to shape time. The notation adapts to reflect the changing musical situation. Manoury's evocative combinations of text, graphics, and traditional notational elements give the flutist an intuitive sense of the shifting sonic and temporal landscape, and of the relationship between flute and computer throughout the work.

7.3.3. Correlating Perspectives: Technology, Performance, and Sound

Thus far, this analysis has focused on elucidation and comparison of the computer's score and the flutist's at several characteristic points in the piece. The technological perspective on *Jupiter* is represented in the follow and qlist scores. The performative perspective is represented in the score and the relationships established by the computer's sounds and interactions. The resultant sonic experience of the entire piece represents an audience perspective and, ideally, should bear a strong resemblance to the composer's conception (mediated by those of the flutist and the technologist operating the computer and mixing the sound in performance). By correlating sound with scores, this analysis will bring together the perspectives that frame the experience of Manoury's composition. The qlists clarify the computer's sounds and behaviors. The notated score indicates the flute's sounds and the interactions with the computer considered most significant by the composer. Sound reveals elements omitted from the score, and possibly hidden in the dense and complex qlists.

The excerpts with notations shown in Figures 7.4 and 7.5 differ greatly, both in visual appearance and programming style. However, analysis of their sonic profiles in the following section will reveal important similarities between the examples, some of which are far from evident in the qlist and the notation. Crucial elements in these sections can be traced back to the opening section of the work. The final section of the work, the primary function of which is to recapitulate the opening, also brings together significant features from the sections shown in all of these examples.

7.3.3.1. Sonic Links Between Different Technologies Perhaps the most striking sections of *Jupiter* are Sections VI and XII, which rely on the relational tactic of sonic dynamics. Here the computer's timbres change actively, fluidly, and often dramatically. As described earlier, the flute's notes do not trigger events; they bypass the score follower and affect the chapo synthesizers directly. Each note influences an ongoing process of timbral transformation, in which spectral envelopes are always opening or closing.

The qlists for these sections reflect their unusual nature. Relatively few note-incipits actually trigger events. Cues are fewer and further between, since each flute note directly affects the chapo synthesis algorithm. Rather than lists of events, the qlists consist mainly of frequency settings for the chapo synthesizer's oscillators, as seen in Figure 7.7. The remaining messages set the synthesizer's wave table number ("chapo-tab") and a reference value for the speed and direction of the amplitude envelope function ("porta"). A comparison of Figure 7.7 with Figure 7.2 shows that the technological means of Section VI are as different from those of subsection III-F as are their notations, excerpted in Figures 7.4 and 7.5. The blank notation of Section VI presents an extreme contrast to the dense notation of Section III. Likewise, the frequency lists in Figure 7.7 are entirely different from the sequenced notes in Figure 7.2.

; 0 9 -----------------------	chapo 18 667.;	chapo 7 550.;
80;	chapo 19 887.;	chapo 8 0.;
chapo-tab 4;	chapo 20 745.;	chapo 9 660.;
porta 512;	chapo 21 965.;	chapo 10 0.;
chapo 0 32.;	chapo 22 823.;	chapo 11 770.;
chapo 1 187.;	chapo 23 1043.;	chapo 12 0.;
chapo 2 261.619995;	chapo 24 901.;	chapo 13 880.;
chapo 3 265.;	chapo 25 1121.;	chapo 14 0.;
chapo 4 123.;	chapo 26 978.;	chapo 15 990.;
chapo 5 343.;	chapo 27 1198.;	chapo 16 0.;
chapo 6 201.;	0 10 ----------------------- 90;	chapo 17 1100.;
chapo 7 421.;	porta 512;	chapo 18 0.;
chapo 8 278.;	0 11 ----------------------	chapo 19 1210.;
chapo 9 498.;	100;	chapo 20 0.;
chapo 10 356.;	chapo-tab 4;	chapo 21 1320.;
chapo 11 576.;	chapo 0 261.619995;	chapo 22 0.;
chapo 12 434.;	chapo 1 220.;	chapo 23 1430.;
chapo 13 654.;	chapo 2 110.;	chapo 24 0.;
chapo 14 512.;	chapo 3 330.;	chapo 25 1540.;
chapo 15 732.;	chapo 4 0.;	chapo 26 0.;
chapo 16 590.;	chapo 5 440.;	chapo 27 1650.;
chapo 17 810.;	chapo 6 0.;	

Fig. 7.7 "Chapo" synthesis qlist example (subsection VI-DEF, cues 9–11; cf. Figure 7.4). (DVD reference 4)

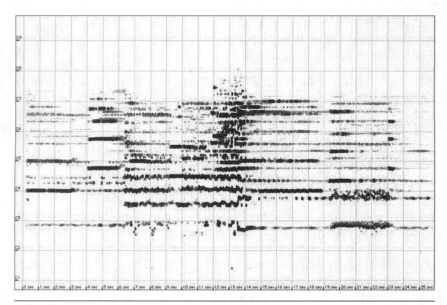

Fig. 7.8 Spectral enveloping (subsection VI-DEF, cues 8–13; cf. Figures 7.4 and 7.7). (DVD reference 4)

Given the extreme disparity between these excerpts in both programming and notation, their sonic similarities are surprising. Figures 7.8 and 7.9 show "peak-graphs" of the excerpts shown in Figure 7.4 and Figure 7.5 above; Figure 7.8 corresponds to Figure 7.4, and Figure 7.9 to Figure 7.5. Peak-graphs (see May 2004) are plots of frequency over time, similar to sonograms, but pitch optimized using Puckette's fiddle~ algorithm (Puckette and Apel 1998). The amplitude of a frequency peak within the spectrum is represented both by the thickness of the line and by the depth of its shade, from gray to black. Frequencies shown are restricted to the range in which fundamentals might reasonably be present and scaled logarithmically so that octaves are of equal size. Peak-graphs in this essay are generated from McNutt's recording of *Jupiter*.

The spectral density and range, the rate and degree of harmonic change, and the typical pitch shapes are visibly similar in these two peak-graphs. Both excerpts present lyrical but fragmented melodies, with a typical gesture of fast outbursts leading to sustained tones. This can be seen in both graphs, with brief regions of chaotic patterns resolving to horizontal lines. The relational tactics are clearly visible in both cases: temporal, sonic, and harmonic extensions (TX, SX, and HX).

Some important differences are also visible. In the excerpt from Section VI, there is a greater tendency to return the same note; thus, horizontal lines

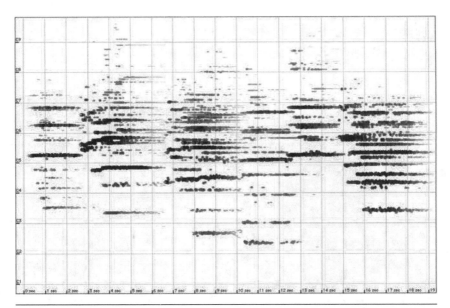

Fig. 7.9 Synthesizer and sampler notes (subsection III-F, cues 65–72; cf. Figures 7.2 and 7.5). (DVD reference 1)

in the peak-graph tend to lie on the same vertical level. In both sections of the work, however, pitch centers shift gradually over time. The flute's fast runs preceding harmonic changes are more clearly visible in Figure 7.9 as dark clusters just before 3 seconds, near 7 seconds, and at 15 seconds. This represents the greater degree of melodic activation in subsection III-F, as well as the rhythmic activation (RA) that the computer's grace-note passages provide at each cue. A type of sonic extension (SX) that recurs through the work is visible from 19 to 23 seconds, focused on C3 and C4 in Figure 7.8. Frequency shifting of the synthesizer output by +6 and –6 Hz (in effect, amplitude modulation) creates this unstable, tremulous timbral "ornament," reminiscent of a trill.

The greatest difference between the two excerpts' sonic profiles is in the envelopes of held notes and chords. Crescendos are clearly visible in Figure 7.8, for example between 4 and 6 seconds. These affect both amplitude and spectrum; new harmonics are introduced as the amplitude increases. They result from spectral enveloping, which adds sonic dynamics (SD) to the catalog of relational tactics in this example. These envelopes contrast with those of Figure 7.9, where clouds of spectral peaks at the beginning of each sustained note decay to held tones. This represents visually the rapid sequences of synthesizer and sampler attacks in this section, which decay to sustained synthesized tones.

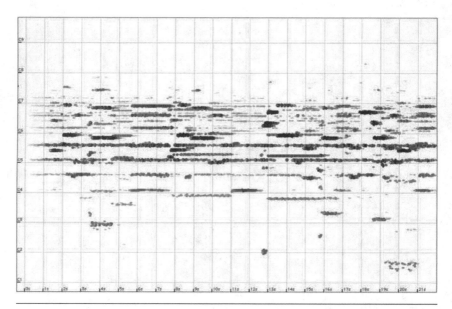

Fig. 7.10 Archetype for Figures 7.8 and 7.9 (subsection I-F, cues 50–67). (DVD reference 5)

These two sections can be seen as developing the same basic musical archetype. That archetype is first presented in subsection I-F, where yet another technology is used: shifting harmonies are generated by shifting the frequency of a pair of held tones. A visual comparison of Figure 7.10 with Figures 7.8 and 7.9 reveals that their timbres and gestures have strong resemblances, despite their technological differences.

Figure 7.10 shows that the activation of timbres in subsection I-F is less than in the later sections, and the movement of the flute line itself is greater. This reflects the context of subsection I-F as part of an exposition of melodic ideas, in a section that focuses on the flute line rather than the computer part. Nevertheless, the shifting harmonic and sonic extensions of the flute line, with flurries of activity in between, can be seen unfolding at a similar pace.

The sustained harmonies seen in Figure 7.10, doubling principal notes of the flute melody, prefigure those of Figures 7.8 and 7.9. Several features of Figure 7.10 are suggestive of Figure 7.8 in particular. Figure 7.10's recurrent C-sharp 4 at 5.5, 11, 16.5, and 20.8 seconds, as well as the constant C-sharp 5-G5 drones, foreshadow the insistent recurrence of C4 in Figure 7.8. The low, tremulous sounds at 3.5 and 19.3 seconds in Figure 7.10 are reminiscent of Figure 7.8's wavering frequency-shifted tones at 19 to 23 seconds. The sonic profile of subsection I-F shows it to be the model for subsection III-F and, even more so, for Sections VI and XII. Each uses a different technological means to explore a related musical terrain.

7.3.3.2. Sonic Links Between Different Notations   A prominent feature of the peak-graph of subsection I-F is the held C-sharp–G dyad that sounds throughout. Held tones (TX) provide similar points of harmonic and timbral reference throughout *Jupiter*. Surprisingly, even though they are a central feature of the work, such temporal extensions are not always clearly notated in the score. Particularly where the texture grows denser and other materials claim the foreground, these elements of the sonic landscape are sometimes minimized or omitted altogether. Table 7.3 in 3.2 above showed an excerpt of the qlist of Section VIII, where spatialized sustained harmonies were combined with a rapid motoric sequence. The notation of this passage, previously examined in Figure 7.6, minimizes the sustained chords; they are shown in a compact form at the bottom of the computer part. Figure 7.11 shows that the sustained harmonies are, in fact, much more prominent than the notation would suggest.

In Figure 7.11, the dancing 32nd notes of the computer's sequenced tam-tam samples are visible primarily in the octave around C7, with shadows in the higher octave and the low range between C3 and C4. They are masked in the middle register by the harmonized chords that grow out of the flute's notes. The fluctuating amplitude seen in both the chords and the tam-tam

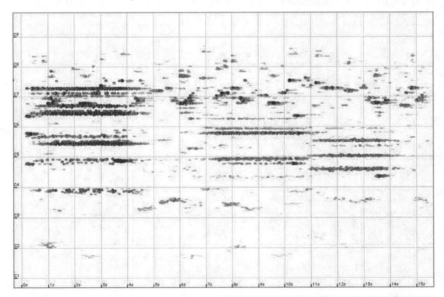

Fig. 7.11 Layered sequence, harmonization, spatialization (subsection VIII-D, cues 8–10; cf. Table 7.3, Figure 7.6). (DVD reference 2)

samples is the result of the sound circulating around a four-speaker array, captured from the front of the hall in this stereo recording. The notation of this excerpt focuses on the motoric sequence that is the focal element in this passage. In the peak-graph, however, the sustained chords appear more prominent. The close relationship of the sustained chords to the flute line is shown by their proximity in the score. This is borne out in the peak-graph, where the chords extend and harmonize the flute's notes.

Sustained tones create sonic connections between even the most extreme developmental sections in *Jupiter*. The graphic notation from Section V, seen in Figure 7.3, bears no resemblance to the precise metric notation of Section VIII, seen in Figure 7.6. The notation in Figure 7.3 describes the computer part with a generalized graphic rather than notating it in detail; it omits all layers other than the interpol sequence and its time scale is enormously compressed, with well over a minute of music represented in one line. The notational strategies in these sections could hardly be more different. Yet, comparison of their peak-graphs reveals interesting similarities. The interpolated sequence visible in Figure 7.12, with a sonic profile closely matching its graphic notation, is realized in tam-tam samples; so are the sequenced 32nd notes of Figure 7.11. As in Figure 7.11, horizontal lines are clearly visible. In this case, they do not change harmony, but represent a continuous B-flat drone. This is quite noticeable to the ear, but is not notated in the score. Also as in Figure 7.11, the drone masks the middle register of the tam-tam samples.

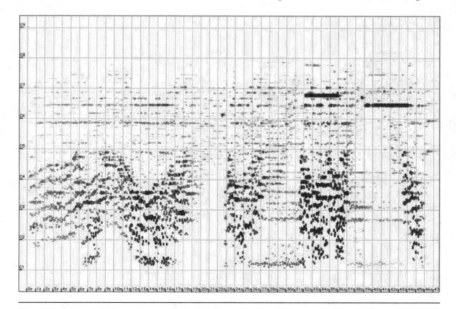

Fig. 7.12 Interpolated sequence with B-flat drone (Section V B, cues 7–11; cf. Figure 7.3). (DVD reference 3)

The amplitude of the drone fluctuates somewhat, because it is produced by processing of the samples rather than the harmonization and reverberation of the flute's notes found in Section VIII. The layers of computer sound in Section V interact with one another and not with the flute. The flute's notes stand out as anomalies floating above the sea of computer timbres.

Figures 7.11 and 7.12, like Figures 7.8 and 7.9, reveal strong sonic links between sections notated and programmed in very different ways. The links between different sections are visible from one perspective, and absent from another. Combining the disparate perspectives of technology, notation, and sound exposes formal relationships within the work that are otherwise hidden. The connections that bind the diverse materials of this work into a unified and coherent whole are manifest in Manoury's technological, relational, and sonic strategies.

7.3.3.3. Recapitulatory Use of Timbre and Technology   Recurrence and recapitulation are central to the form of *Jupiter*; these tendencies can be seen from every perspective. Sections focusing on the solo flute consistently recur: Sections I, IV, VII, XI, and XIII all share this tendency. Each succeeding "flute-centric" section responds to the musical challenges of the intervening "computer-centric" sections. Section XIII, the conclusion of the work, recapitulates aspects of the opening while weaving in elements from the intervening sections. Its score emphasizes its relationship to the opening; its peak-graph and qlist reveal subtle orchestrations that refer to sounds from various parts of the work.

In subsection XIII-B the flute is accompanied by a harmony gradually built from the flute's notes. The notation, shown in Figure 7.13, reveals nothing more. Infinite reverberation and paf synthesis are orchestrated to produce these temporally extended pitches, as at the opening of the piece. However, a glance at the peak-graph in Figure 7.14 suggests that there is more going on than the score reveals. Just before 7 seconds and again around 17 to 19 seconds quavering instabilities can be seen in the spectrum. Looking closely

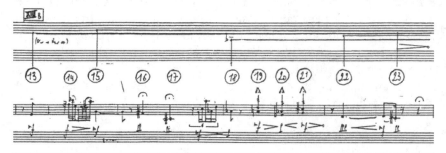

Fig. 7.13 "Flute-centric" notation (subsection XIII-B, cues 13–23) (reference used with permission). (DVD reference 6)

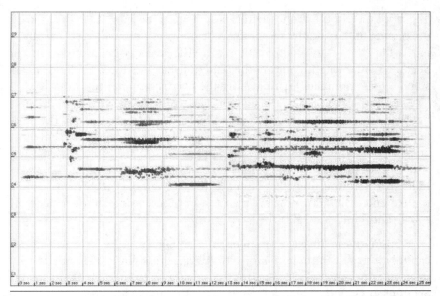

Fig. 7.14 Orchestrated "flute-centric" sound world (subsection XIII-B, cues 13–23). (DVD reference 6)

at the qlist, shown in Table 7.4, it is easy to see the detailed orchestration of this section and explain the discrepancies between score and peak-graph. The computer's sustained tones are seen to be embellished by frequency shifting, harmonizer "detuning" and octave shifting, noise modulation, and spatialization.

The subtle changes of timbre through this section do more than simply embellish the musical line and harmony; they serve a structural function, introducing faint echoes of the timbres in preceding sections of the work. The drones and persistent harmonies create a link with much of the piece, including such extremes as Sections V and VIII, as discussed above. The frequency shifting at cue 16 of Section XIII recalls the tremulous frequency-shifted timbres heard in Sections III and VI. The doubled A-flat in the lower octave invokes the registral expansion of the central sections. This is a special moment, since all other single-note harmonizations in *Jupiter* are at the unison. These are small details, but they have a large effect: they reflect upon the vast sonic terrain that has come before. Subtle digital orchestration adds nuance and meaning to the computer part and creates connections through the extended form of the work.

7.3.4. From Orchestration to Form

The orchestration of technologies, relationships, and sounds over time gener-ates much of the form of *Jupiter*. Its thirteen large formal sections have clear

Table 7.4 Qlist Excerpt. Orchestration of Subsection XIII-B, Cues 13–20 (slightly edited). (DVD reference 6)

Message	Meaning
0 13 ------------------- 130;	
oto2 127; rto2 112; fto2 107;	send output from paf synthesizer, reverberator, and frequency shifter to the speakers (at different levels)
fnois 19;	set the noise modulator (no output yet) to a fairly low modulation index
oto4 127; rto4 112; nto4 97; spaton 1; spatinc 5;	set up the spatializer: send it signal from the paf synthesizer. reverberator, and noise modulator, and send it spinning slowly around the 4-speaker array
ampl 127 1000;	fade paf synth 1 (doubling flute E4) up to full output over 1 second
rgate 126; revfb 127; 200 rgate 0;	capture and hold the first 200 ms of the flute's E4 in the infinite reverberator (reverb∞)
0 14 ------------------- 140;	
rtof 127; fneg 127; fsfre 64;	Send the reverb∞ signal to the frequency shifter; set this to a shift of -64 Hz, at full output
0 15 ------------------- 150;	
amp2 127 1000; rtof 0; rgate 126; revfb 127; 400 rgate 0;	fade paf synth 2 (doubling flute G4) up to full output over 1 second turn off the send from reverb∞ to frequency shifter capture and hold the first 400 ms of flute's G4 in the reverb∞, creating an m3 dichord with the previous reverb∞ note (E4) and doubling the paf synthesis
0 16 ------------------- 160;	
dtof 127; rtof 127; fto2 127 100; fto4 113 100; fneg 127; fsfre 6; fpos 127;	Send the direct flute and the reverb∞ to the frequency shifter; set this to a shift of +6 Hz and -6 Hz simultaneously (this is the amplitude modulation effect observed in III-F and VI-F, which detunes partials slightly to create a "fluttering" vibrato-like sound); fade the frequency shifter output up over 100 milliseconds; send frequency shifter output to speakers and spatializer
0 17 ------------------- 170;	
rtof 0; dtof 0; fneg 0; rtof 0; fpos 0;	silence the frequency shifter's "vibrato" by shutting off its inputs and outputs
0 18 ------------------- 180;	
amp3 127 10; vamp3 3 1000; vfreq3 50 1000;	fade paf synth 3 (Ab3) up to full output, very quickly; gradually introduce a slight vibrato over the course of one second

Table 7.4 Continued

Message	Meaning
noise3 51 ;	fade noise modulator output up to a moderate level (affects paf synth)
trans0 -1200; hamp2 0;	set up the harmonizer to do just one voice of harmonization, transposing down an octave; silence the other three harmonizer voices
hamp3 0; hamp4 0;	
dtoh 127; htor 127; dtor 0;	reroute the flute output: previously flute → reverb∞, now flute → harmonizer → reverb∞
rgate 117; revfb 127; 300 rgate 0;	capture and hold the first 300 ms of the flute's Ab4, transposed down to Ab3 by the harmonizer. in the reverb∞, thus orchestrating and sustaining the flute's note in the lower octave and adding it to the chord
0 19 ------------------- 190;	
hto2 138 500; hto4 134 500; rtoh 127; dtoh 0; htor 0;	reroute the harmonizer and reverb∞: instead of the direct flute, send the reverb∞ (holding three notes) to harmonizer; stop sending harmonizer to reverb∞ to avoid feedback; send harmonizer output to speakers and spatializer
100 hwind 67; hampl 127; hamp2 127; hamp3 127; hamp4 127; hfrel -18; hfre2 -6; hfre3 16; hfre4 17;	after a delay of 100 ms (to allow the sound in the harmonizer and reverb∞ to clear after the rerouting of signals) set the harmonizer to full output, with different slight "detunings" set as transpositions for each voice; this creates a chorus effect, adding to the complexity of the chords still being played by the reverb∞
0 20 ------------------ 200;	
rtoh 0;	silence the harmonizer's chorus effect

and distinct characters, which can be observed in their notational looks, technological means, and sonic profiles. Subsections within the thirteen sections also present contrasts, many of them quite strong. The first section of the piece is the most varied; it presents a series of musical archetypes that are the seeds of the larger form of the work. After this exposition, each is developed in different ways in the succeeding sections.

Analysis of form often focuses primarily on the elements of harmony and motive. This would be an effective approach to *Jupiter* as well. Even more striking, however, is that the orchestration of relational tactics, behavior types, and timbres provides a clear model of the work's form.

7.3.4.1. Formal Archetypes and Their Development Table 7.5 shows key elements of each subsection (opening solo and A–G) of Section I. In the top row, the vertical position of names shows the conceptual distance between flute and computer—in subsections listed at the top the music is entirely flute-centric, while at the bottom the distance between flute and computer is substantial. In the next row, the start time of each subsection is given. Below this, capsule descriptions of the characteristic musical behaviors of each subsection are given; these are amplified in the analysis below. Next, the relational tactics proposed in 7.3.1.2 are used to describe the computer's typical role in each subsection: temporal extension (TX), rhythmic activation (RA), harmonic extension (HX), or sonic extension (SX). Finally, the technologies used to generate the sonic materials in each section are listed, with the chain of processing given through indications (in parentheses) of the sources processed by each module. Abbreviations of the computer's sonic resources refer to the list in 7.3.1.1. The most characteristic sonic features of each subsection are shown in bold face.

The changing timbral and behavioral distance between flute and computer in Section I is reflected in the fluctuating shapes, textures, and vertical ranges visible in Figure 7.15, a peak-graph of the entire section. The time-points in the second row of Table 7.5 are marked by clear sonic changes visible in Figure 7.15.

The opening flute solo concludes with a C-sharp 4 at 17 seconds. This is the first defining pitch of Section I, and it is repeated through subsection

Table 7.5 Archetypal Behaviors in Section I

sub-section	opening	I-A	I-B	I-C	I-D	I-E	I-F	I-G
start time	0:00	0:17	0:50	1:09	1:24	1:43	2:03	2:50
flute gestures	lyrical melody	iteration (C#4)	iteration (G4)	iteration (C#4)	incipits	lyrical melody	lyricism/ iteration	motoric rhythm
tactics of relation	(solo)	TX HX	TX SX RA	TX HX	TX HX RA	(solo) at end: TX	TX HX SX	TX SX
sonic resources	(none)	**harm(f)** **+ paf** rev∞(h) [held into IB] fshift(r)	**harm(f)** paf rev∞(h) **fshift(r)** noise(p) spat(n,p)	**harm(f)** **+ paf** rev∞(h) [held into ID] spat(r,p)	**harm(f)** **+ paf** rev∞(h) spat(r,p)	at end: rev∞(f) + paf [held into IF]	harm(f) paf rev∞(f) **fshift(r)** **noise(p)** spat(n,p)	paf rev(f) **fshift(r)** **noise(p)** spat(n,p,s)

*The sources sent to each signal processor are abbreviated as single letters in parentheses: f = flute, h = harmonizer, r = reverberator, p = paf synth, n = noise, s = frequency shift; a "+" sign indicates doubling

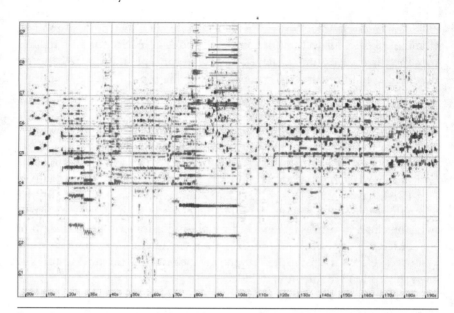

Fig. 7.15 Peak-graph of Section I.

I-A. In this subsection, the harmonizer is applied directly to the flute sound, extending it harmonically but not temporally or timbrally. Layered with this harmonic extension (HX), selected note-incipits trigger the reverberator to capture and hold the harmonizer's output. This creates extended drones (TX) that support and color the flute line. The effect is reminiscent of recitative, with harmonies accompanying and amplifying the solo line. Patterns of arpeggiation begin to grow out of cue notes beginning around 34 seconds, but rapidly devolve into harmonic support. Orchestration of timbres is already evident here; the infinite reverberator's drones are doubled in unison by paf synthesis. Frequency shifting added at the end creates a timbral transition into the start of subsection I-B, which begins at 50 seconds. Harmonic and behavioral continuity is provided by the drones in the reverb∞, which sustain the last harmony of subsection I-A throughout subsection I-B.

In Section I-B, the flutist iterates the second defining pitch of Section I, G4. The computer meanwhile generates melodic segments (RA, HX) through sequenced changes of transposition in the harmonizer. These patterns are timbrally modified (SX) by frequency shifting, which also extends the computer's melodies into a wide and chaotic registral span. The computer's rhythmic activity takes the foreground, but the flute reclaims it with a fast staccato introduction to subsection I-C, a short passage beginning at 69 seconds that echoes the behaviors of subsection I-A.

At the end of subsection I-C a transition is again created by sustained harmonies held throughout subsection I-D. Here, at 84 seconds, the computer's rhythmic and harmonic independence increases. The flute's short notes and melodic fragments cue 32nd note flurries in the computer. Selected high pitches from these flurries are held, building an increasingly complex sustained harmony (TX, HX) as subsection I-D unfolds.

The dense harmony fades at 100 seconds, setting the stage for subsection I-E. This solo flute passage hearkens back to the opening flute solo. At the end of this solo, the flute's C-sharp 4 and G4 are sustained by the reverb∞, creating a harmonic connection to earlier sections. The drones are once again held through the next subsection and are doubled by paf synthesis. In subsection I-F, starting at 123 seconds, the flute's line is still soloistic, but now continually returns to the low C-sharp pedal tone. The accompanimental relationship here is again recitativelike, with harmonies that closely follow the flute's rhapsodic rhythm. The computer follows the flutist's grace notes closely, emphasizing these articulations through extensions of harmony and timbre (HX, SX). While rhythmically close to the flute, the computer's harmonies and timbres are much further from the flute than before. Frequency shifting, used earlier in subsection I-B, transforms the sustained C-sharp–G tritone into a series of rapidly changing harmonies that traverse extreme registers and skewed overtone structures. The contrast of the computer's sounds with the flute line is extreme, even though the two are nearly in rhythmic unison.

Subsection I-G, at 170 seconds, presents a new and different musical behavior. Here, motoric 32nd notes in the flute are reminiscent of the computer's passagework in subsection I-D, but in longer continuous lines. This prefigures the motoric coordination (MC) of later sections. The computer is less active here—timbre, not time, is the domain of its independence. In addition to sonic extension in the form of frequency-shifted reverberation of the flute's sound, the computer provides temporal extension of selected flute pitches by doubling and sustaining them with paf synthesis. The timbral envelopes of the synthesized notes have a distinct character, with sharp and spectrally rich attack–decay phases (particularly visible in the octave above C7 between 170 and 183 seconds). The synthesized attacks stand out strongly before decaying into timbres that echo and support the flute line; they prefigure the sonic dynamics (SD) of later sections.

Sustained harmonies, melodic continuity, spatialization, and the recurrent C-sharp–G tritone, weave the subsections of Section I together, as do the various internal resemblances described above. At the same time, each subsection presents a distinct field of timbres and relations between flute and computer. These archetypal models are developed in later sections. In Section II the flute part fragments and extends the melodic materials presented at the opening of Section I. Fragmentary gestures alternate with rapid figures leading to either longer notes or rests. The latter extend the iterative behaviors of subsections I-A and I-B into new melodic regions. The computer follows suit, presenting longer segments of fast motoric rhythms. Thus, the flute line's fragmentation is matched by increasingly active accompaniment by the computer. This developmental strategy itself mirrors the unfolding of the first four subsections of Section I. In Section III, the musical gestures of Section II are further developed. The relational strategies used in Section II are simultaneously extended to include elements of other archetypes. The incipit-response patterns seen in subsections I-B and I-D are extended. Elements of subsections I-F and I-G are also developed here and woven together into a new texture at subsection III-F.

The return to lyrical solo passages in Sections IV and VII, accompanied by temporal extension of flute notes, hearkens back to the opening and to subsections I-A, I-C, and I-E. Section XI extends the model of an accompanied solo with further orchestration and harmonic support from the computer. The flute opens Section XIII with an inversion of the opening solo melody, which introduces a foreshortened and enervated echo of Section I. The music briefly recalls several of the initial archetypes, and a few elements of their development through the piece, before subsiding to the central C-sharp–G tritone of the opening.

Even the computer's most independent roles are outgrowths of the basic relationships established in Section I. The computer's independent behaviors in Sections V and IX are a radical intensification of the tactic of rhythmic activation used in subsections I-B and I-D. This is combined with extreme sonic and harmonic extension, as in subsection I-F when long rhythmic passages inhabit new timbres and registers that contrast strongly with the flute. While these sections are radically different from the opening, elements of their sounds and behaviors can still be traced back to archetypes in Section I.

In a strategic sense, the interpolation engine used in Sections V and IX actually positions the computer part much closer to the flute line than it would appear. The shape, speed, and trajectory of the interpolations mirror the flutist's interpretation of figures in Sections II and VII. If the flutist's performance is faster or slower, more regular or irregular, the interpolated sequences will follow that tendency. In this way, the flutist is given authority in one section to control the real-time composition of another. The timbres in Sections V and IX obscure the close relationships between the flute's interpretation of certain gestures and the computer's reinterpretations of them. These similarities are also hidden by the removal of the computer's recording of gestures from their re-creation, since they occur in completely different sections of the piece. After just a few rehearsals, however, the flutist is entirely aware of these connections (the points where gestures are recorded are clearly notated in the score).

The other cases of extreme development in the middle sections of the work are easier to relate to the opening. The musical gestures of Sections VI and XII resemble those of subsection I-F, as observed in 7.3.3.1. The distinctive timbral envelopes of the synthesizer notes in subsection I-G also foreshadow the sonic dynamics of these sections. The motoric coordination that characterizes Sections VIII and X is an extension of the computer's short motoric sequences, heard in subsection I-D, combined with the model of extended motoric passagework presented by the flute in subsection I-G. Such connections can be found on a larger formal scale as well. The timbral world of Sections VIII and X, focusing on samples inhabiting a wide registral span, is informed by the new timbres introduced in Section V. Connection, contrast, and combination produce a formal plan that is highly architectural in its sectional design, but still fluidly integrated.

7.3.4.2. Formal Plan and Self-Similarity   Each musical archetype presented in *Jupiter* corresponds to a particular set of relationships between the flute and the computer. Within Section I, similarities and contrasts between subsections create a hierarchy of relationships, as shown in the top part of Table 7.5. This can be seen as a microcosm of the relationships between sections in the larger form: the design of the thirteen sections of the piece is an expansion of the subsectional design presented in Section I. The primary structural difference is the recapitulatory behavior discussed in 7.3.3.3. Table 7.6 summarizes the work's large-scale organization. The similarity of the flow of relationships between flute and computer within Section I (Table 7.5) and in the larger form (Table 7.6) can be seen in the pattern of relationships between flute and computer (represented by vertical position) over time.

Table 7.6 Formal Plan: Hierarchy of Sectional Identities

	I	II	III	IV	V	VI	VII	VIII	IX	X	XI	XII	XIII
I ACE	I	II		IV			VII				XI		XIII
I BD			III		V				IX				
I F						VI						XII	
I G								VIII		X			
primary	TX	HX	RA	TX	IB	HX	TX	MC	IB	MC	TX	HX	TX
flute/cptr	HX	RA	SX	SX	HX	SX	SX	HX	HX	SX	HX	SX	HX
relationships	RA				SX	SD		SX	SX		RA	SD	
								→IB		→IB		→RA	

Relational tactics: TX = temporal extension, RA = rhythmic activation, HX = harmonic extension, SX = sonic extension, MC = motoric coordination; IB = independent behaviors, SD = sonic dynamics; → indicates a transition to another tactic, moving into the following section.

In the top portion of Table 7.6, the hierarchy of relations between flute and computer is visible. As in Table 7.5, higher vertical positions are more flute-centric and lower ones, more computer-centric. Closely related sections appear at similar vertical positions, also as in Table 7.5. Archetypes from Section I associated with the various sections are listed to the left of this graph in order to make explicit the relationship between Section I and the larger form. In the lower portion of the table, the most typical relational tactics of each section are shown; their similarities and differences parallel the relationships between sections.

7.3.4.3. *Form as a Function of Digital Instrumentation*   The preceding tables focus on behavioral relationships. It is also possible to assess the large-scale form of Jupiter in terms of timbre by determining which instruments within the digital orchestra are used in each section. Since instruments also imply characteristic interactive relationships, as observed in 7.3.1.2, parallels to Table 7.6 should be expected in such an assessment.

Table 7.7 shows an overview of form as a function of instrumentation. Instrument types are listed from top to bottom in increasing order of the conceptual distance from the flute line they tend to establish. A shape can easily be seen, with the instruments of Sections I, IV, VII, XI, and XIII tending to inhabit the top half of the table, and Sections V, VI, XIII, IX, X, and XII tending toward the bottom. This is further clarified in the bottom two rows. By assigning values from 1 to 14 to each row of the table from top to bottom, summing the row values of the elements in each column, and then dividing by the number of elements in the column, the "vertical scores" at the bottom of the table are obtained (for ease of reading, they are scaled by a factor of 10 and rounded to the nearest integer). These scores approximate the conceptual distance between flute and computer in each section. A graphic display of the "vertical scores" is given in the bottom row; its shape closely resembles that seen in the top portions of Tables 7.5 and 7.6.

The "vertical scores" in Table 7.7 illustrate the close relationship between Sections I, IV, VII, XI, and XIII; all have scores in the mid-30s. The gradual expansion of the composition's sonic and relational territory through Sections II and III is visible in their increasing scores. The sudden jump to a score of 67 at Section V represents that section's extreme difference from what came before. The sections involving independent behaviors, sonic dynamics, and motoric coordination all have scores in the 60s and 70s. The correlations between numeric scores in Table 7.7 and vertical positions in Tables 7.5 and 7.6 show a well-defined and consistent architecture in both relational and timbral behaviors.

Table 7.7 Technologies Used and Sectional Identities

	I	II	III	IV	V	VI	VII	VIII	IX	X	XI	XII	XIII
fl→rvb∞	X	X	X	X			X		X		X		X
fl→harm → rvb∞	X	X	X	X		X		X		X	X	X	X*
paf synth	X	X	X	X	X		X						X
freq shifter	X	X	X	X	X	X			X		X	X	X
noise mod	X	X		X	X	X		X		XX			
spatializer	X	X		X	X		X	X	X	X			X
fl phase mod				X	X						X	X	
samp: flute note		X	X										
add synth			X										
syn/samp →harm			X			X	X		X	X	X		X
samp: tongue ram											X		
samp: tam-tam					X			X					
samp: pno chord									X				
chapo synth						X						X	
vertical score	35	41	53	35	67	74	37	75	65	73	35	70	35
graphic view of vertical score	▮	▮	▮	▮	▮	▮	▮	▮	▮	▮	▮	▮	▮

* in Section XIII, the routing more often used is fl→rvb∞→harm.

7.3.4.4. Form, Tradition, and "Backward Compatibility" *Jupiter*'s formal tendencies can also be measured in terms of performance by comparing the form and its component sections to traditional practice. The concerto-like relationship between soloist and orchestra is increasingly upset in the sections with higher "vertical scores" in Table 7.7. Fewer and less intricate cues follow the flute line, the temporal correlation between the flute and computer is generally weaker, and the notations become more generalized and nontraditional.

This tendency leads to crises at the ends of Sections IX and X, where the computer breaks into wild solo passages. These consist of rapidly sequenced runs of samples sweeping in rapid glissandi through registers. Their sonic results are shown in Figure 7.16. These striking passages invert the norm of a classical concerto by giving the cadenzas to the digital orchestra. The flutist gets no cadenza. The extended solo passage in the middle of Section VIII, mentioned in 7.3.1.4, is simply an extension of the computer's motoric music before and after, lacking the freedom of a cadenza. The flutist's role in Section VIII, and to a lesser degree section X, is to follow and accompany the computer. This is the height of transgression against the expectation of a concerto, though it is not without precedent in the traditional literature (consider, for example, the recapitulation of Mendelssohn's *Violin Concerto*).

The formal model of *Jupiter* is remarkably classical in its organization into well-defined and hierarchically related sections. The presentation of

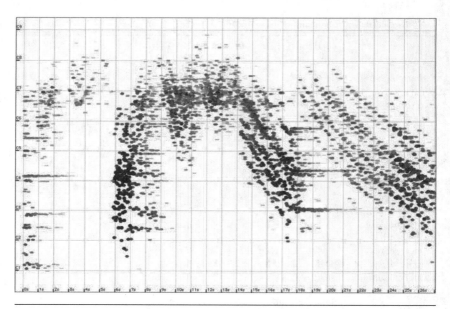

Fig. 7.16 First computer solo (subsection IX-C, cue 13). (DVD reference 7)

archetypes at the beginning that are extended in later sections is not unlike the model of exposition and development in a classical sonata form. There is also a recapitulation in Section XIII, as described in 7.3.3.3. The metaphor of soloist, orchestra, and conductor proposed by Manoury and examined in detail throughout 7.3.1 evokes the model of a classical concerto.

As observed earlier, the alternation of focus between solo flute and digital orchestra is reminiscent of ritornello form. The roles of soloist and accompaniment are inverted in the central sections of the work, further removing these sections from traditional practice. In fact, over the course of the work it becomes clear that the normal solo-ritornello alternation is completely reversed. The ritornelli are given to the solo flute in Sections I, IV, VII, XI, and XIII, instead of to the digital orchestra. These are the only sections that evoke a feeling of return, and they open and close the work as ritornelli normally would. The computer's only evident repetition is its transgressive pair of cadenzas at the ends of Sections IX and X, which certainly do not function as ritornelli.

The shifting relationships between the notated score and traditional practice also indicate the work's form. The least traditional notations, discussed in 7.3.2.2, are seen in the sections that show the greatest separation between flute and computer in Tables 7.6 and 7.7. Harmonic tension and instability in a classical sonata form tend to increase through the central development section. In *Jupiter*, relational tension between flute and computer and notational distance from tradition follow a similar trajectory. In this respect, the work's form is "backward compatible." While pushing the envelope of technology and creating a new mode of live electronic music performance, Manoury drew upon classical expectations to develop a hierarchical structure of interactive relationships which resonates strongly with a performer's experiences in traditional repertoire.

7.4. Summary and Conclusions

That *Jupiter* is a real-time interactive work creates special opportunities for analysis. It is multiply documented in the interrelated perspectives of score, software, and sound. Analysis from all of these perspectives provides valuable insights into how the work was made, how it communicates, and what its crucial musical relationships are. Correlation of the patch, computer scores, notated scores, and sonic results allows for analytical depth and clarity. Impressions from one perspective can be verified through comparison with another. This approach reveals a work that is highly structured and unified, despite its great internal variety. Elements of sound, notation, and technology are strategically deployed to different sections, but they are subtly layered, combined, and reinvented over time. The first section is the source of musical archetypes developed later in the work; the relationships between succeeding sections in the form recontextualize and reinvent these archetypes.

Orchestration is a crucial metaphor for the deployment and layering of relationships and timbres in *Jupiter*. This analysis has focused on the orchestration of timbres and interactive relationships to construct a strategic model of form. A more traditional approach focusing on harmony, rhythm, and pattern could surely be the basis for a parallel analysis; elements of this approach have occasionally been suggested in this essay. From any perspective, *Jupiter* is remarkable in the depth of connections, the clarity of strategic planning, and the nuanced execution that characterize all aspects of the work.

Jupiter demonstrated that real-time interaction based on pitch tracking and score following could form the basis for a substantial work. It grew in subtlety and complexity as it adapted to several generations of hardware and software. This demonstration of IRCAM's technology through the decade from 1987 to 1996 is still remarkable nearly a decade later—not so much for its technological means as for their orchestration into a nuanced and coherent work that builds a bridge between the classical past and the technological future.

References

Chadabe, J. *Electric Sound: The Past and Promise of Electronic Music.* Upper Saddle River, NJ: Prentice-Hall, 1997.

Déchelle, F., M. DeCecco, M. Puckette, and D. Zicarelli. "The IRCAM 'Real-Time Platform:' evolution and perspectives." In *Proceedings of the International Computer Music Conference,* 228–229. San Francisco: International Computer Music Association, 1994.

Favreau, E., M. Fingerhut, O. Koechlin, P. Potacsek, M. Puckette, and R. Rowe. "Software Developments for the 4X Real-Time System." In *Proceedings of the International Computer Music Conference,* 369–73. San Francisco: International Computer Music Association, 1986.

Feldman, M. *Essays.* Kerpen: Beginner Press, 1985.

Lindemann, E., M. Starkier, F. Déchelle, and B. Smith. "The Architecture of the IRCAM Musical Workstation." *Computer Music Journal* 15, no. 3 (1991): 41–50.

Lippe, C. "A Look at Performer/Machine Interaction Using Real-Time Systems." In *Proceedings of the International Computer Music Conference,* 116-17. San Francisco: Computer Music Association, 1996.

———. "Real-Time Interactive Digital Signal Processing: A View of Computer Music." *Computer Music Journal* 20, no. 4 (1996): 21–24.

Manoury, P. *Jupiter.* Paris: Editions Durand, 1992.

———. "*Jupiter* and *Ultima.*" *Program Notes.* Toronto, Canada: Music Gallery, 2002. Available online: <http://www.interlog.com/~nmc/2002-2003.pdf>

May, A. *PeakGraph* (Max/MSP patch). 2004. Available online: <http://spot.colorado.edu/~aamay/PeakGraph.zip>

McNutt, E. *pipe wrench: flute and computer.* CD. Electronic Music Foundation, 2001.

———. "Performing Electroacoustic Music: A Wider View of Interactivity." *Organized Sound* 8, no.3 (2004): 297–304.

Puckette, M. "Combining Event and Signal Processing in the MAX Graphical Programming Environment." *Computer Music Journal* 15, no. 3 (1991): 68–77.

———. "FTS: A Real-Time Monitor for Multiprocessor Music Synthesis." *Computer Music Journal* 15, no. 3 (1991): 58–67.

———. "Formant-based audio synthesis using nonlinear distortion." *Journal of the Audio Engineering Society* 43, no. 1 (1995): 40–47.

———. "Pure data." In *Proceedings of the International Computer Music Conference,* 43–46. San Francisco: International Computer Music Association, 1997.

——— "Max at 17." *Computer Music Journal* 26, no. 4 (2002): 31–34.

Puckette, M., and T. Apel. "Real-time audio analysis tools for Pd and MSP." In *Proceedings of the International Computer Music Conference,* 109–12. San Francisco: International Computer Music Association, 1998.

Puckette, M. and C. Lippe. "Score Following in Practice." In *Proceedings of the International Computer Music Conference,* 182–85. San Francisco: International Computer Music Association, 1992.

Puckette, M., P. Manoury, C. Lippe, M. Battier, T. Mays, and L. Stuck. *PureData Repertory Project: Philippe Manoury, Jupiter.* 2003. Available online: <http://crca.ucsd.edu/~msp/pdrp/latest/patch/manoury-jupiter>

Rowe, R. *Interactive Music Systems: Machine Listening and Composing.* Cambridge, MA: MIT Press, 1993.

Vercoe, B. "The Synthetic Performer in the Context of Live Musical Performance." In *Proceedings of the International Computer Music Conference,* 185. San Francisco: International Computer Music Association, 1984.

Welsh, J. *The Music of Stuart Saunders Smith.* New York: Zinn Publishing, 1995.

DVD References

Number	File Name	Description	Media Type
1	Fig.7.2 + 7.5 + 7.9.aif	Section III, cue 66; examined in Figures 7.2, 7.5, and 7.9	Stereo AIFF
2	Figs. 7.6 + 7.11 + Tab. 7.3.aif	Section VIII, cue 8; examined in Table 7.3 and Figures 7.6 and 7.11	Stereo AIFF
3	Fig. 7.3 + 7.12.aif	Section V, cues 7-11; examined in Figures 7.3 and 7.12	Stereo AIFF
4	Fig. 7.4 + 7.7 + 7.8.aif	Section VI, cues 8–13; examined in Figures 7.4, 7.7, and 7.8	Stereo AIFF
5	Fig. 7.10.aif	Section I, cues 50–67; examined in Figure 7.10	Stereo AIFF
6	Fig. 7.13 + 7.14 + Tab. 7.4.aif	Section XII, cues 13–23; examined in Figures 7.13 and 7.14 and Table 7.4	Stereo AIFF
7	Fig. 7.15.aif	Section I (complete); examined in Figure 7.15	Stereo AIFF
8	Fig. 7.16.aif	Section IX, cue 13; examined in Figure 7.16	Stereo AIFF

Notes

1. Philippe Manoury and Miller Puckette were generous in their explanations of and comments about aspects of the research that resulted in the analysis presented in this chapter. Many of their insights have been incorporated into this essay and the author is deeply indebted to both of them. Elizabeth McNutt contributed profoundly on the subject of performing *Jupiter* and the author would like to thank her for the permission to use her recording of the work in the graphic and audio examples presented in this chapter. Many thanks to Daphne Leong and Mary Simoni for their thoughtful commentary and editorial assistance.
2. This process has been extensively described in the literature, notably Vercoe (1984); see also Puckette and Lippe (1992).

8

Barry Truax's *Riverrun*[1]

MARA HELMUTH

8.1. Introduction

Listening to *Riverrun* by Barry Truax more closely connects the listener to the physical world through a metaphor of water sounds, creating an experience related to that of a natural wonder. While the work was created with real-time synthesis, it is heard as a river soundscape. The flexibility and power of granular synthesis techniques give the composition its fluid and timbrally diverse character. Granular synthesis techniques resemble some natural phenomena, but the power of the work goes beyond technique. Immersed in evolving complex timbral textures with many transformations and only a few distinct borders, the listener perceives anew his or her relationship to the environment.

Riverrun is a slowly transforming sonic environment. It does not have the concise phrases and active harmonic rhythm of classical music, or even the sculptured quickly unfolding gestures of much recent electroacoustic music. The events evade precise descriptions in traditional musical terms. Densities, timbral qualities, and stochastic layerings make up a fluid, transforming entity with such internal subtlety that it is only understood on a large time-scale. Thus, each section is like a phrase in which intense microlevel activity reflects complex natural processes.

Key aspects of this comparatively new genre of electroacoustic music—stochastic material, various types of transformation, and use of space—are explored within the soundscape. Each of these aspects questions the lines between inner and outer, or creates conditions that encourage attention to changes in sound worlds and to interactions of many aspects of sound, rather than identification and recognition of distinct sonic entities. Instead of clearly defined motivic pitch or rhythmic units, probability states create tendencies, likelihoods, and spontaneous-sounding textures resembling a stream or waterfall, with indistinct boundaries. One can be in or merge with this liquidity; it is not distinct from the listener. During transformations, movement in a rising pitch band, a convergence of grains to a pitch, or a change in density seems to modulate the listener's position as well as the sound—one is in/by/ near a rich, low frequency, a helicopter-like pulsing, or rising with a spectral band, or feeling the pitch convergence as a focusing vibration within. In spatial play the point is even stronger: the listener is approached, surrounded, or completely encompassed by the dense, enlivening textures. Truax's interest in encouraging "a different mode of listening" (1988, 25), is fulfilled in the listener's relationship to the music, its context, and its time.

8.2. Background

Riverrun was originally a four-channel, twenty-minute long work completed in 1986, and was released on compact disc in stereo (Truax 1987a). A commission by the Music Section of the Biennale di Venezia, *Riverrun* was completed with the financial assistance of the Canada Council. The first performance was in 1986 at the International Computer Music Conference in The Hague. In 1991 it received the Magisterium award in the International Competition of Electroacoustic Music in Bourges, France. In 2004 Truax made an eight-channel version, which was premiered on an exceptional sound system in April 2004 in Belfast at the Sonic Arts Network's 25th Retrospective Concert at Sonorities Weekend.

The author met with Truax in July 2004 at his home studio in Vancouver, British Columbia, where he demonstrated the software used to create *Riverrun* on the PDP 11, DMX-1000, and MTU interface; the system still ran. Audio output was not produced due to a very recent problem with a blown audio chip, which has since been fixed. The author was impressed with the flexibility built into a real-time system with such an apparently simple method of control as alphanumeric characters. Truax has used the system, with additional newer programs and the AudioBox audio interface, as a strong component in recent works. The longevity of this two-decade-old system is unusual in a field in which hardware and software may be reinvented every few years, and it has allowed him to focus on composition and expanding existing capabilities rather than learning new systems and porting software. The eight-channel version of Truax's *Island,* and *Temple,* both from sampled sources, were also heard during this meeting. They seemed more closely related to *Riverrun* in textural, gestural, or timbral aspects than many other of the composer's works, which involve primary components of voice with text, even if rich granular textures between or behind vocal phrases are heard.

"riverrun" is the first word of James Joyce's *Finnegans Wake* (1939), and the composition reflects the spontaneity and sound-oriented focus of this literary work. The word also refers to the soundscape the piece brings forth. In *Acoustic Communication* (2001) Truax defines soundscape composition as when (1) the listener can recognize the source material after transformations; (2) the listener's knowledge of the context is drawn upon to understand the work; (3) the composer's knowledge of the context directs the composition of the work; and (4) the work deepens the listener's understanding of the world (240). Aside from the fact that *Riverrun* is created from synthesis, and, therefore, the "source material" undergoing transformation is actually an abstract technique, granular synthesis, *Riverrun* fits his definition on all counts.

The piece is not programmatic, in the sense that specific sounds of a river correlate to sounds in the piece, but the sonic activities in the piece were inspired by the idea of a river such as British Columbia's Fraser. This river moves through narrow Fraser Canyon and through Hell's Gate, becomes broad and quiet in the delta region where it splits into several flows, and finally merges into the Pacific Ocean in Vancouver, Truax's home. The moving soundscape traverses the metaphorical river, and spectral activities refer to aspects of the river—droplet originations, dripping, thundering through canyon walls, and widening into a large placid delta. Even visual aspects are incorporated, as Truax described the sound the author had heard as cricket-like as signifying to him the "sunlight glistening off the water" (Truax 2004c).

The composition was created with real-time granular synthesis on a Digital Equipment Corporation PDP 11 with a DMX-1000 Digital Signal Processor. Thirty pages of assembler code for the GSX program controlled grain parameters and responded to user commands, and DMX-1000 microcode generated synthesis. Truax performed stereo sequences of the piece by hitting alphanumeric keys and recorded the material to eight-channel tape. A brief discussion of granular synthesis follows.[2]

8.2.1. Granular Synthesis

Granular synthesis techniques involve creating complex sounds from tiny units of sound. The physicist Dennis Gabor first proposed a model of sound as acoustical quanta that took into account the time pattern as well as the frequency pattern (1957, 591–94), in contrast to existing models of sound based on Fourier analysis. These quanta could describe any sound. Iannis Xenakis was influenced by physicist Abraham Moles and Werner Meyer-Eppler's work incorporating Gabor's ideas (Roads 2001, 62–64). Xenakis (1971) invented the term *grains of sound* and described a theory for composing with grains, and in 1959 created *Analogique A-B*, an analog tape composition created from cutting up recorded sine tones into fragments (Xenakis 1971, 79–109). Curtis Roads implemented digital realizations of granular synthesis (Roads 1978, 61–62; 1985, 149–58) and created several tape compositions using the technique. After having worked with stochastic processes and timbre, often using frequency modulation techniques (Truax 1979, 30–39; 1977, 68–82; 1982. 72–77), Truax developed interactive methods of composition with the DMX-1000 on the PODX system (Truax 1977, 1988b,138–45), including a real-time implementation of granular synthesis. Truax's *Riverrun* was probably the first piece created entirely with a real-time implementation and the most influential early work created with the technique. He said, "granular synthesis seemed to break through into a new domain of richness and 'corporeality' or what I now call the 'volume' (i.e., perceived magnitude) of the sound, hence the analogy to large scale environmental sounds like waterfalls and cataracts" (2004b). In recent decades many composers have worked with granular synthesis techniques in various software applications.

A grain is a short segment of sound. Its waveform may be synthetic, often a sine wave, a frequency modulated sound, or a sampled sound. The grain envelope, necessary to avoid hearing a click on each grain, can be Gaussian, or made of straight line segments, as on the PDP 11 for efficiency. The parameters for each grain are its frequency (or register), rate (time between grains or between start points of grains), duration, and an optional amount of variation in these parameters, which may be described by probability distributions. Regular grain rates can produce heard frequencies, while the frequency of the waveform inside the grain may affect timbre. Grains may be .001 second in duration, although composers often work with longer grains. The densities may also range from very low with a discontinuous series of grains, to a "fused" texture—heard as continuous—to thick, cloudy textures with many thousands of overlapping grains.

A contiguous series of sine wave grains at the same pitch, with the frequencies in phase and at a constant rate, performs amplitude modulation of the original grains, producing sidebands above and below the original frequencies. Often, however, probabilities are used to control variation in the rates, frequencies, and durations of grains, producing complex results of varying densities. This stochastic granular synthesis can generate highly diverse musical results due to phase relationships between grains, and other aspects. Granular synthesis implementation strategies may produce highly individual kinds of sounds. Since many natural sounds, such as water and thunder, have a stochastic component, they may be emulated with granular synthesis. Truax has described the "paradox" of granular synthesis as very rich textures being based on "trivial" grains of sound (1988b, 25).

Granular synthesis techniques provided the musical materials for *Riverrun*, and generally engendered complex states of multiple events rather than lines of individually heard notes at precise time points. In *Computer Music Journal*, Truax detailed the techniques used in *Riverrun*, summarized below (1988b, 14–25). Grains were composed of additive synthesis or frequency-modulated (FM) sound, with three-part straight-line envelopes. The attack and decay portions of the envelope ranged from 1/2 to 1/16 of the grain duration, and defaulted to 1/4. With FM-based grains, the same envelope controlled amplitude of both the carrier and the modulator frequencies, producing palendromic grains with the highest modulation index and, therefore, richest timbre in the sustained portion of the grain. According to Truax, some of the FM ratios were based on John Chowning's FM vowel sounds, particularly in the beginning of Section 2 with the pulse that disintegrated. The DMX-1000 could produce up to twenty simultaneous "voices" (each producing one grain at a time) of additive synthesis grains, or up to eight voices of FM grains. Half of the voices were assigned to each of two channels, producing stereo output. A variable delay time might occur between grains. The shortest grains produced by the scheduler were eight milliseconds (ms) in duration, generating 125 grains per second (gps) per voice. Amplitude modulation from the grain envelope sometimes produced sidebands, and the gradual changes in grain duration resulted in tuning changes, with glissandi in and out of harmonic relationships to the grain frequency and to other simultaneous layers. Grain densities in the piece were often high, at 100 to 2000 gps. Listings of grain parameters for objects in the piece are found in the Appendix.

Truax used uniform random distributions to control the grain parameters, producing a stochastic music based on probabilities (Truax 2004a). The following control variables specified grain parameters for *Riverrun*: (1) center frequency and frequency range; (2) grain duration and duration range; and (3) delay time between grains. For additive synthesis, the number of voices with each of three waveforms and the total number of voices were also under user control. With FM, average modulation index, index range, and total number of voices were also available. These control parameters for the granular objects, also called presets, were under individual keystroke control. Ramps, or patterns of change in the parameters of the presets, were also stored and combined with the presets to elicit transformations, and initiated with keystrokes. The ramp value in milliseconds specified the time after which the value would change by the incremented amount. Tendency masks, which Truax developed later to allow independent control of ramps for different parameters, had not been implemented yet, so each stereo layer had linked ramps in *Riverrun*. Within a sequence, then, the same ramps operated on all parameters, but ramps could move in opposite directions by using positive and negative increments for different parameters. A parallel processing programming strategy allowed all of these control processes to operate compatibly in real time, and with access to data that described the current state of synthesis. The hierarchy of control levels developed for this piece allowed the user to enter a new value for a parameter, increment a parameter, increment a group of "synchronized" parameters, initiate highly controllable ramps on synchronized variables, and modify overall amplitude levels. Presets could be stored during a ramp in performance and later retrieved and edited without interrupting synthesis. Each of the four stereo tracks of the sequences making up *Riverrun* was performed with real-time control and recorded to tape beginning at the same point on the tape, to achieve an octophonic texture. Only a few modifications were made to the tape after real-time synthesis; these included doubling the speeds of sequences M and J generating higher frequency layers for some iterations. While the control method was simple keystrokes, this highly developed system generated enormously varied and powerful material in real time.

Looking at the computer code, one is struck by its efficiency compared to the numerous levels and complex object-oriented constructions often used today: Only 256 assembler instructions of controller code generated the grains themselves. Traux writes:

> Since 12 lines of microcode defined a "voice" or grainstream layer with a fixed waveform, 20 such layers could be generated in real time; in the case of FM grains, 30 lines of code generated each of the 8 layers. Precise timing of events was handled every 1 ms with an interrupt routine on the PDP-11 involving a few hundred lines of assembler code, with the remaining code handling user commands, printouts to the screen, generation of grain parameters, and managing presets and ramps. FORTRAN routines were used for file management. Because of the efficiency of the granular controller being written in Macro assembler, it used less than 7400 words of memory, and because of the overlay strategy used by the PDP, the entire program, including system requirements, ran comfortably in 64 kilobytes of memory. (2004e)

The small amount of memory available meant that samples had to be efficiently used when using sound sample sources. The access time for the RLO2 disks was actually rather fast for its time, allowing 50 kHz reading of samples, and 40 kHz randomly accessed individual blocks (Truax 2004d). Debugging the DMX code had to be done only through the digital to analog converter by listening to or analyzing the results; so, Truax developed a layered approach, building one voice at a time. The system had a particular set of timing characteristics, probably due to a slight performance delay. If twenty grain streams are synthesized at the same time, the twentieth grain begins slightly later than the first. According to Truax, this delay gives the system a particular "sound" appropriate for his music that he has not been able to duplicate with other configurations.

Fig. 8.1 Barry Truax at his home studio July 2004, with PDP 11 screen on right (photo by Mara Helmuth). (DVD reference 1)

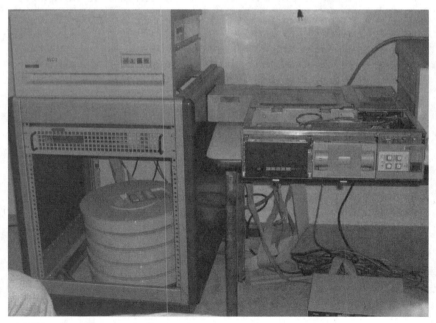

Fig. 8.2 Truax's PDP 11 with the DMX-1000 in a room adjoining the studio (photo by Mara Helmuth). (DVD reference 2)

194 • Mara Helmuth

8.3. The Analysis

8.3.1. Formal Organization of Work

Riverrun can be divided into five sections, seen in Figures 8.3 and 8.4. The first and last sections are related sonically; they are created from varying densities of grain layers that evolve over time, giving the piece an overall arch form. The higher spectral patterns of parallel ascending and descending bands revealed by the sonograms are common to these sections. Section 1, from 0:00 (minutes:seconds) to 5:35, begins with sparse distributions of individually heard grains (Sound 1, DVD reference 4), which gradually become denser through the increasing rates and additional layers of sequence A. At the end, Section 1 focuses on the unique place in the piece where local rhythm is present, where simultaneous grains are heard periodically for a short time, and where distinct pitches (G, B, and D) emerge. For much of the work, the interval G D and its implicit tonality provides a basic stage on which complex timbral evolution is played out. The timbral activity expresses a metaphor for the sounds of a river, sometimes characterized in the text portion of the complete analysis. Regarding important pitches, Section 1 emphasizes G. (Note that most pitches are microtonal and only approximately described by pitch class or notation.) The primary pitches at the beginning of Section 2 are D and A, and Section 2 contains more densely fused textures (Sound 2, DVD reference 5).

Section 2, from 5:35 to 8:48, and Section 3, from 8:48 to 10:57, are both arch forms; each of these sections begins and ends with pitched material and becomes dense and unpitched in the middle, as in Sounds 3 and 4 for Section 3. The entrance of the high D in Section 2 confirms a "modulation," or a shift of emphasis to D, while Section 3 returns to G and D. Sections 3 and 4 lack the higher spectral activity and clarity of the other sections. Some of the most dense and complex timbral material is in Section 4, which extends from 10:57 to 14:08, and also is an arch form. Sequence I and the bass ostinato sequence K emphasize 125 Hz (B), 200 Hz (G), and their harmonics. Around 13:30, pitch bands similar to Section 5 occur from 400 to 2200 Hz. Section 5, from 14:08 to 19:54, contains glissandi sliding in and out of perfect intervals, each of which feels like an arrival point on D and A, occasional "mediant" (B) emphasis, and ultimately G and D. Very low pitches come into tune with higher layers, while sidebands at 50 Hz intervals provide timbral complexity. Higher spectral activity ("twitter" or cricket" sounds of sequence M) are arranged in diamond-shaped patterns with both vertical (frequency axis) and horizontal (time axis) symmetries.

Sound 1 *Riverrun* Section 1 excerpt, 0:20–0:25, with individual grains. (DVD reference 4)

Sound 2 *Riverrun* middle of Section 2, 7:30–7:40. (DVD reference 5)

Sound 3 *Riverrun* beginning of Section 3, 8:49–9:05.(DVD reference 6)

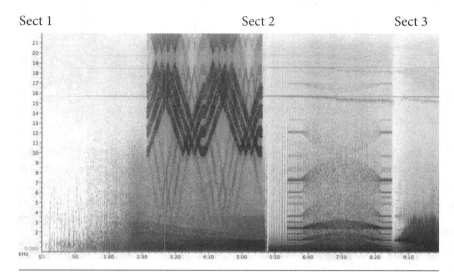

Fig. 8.3 Sonogram of *Riverrun*, 0:00–10:00. (DVD reference 3)

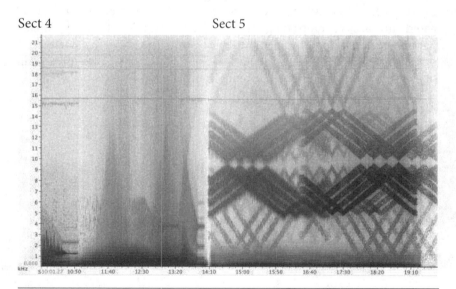

Fig.8 4 Sonogram of *Riverrun*, 10:00–20:00. (DVD reference 7)

Sound 4 *Riverrun* ending of Section 3, 10:32–10:48. (DVD reference 8)

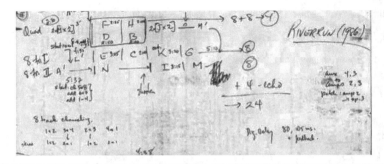

Fig. 8.5 Truax's diagram of the work, indicating sequences of material and source tapes for mixdown (Truax 1986a). (DVD reference 9)

Frequencies that exceed the Nyquist, which is one half the sampling rate, produce foldover in digital systems, as the waveform cannot be accurately represented. The frequency X above the Nyquist "folds over" to the Nyquist minus X. Foldover can be seen in sonograms as shadowy lines for frequencies above 10 kHz, except for the M and J sequences in Sections 1, 4, and 5, which were played at double speed, putting the foldover frequency at 20 kHz. However, this foldover is probably not very audible (Truax 2004c).

Riverrun is composed of four stereo pairs of channels, mixed from as many as thirty-two channels of sound on two, eight-channel tapes (rows 3 and 4 in Figure 8.6), and a quad premix (rows 1 and 2). A performed keystroke triggered entrances of ramps on granular objects. Examples of granular object parameter starting points are in the table below. (The object name letters do not correspond to the named sequences from Figure 8.6.) Additional grain object parameter listings may be found in the Appendix.

	Section 1	2	3	4	5
Quad Premix Tape	2x[Mx2]	F	H	2x[Jx2]	M'
		D	B		
8-ch Tape #1	L'	E	C	K	G
8-ch Tape #2	A'	N	I		M

Fig. 8.6 Simplified diagram of materials based on Truax's diagram. Rows indicate original source tape contents, and columns indicate sections of the work. Sequences J and M were played at double speed where noted with "x2," creating sequences an octave higher than originally synthesized. " ' " indicates a reversed tape layer. (DVD reference 10)

Table 8.1 Grain Parameters for Some of the Objects Found in *Riverrun* (Truax 1986a)

Obj.	No.	Freq	Freq Range	Dur.	Dur. Range	Delay	Ramp	Max. M.I.	M.I. Range
B	4	300	8	20	1	0	1000	3	2
N	5	100	5	10	0	0	100	3	2
D	6	100	5	20	2	0	100	3	2
F	12	250	5	8	2	0	1000	1	4
H	14	750	5	8	2	0	1000	1	4
E	16	0	150	20	1	1	2000	1	0
K	17	0	200	20	1	1	2000	1	0
L	18	0	250	20	1	1	2000	1	0
F	28	200	2000	8	12	0	1000	1	0
G	29	200	2000	8	0	250	400	1	0

A sequence designated by a letter in Figure 8.6 may refer to several granular objects or presets. For example, sequence F indicates object B (no. 4) in channels 1 and 2, object V in channels 3 and 4, object Z in channels 5 and 6, and object X in channels 7 and 8. This distribution of sounds is only one of the four sequences heard in Section 2. The objects are preset starting values, which are generally altered by ramps during the sequence. In an example from Truax's notes (1986a), sequence F ramps incremented frequency values by 2 and 5 Hz, and durations by 1 and 2 ms. Ramps were sometimes paused or run in reverse direction when certain values were reached or specific tape counter numbers were reached.

8.3.2. The Compositional Process

Fourteen sequences, most of which were eight-channel and lettered A through N, were recorded from real-time performance to tape. A sequence often contained four objects, one on each stereo pair of channels, and had a particular set of sonic qualities according to their parameters. A brief description of the sequences summarizing Truax's notes, with the author's aural impressions at the end of each description follows. Octave point pitch class notation is used here, with the integer indicating the octave (8.00 = middle C), and the decimals indicating pitch class (.01 to .12 represent C sharp to B natural). Most pitches are microtonal, and may be notated with a "+" to indicate a sharp pitch.

> A—Section 1—Frequency 200, frequency RNG 2000, duration 8, duration RNG 12, some with FM c:m 2:1, 7:5 carrier waveforms 4–6, modulator waveform 1(sine). Objects X, V, B, K. Reversed (Truax 1986a). Heard as sparse opening grains becoming denser.

B—Section 3—100 Hz and harmonics, rapid changes to large durations and back. Objects X, V, B, K (Truax 1986a). Heard as G+ (7.073) to descending grains to low G+ (7.073/6.073).

C—Section 3—same as B, with FM c:m 1:3. Objects X, V, B, H (Truax 1986a). Heard as G+ (7.073) to descending grains to low G+ (7.073/6.073).

D —Section 2—75, 150, 225, 300 Hz with slow changes, increment on delay and on frequency in middle of sequence and back. Objects Z, X, V, B (Truax 1986a). Heard D.

E—Section 2—same as D with FM c:m 1:1 (Truax 1986a). Heard A (8.09) and D (9.02).

F—300 Hz and octaves, expanding ranges and back, 50 ms duration. Objects B, V, Z, X. Ascending ramps on delay and back. Incremented frequency by 2, frequency RNG by 5, duration by 1, duration RNG by 2, delay by 1, ramp by 2. Waveform 2 in 4 voices, Waveform 3 in 6 voices (Truax 1986a). Heard high D+ octaves at beginning and end.

G—Section 5— 50 and 50 Hz modulator, expanding range through harmonics. FM c:m 1:1. Objects P, O. Frequency increment 2, ascending ramp to 100, descending to 2. Duration increment 1, ascending to 25, 30, 40, descending to 30, 25, 20, pausing on tuned values. Duration range increment 1, ascending to 40, descending to 2. MI 2, 3, 4, and 5. Waveforms 1, 2, 3, and 5 modulated by 1(sine) (Truax 1986a). Heard as shifting to and from low G+ and high D.

H—Section 3—1200 Hz and low modulator/watery texture, with FM c:m 150:1, 200:1, 50:1. Object Z. Waveform 1 (sine). Increments on frequency 2, MI 1, MI RNG 1. Ramp on MI to 500 back to 1. Duration range and delay decrease, then back (Truax 1986a). Heard as beginning and ending on high D.

I—Section 4—Wide range of frequency and duration, to narrow and denser. 125, 250, 375, and 750 Hz with FM c:m 2:1, 4:1, 6:1, 12:1, carrier waveforms 4–7, and modulator waveform 1(sine). Objects P at start, reaching objects X, F, G, H (Truax 1986a).

J—Section 4—100, 150, 200 Hz. Infrasonic, expand frequency, duration, MI RNG and back with FM c:m 1:2, carrier waveform 5, modulator 1. Objects Z, X, V, ch. 1–6. Incremented frequency by 1 or 2, duration by 1, duration RNG by 1, MI by 1, MI RNG by 1 (Truax 1986a). Heard as B (7.11) with noisy low bubbly sounds.

K—Section 4—bass ostinato with MI ramp. Objects numbered 1–18, based on 200 Hz with freq RNG of 10. Durations were multiples of five between 15 and 30 ms and delays of 5, 10, 15, and 20, together forming modulation periods of 15 to 45 ms. MI of 200/N for N = 3,4,5…,9 produced c:m 3:1, 4:1, 5:1,…9:1 Ramp 2000 (Truax 1986a). Heard as a low pitch, becomes dense and thick, ending on G.

L—Section 1—250 Hz with FM c:m 1:1, carrier waveform 4–7, modulator waveform 1(sine). Objects Z, X, V, N. Increased number of voices from 0 to 8. Incremented frequency by 3, MI by 1, MI RNG by 1, duration by 1. Reversed (Truax 1986a). Heard increasing densities.

M—Sections 1 and 5—high frequency texture, at 5000, 6000, 7000, 8000 Hz ascending then descending ramps. Objects P, O, I, U. Incremented frequency by 10, duration by 1. Duration 50 to 100 to 10 to 100 ms. Tape speed is doubled in Section 1, so frequencies are doubled also. Reversed in Section 5. Heard as "sun glistening off water" (Truax 2004c). Heard as "crickets," "twitter."

N—Sections 2 and 3—500 Hz, frequency RNG 5000, duration 8 ms, delay 1000, ramp 1000 some with FM c:m 2:1, 7:5, 9:7, carrier waveforms 4–6, modulator 1(sine). Incremented frequency RNG by –2, duration by 1, duration RNG by 2, delay by –1 (Truax 1986a). Heard as pulse, fast then slower, asynchronizing over several minutes into long grains.

Sequences A, L, and M were reversed after recording to tape. It was easier to begin generation with synchronized sequences and let them become unsynchronized; so, when the opposite effect was required, the tape was reversed.

8.3.3. Stochastic Transformations

Texture is primary in *Riverrun*. Intensity often builds through the entrance of a grain layer with different parameters or lessens as layers drop out. Individual sequences usually transform gradually due to ramps on frequency and duration parameters. While the system had the capability to make abrupt changes such as modifying the carrier:modulator ratio or the waveform in real-time performance, Truax avoided such sudden changes in *Riverrun* to preserve continuity and maintain the river metaphor. The sonograms in the complete analysis, with the text descriptions, are one way to expose characteristics of the stochastic states and their changes.

Even the very sparse opening contains seemingly randomly distributed midrange frequency grains, which can be heard individually but are grouped by the mind into units of several grains until the density becomes high enough for the grains to be heard as a stream. Just after this point, one minute into the piece, a set of sustained pitches or a stream of grains (shown in Figure 8.7) is heard for several seconds in duration, as if to mark the recent change in texture from individuated to continuous. It also marks the entrance of a new midrange sequence and denser texture with faster, more constant grain rates. Such sustained sounds were an idiosyncrasy of the system: when a global amplitude ramp ran, the background process producing new random values was bypassed, meaning random grain variations were avoided for that time period (Truax, 2004c). The appearance of the brief sustained

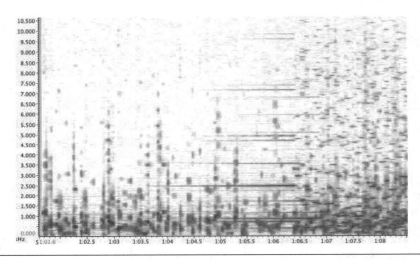

Fig. 8.7 *Riverrun* sonogram, point of first sustained pitch material at 1:03. (DVD reference 11)

Sound 5 *Riverrun* Section 1 excerpt,1:02 to 1:08. (DVD reference 12)

sound punctuates the entrance of the grain layer with a brief opposition to overall gradual change.

Interplays such as these, between simple and complex elements, exposing tiny units versus mass dynamics, occur at various points in the piece. At 2:35 a group of frequencies heard as a timbre enter, sustain for about two seconds, and then widen into bands of grains, as shown in Figure 8.8.

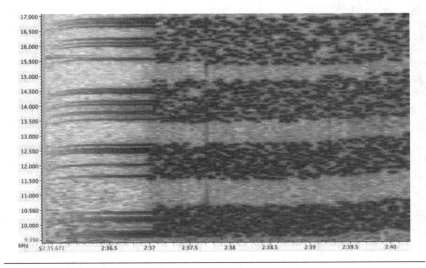

Fig. 8.8 Sonogram of *Riverrun* at 2:35.

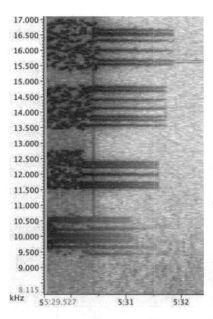

Fig.8.9 Sonogram of *Riverrun* at 5:30.

The converse dissolution of grain frequency bands back into the more focused timbre occurs near the end of Section 1 at 5:30, as seen in Figure 8.9.

At 11:00 to 11:30, longer grains are heard individually as noisy and unpitched in an additional foreground layer, in an increasingly dense texture. The ending of the piece dissolves into unpitched midrange grains; it becomes sparser and sparser, like a retrograde of the opening material but with more emphasis on the moving higher spectral bands.

Since the materials are characterized by stochastic states, they may change gradually over time by increasing in density or moving in frequency range. Grain rates affect the pitches, densities, and microlevel rhythms perceived. Since any of the parameters may change gradually, the resulting sense is of timbral evolution between states that may seem more or less stable. States that seem stable are sometimes characterized by pure intervals—such as the perfect fifth, perhaps with an obvious microlevel rhythm that accents the interval arrival, or with a widening of register by adding the pitch in a different octave.

A pitched band may diverge into an unpitched band of grains, losing a sense of pitch and revealing a continuity of discontinuity. These watery textures have so much timbral vitality and variety that the listener feels as though s/he has left the safe shore of pitch for a stormy sound voyage. Conversely, layers may converge from unpitched sound into focused grain pitches or grain rates heard at a particular pitch. Sections 2 and 3 exhibit these transformations from pitched to unpitched to pitched material through divergence and convergence (seen in Figures 8.3 and 8.4, Sounds 3 and 4). In Sound 6 (DVD reference 13), the dense Section 4 textures focus into more pitched material based on B (7.11) and then the lower G (6.07) is heard.

Sound 6 *Riverrun* Section 4 excerpt,13:35–14:00 (see complete analysis for detailed sonogram). (DVD reference 13)

The drone in Section 5 (sequence G) slowly moves up and down in pitch as seen in the sonogram in Figure 8.10.

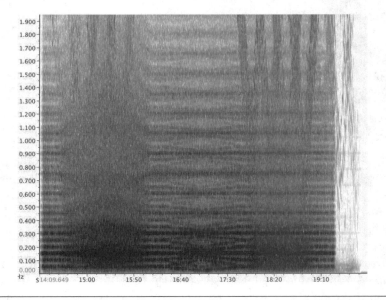

Fig. 8.10 Sonogram of lower spectral activity of Section 5 from 0 to 1.9kHz. (DVD reference 14)

Sound 7 *Riverrun* Section 5 excerpt, 14:10 to 16:10, drone transforms gradually from Figure 8.11 sound to less focused bands of sound and then back. (DVD reference 15)

Grains based on 150 Hz, with a 1:1 C:M ratio for FM, produce sidebands at 300 Hz, 450 Hz, and higher, with modulation indices between 1 and 4. The modulation index and waveform vary for each stereo channel pair. Grains have durations that are ramped between 20 and 40 ms, also producing amplitude modulation. The combination of AM and FM distortion produces frequencies every 50 Hz with the strongest at 150 and 300 Hz, as seen in the sonogram in Figure 8.10 at 14:10 (Sound 8.7, DVD reference 15), 16:10, 17:50 and 19:10. The low "chord" found at these times can be approximated by the pitch notation in Figure 8.11.

Fig. 8.11 Approximate notation for the Section 5 drone based on 150 Hz at 14:10. Parentheses indicate less strong components.

The pitch 150 Hz (7.0237) is actually equivalent to about 37 cents or 3 Hz above the D below middle C, (as are its sidebands), so the "+" sign is used to denote this microtonal aspect. The sequence G "slowly ramps the duration parameter from 20 ms (50 Hz modulation) to longer durations, but pauses on the significant (i.e., tuned) modulation values of 25, 30, and 40 ms. This is so slow that the listener only gradually realizes the drone is changing and coming "into tune" on some very low "chords" (given that the duration and frequency ranges are also changing slowly, the chord is usually blurred except when those ranges come back to low values)" (Truax 2004c). These "blurred" moments occur because when the duration and frequency ranges are larger, there is more variation in the frequencies produced. The less distinct moments in the low drone around 15:10 and 18:20 are also synchronized with the higher frequency sequence M, which attains its limit of 9 kHz, as seen in Figure 8.2, providing a sense of connection between sound layers. The modulation values of 20, 25, 30, and 40 ms correspond to pitches very low G+ (5.0735, 50 Hz), Eb/E (5.0349, 40 Hz), C (5.0016,), and G+ (4.0735). When the modulator descends, the sidebands move closer to the carrier, as at 16:40 in Figure 8.10, when the sidebands at 100 and 200 Hz move inward toward the 150 Hz carrier. The gradual detunings create tension that is released when layers again synchronize harmonically and produce arrival points such as at 16:00. The dense layers and slow changes of this section relate to the expansive delta section of a river.

8.3.4. A Unique Transition

While much of the time the piece is concerned with gradual transformations with only microlevel pulses, there is one point of singularity at the end of Section 1 that contains clear rhythmic events, shown in Figure 8.12. After a buildup of intensity in layerings, grains appear to group around regular attack

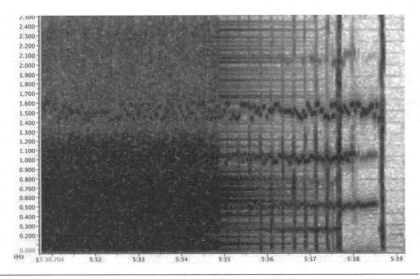

Fig. 8.12 *Riverrun* sonogram at 5:30, end of Section 1. (DVD reference 16)

Sound 8 *Riverrun* excerpt 5:30 to 5:45. (DVD reference 18)

points at 5:35, in a .25 second pulse, which three seconds later, changes to a pulse every one second, as seen in Figure 8.13. This unpitched pulse appears to be created from frequency modulated grains with no variation in grain rate. The slicing pulses of simultaneous grains appear to shift out of phase slowly, leaving attacks that are less and less clear, and, one minute later the pulse has become extremely subtle. The pulse maintains momentum through

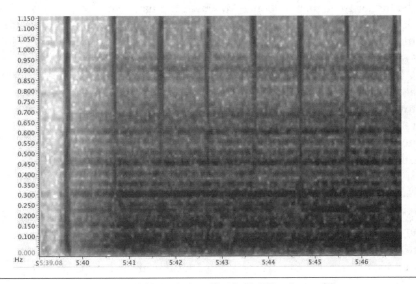

Fig. 8.13 *Riverrun* sonogram at 5:39, beginning of Section 2 (DVD reference 17)

the elision of Sections 1 and 2, and prepares the listener for the upcoming dense, fused textures.

What are the reasons for only one occurrence of a clear pulse? This sharp edge in a virtual sea of contrasts can be heard as the possibility that even something so precisely constructed and extremely unlikely may occur. The author wondered if it might signify the presence of human life in the universe? Could it suggest the straight lines of a city occurring amid the forests and streams of a natural world? The pulse then falls apart into a randomly complex texture. Only by seeing the brief but uncompromising precision of a rectangular cityscape can one completely understand the beauty of the sunset through the complex patterns of tree branches. Alternatively, this point could be heard as a magnification and quantization of the underlying grain rates from granular material used in the piece. Truax explained that the regularity was inspired by water dripping sounds, and prepares the listener for the "powerful fused textures that follow—with the image that the river has now become something incredibly powerful through the transition" Truax 2004c").

8.3.5 Spatial Aspects

The piece was originally generated in four stereo pairs of channels, each recorded onto eight-track tapes by rewinding the tape to synchronize pairs, then mixed to quadraphonic, and finally to a stereo version. The eight-channel version keeps the original eight channels discrete, and the 80 and 105 ms delays (heard most clearly in the rhythmic section between Sections 1 and 2) used to fuse the sound in the original version, were eliminated. In the eight-channel version all eight tracks of the original four stereo pairs are on discrete channels, and the same additional tracks (totaling up to thirty-two) were mixed down to the final eight. The octophonic version of *Riverrun* has a speaker arrangement as follows:

8	1	2
7	L	3
6	5	4

Fig. 8.14 The eight-channel speaker arrangement, with listener position in center. (Truax2004a)

Throughout most of the piece quite different grain distributions and sometimes different pitches, are heard in separate channels. Often channels 1, 3, 5, and 7 have different kinds of activity than channels 2, 4, 6, and 8. For example, at the fifth minute channels 1, 3, 5, and 7 have various thick full bands while channels 2, 4, 6, and 8 have narrower, subtler bands. In the beginning of the work individual grains are heard as separate events in channels 2, 4, 6, and 8. Particularly when grains are sparse, the location jumps between individually heard grains produce a syncopated contrapuntal quality. Channel 4 has regular pulses of groups of grains occurring approximately every 2.5 seconds. The listener can hear the sound in channel 8 as a recurring rhythm, which could be notated as approximately a whole note + quarter note, then a quarter note that is randomly altered, sounding syncopated but persistent during the beginning of the piece. During the second half of the first minute, as density increases grain groupings enter in channels 1, 3, 5, and 7, completing the entrance of all eight channels.

In Section 2, channels 1, 3, 5, and 7 contain streams of grains focused in the lower spectral regions, while channels 2, 4, 6, and 8 also contain surprisingly regularly patterns of upper spectral activity (see Figures 8.15 and 8.16, DVD references 28–35; Sound 9.1 to 9.8, DVD references 20–27). At 3:00 (Sound 9, DVD reference 19), channels 1, 3, 5, and 7 present granular material with audibly different frequency ranges: channel 1 has midrange fast grains; channel 3 has a more constant stream with more higher frequencies than 1; channel 5 is similar to 3 but has more constant stream; channel 7 is similar to 1 but has a narrower range with some almost percussive knocking sounds, probably a result of shorter grains and more variation in rates. The other four channels contain high frequency sounds ("crickets" or "twitter") from 8 to 22 kHz. Channel 2 contains the highest frequency sounds of this type, all around 12 to 22 kHz, while channel 4 contains lower, 5 to 17 kHz, sounds, and channels 6 and 8 contain the widest distributions of this "twitter" from 5 kHz to 22 kHz. Channels 4, 6, and 8 also contain some low- to midrange sparsely placed large grains, which punctuate the texture, seen most clearly in the channel 6 sonogram.

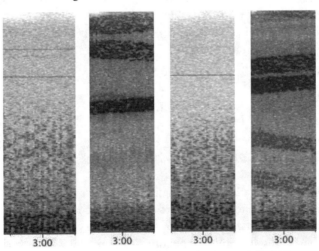

Fig. 8.15 Channel 1–4 sonograms for a two-second duration around 3:00(DVD references 28–31). (Sound 9.1 to 9.4, DVD references 20–23)

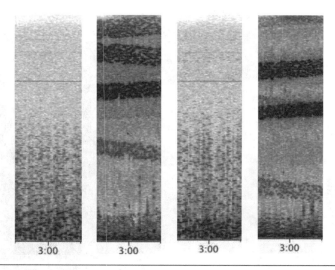

Fig. 8.16 Channel 5–8 sonograms for a two second duration at 3:00 (DVD references 32–35). (Sound 9.5 to 9.8, DVD references 24–27)

Sound 9 *Riverrun* excerpt, 2:59 to 3:01, in eight channels. (DVD reference 19)

Sound 9.1 to 9.8 *Riverrun* excerpt, 2:59 to 3:01, for channels 1 to 8. (DVD references 20–27)

Throughout Section 2 (Figure 8.17) these bands of upper spectral grains move in parallel glissandi up and down, sometimes with "reflections" or foldover below the primary pattern.

When grain frequencies and rates produce material with more than one pitch, they are also often distributed between channels. For example, at the end of Section 1 at 5:30 all channels, except 2, play stochastic streams of grains (Sound 11.1 to 11.8, DVD references 48–55). Channels 4 and 6 have bands narrow enough to be heard as pitched: channel 4 at B 8.11 to A 8.09, and channel 6 at B 7.11 to C 8.00. Channels 2 and 8 have the fast (.25 second) unpitched pulse. The "chord" heard at 5:37 is heard in channels 1 (G 7.07), 5 (B 7.11 and E 7.04), and 7 (B 7.11 and C 8.00). As Section 2 begins, the pulse occurring every second is in all channels, although not at the same frequencies. Sustained pitches enter after the pulse is established with D (8.02) in channels 1, 6, 7, and 8; A (7.09) in channels 2 and 4; and low D in channels 3 and 5. This means that the listener hears low D in the rear channels, A on the right, and D (8.02) in front and left.

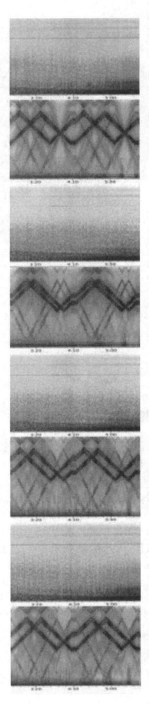

Fig. 8.17 Sonograms of channels 1-8 for Section 2. (DVD reference 36)

Sound 10 *Riverrun* excerpt, 7:30 to 7:40, in eight channels. (DVD reference 37).

Sound 10.1 to 10.8 Individual channels 1 to 8. (DVD references 38–45)

Sound 11 *Riverrun* excerpt, 5:35–5:45, in eight channels. (DVD reference 47)

Sound 11.1 to 11.8 *Riverrun* excerpt, 5:35–5:45, for channels 1 to 8. (DVD references 48–55).

Near the end of Section 2 there is a convergence from frequency bands to heard pitches. At 8:32, Channels 1, 2, and 4, which already have an A component (7.09), move toward A (8.09), while channels 3, 5, 6, 7, and 8 converge on D (8.02). Again A is centered more on the right-front space, while D is heard on the left.

The upper spectral activity in Section 5 from 14:20 to 16:30 is placed in discrete channels—each channel has grain streams in different registers with its distinct motion up and down, as in Figure 8.18. Often harmonics appear as a reflection above the bands of grains, and sometimes symmetrical motion ("contrary motion") occurs as a secondary band descends and the primary band rises. These bands are not heard as individual lines, however, but as large-scale transforming gestures that contract and expand. At 16:30 various channels contain similar activity rather than discrete activity as was the case earlier in Section 5. At this point the shifting in and out of perfect intervals of the 4th and 5th heightens tension, and the listener is encompassed by grain streams that are no longer localizable.

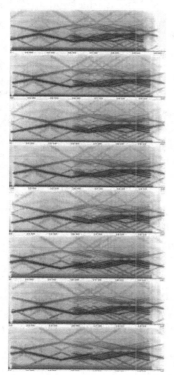

Fig. 8.18 Sonograms of channels 1–8 for Section 5. (DVD reference 46)

When channels are listened to individually, the listener can be surprised by the differences, as the multichannel texture seems integrated. The sense of being overwhelmed by the piece, experienced by many listeners, may be due to this textural/spatial depth.

Truax describes the spatial aspects of the Belfast premiere of the eight-channel version of *Riverrun*:

> The Belfast performance/premiere was fantastic. Their rig is 40 high quality Genelec and Myers speakers arranged in 5 (!) height levels, each with 8-channel surround. Two levels are suspended above the audience, and two below given that the floor is a grid, with a moveable set around the audience (which I positioned as in the first diagram). Then, during the live diffusion, I controlled the 5 levels, starting with just the very high ones, gradually adding in the mid and ground levels, and saving the below ground ones for the big middle sections, which created an immense sense of physicality. In Section 4 (with the scored sequence), I started below, then piled up the higher levels, and in the last section started with high and low combined and gradually filled in the middle. An absolutely amazing effect! ("Re: speakers")

The use of the vertical component increased spatial depth in an already complex diffusion.

8.3.6. *The Analysis Format*

The following multidimensional graphical analysis was done in a way similar to the author's previously analyzed works (Helmuth 1996, 77–102) and contains five levels of representation: (1) text description, (2) event groupings, (3) pitch, (4) amplitude, and (5) sonogram or sound spectrogram. In the first level the text describes anything not covered in the other levels, including sections, timbral descriptions, and arrival points. Sound examples are indicated by #N, with N being the example number. Level 2 indicates section beginning and end points, with square brackets, and "phrases," or segments of sound heard as a continuous unit, with slur notation. These lower level event groupings may be sounds that enter, noted by the beginning of the slur, sustain for some period of time and end, indicated by the end of the slur. There may be several levels of slurs indicating "phrases" and "subphrases." *Riverrun's* continuous character means that these units are often rather subtle. Sometimes a noticeable entrance will fade into and fuse with an existing texture, in which case the rising slur will merge with the upper level slur, and not emerge again. Important pitches are notated on a staff on level 3. The same pitch may be heard in several octaves, but here the most important register is indicated. If several pitches are heard as an important timbre, they may also be represented on the staff notation. This notation may resemble Schenkerian analysis, but it is not. The fourth level is an amplitude graph from the positive side of a soundfile editor display. While this does not correct for human perception bias in certain frequency regions, it does indicate signal strength over time. The sonogram on the fifth level displays frequency content over time, and is often the most revealing component of the analysis, giving strong clues about active registers, gestures, texture, and timbre.

The pitch and grouping notation graphics were done in Sibelius, while the amplitude and sonograms were done in Cornell's ornithological software, Raven. Sound examples were created by mixing excerpts of the eight-channel version to stereo. The 2004 eight-channel version of the work was used for the analysis. Sonograms were created from a mono mix of the eight channels, except where noted that channels were individually analyzed.

Multidimensional Analysis of Riverrun by Barry Truax. (DVD references 56–95)

Sound 12. *Riverrun,* stereo mix of eight-channel version. (DVD reference 96)

Section 1 Sparse individual midrange grains distribution between ch 2, 4, 6, 8, "droplets", #1 (DVD reference 4)

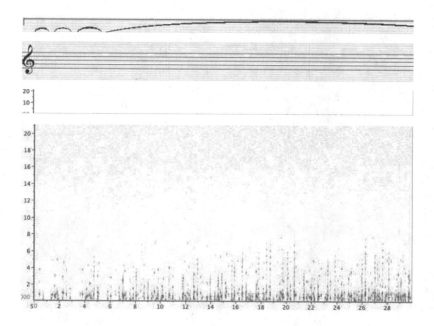

grains in all eight channels   density increasing to nearly continuous

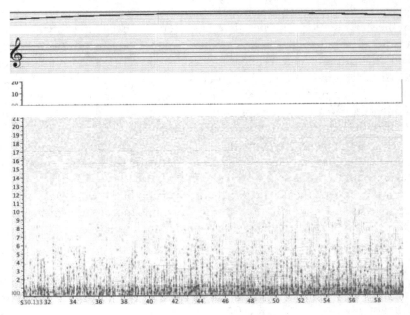

#5 sustained pitches mark entrance of a new layer with higher partials (DVD reference 12)

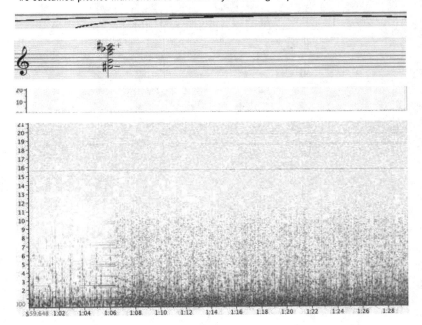

subtle entrances of wider register layers

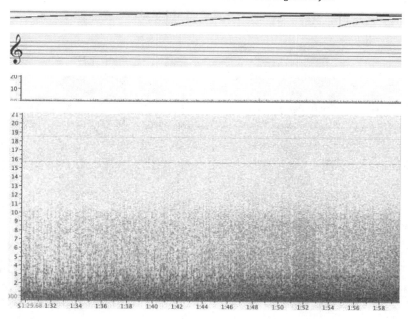

single large grains protrude from dense texture   more thickening of mid-range

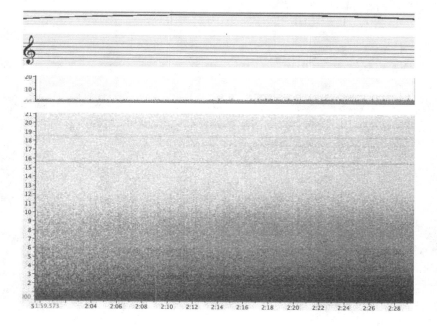

"crickets" microrhythms   scratchy

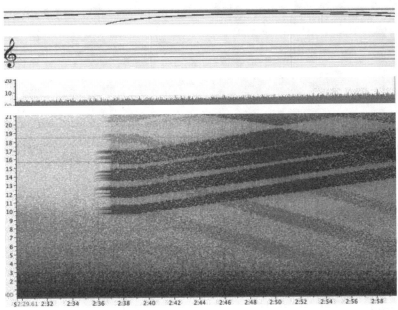

#9 to 9.8   "cricket" swells
(DVD references 19–27)

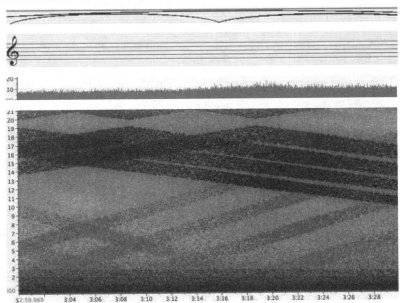

rising "twitter"

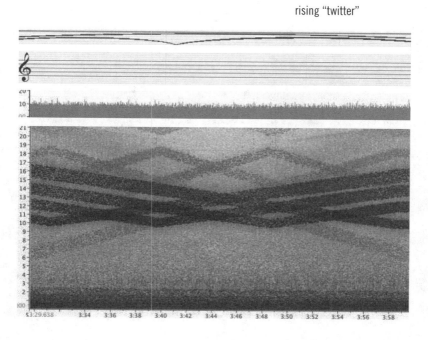

pulse   low ch 8 pulse, high descending converge   high rising   louder rushing in front channels, then rear

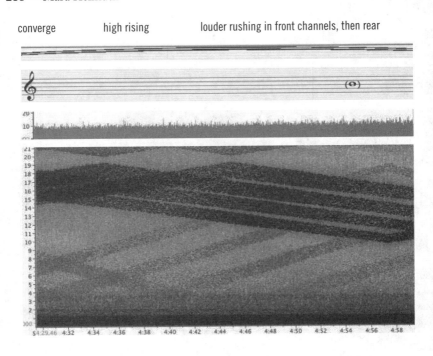

high rising   high flattens   building intensity, front high layer, low layer

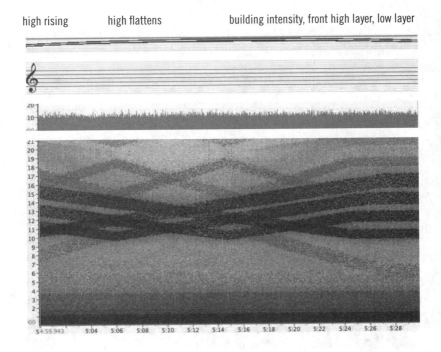

#8, #11.1 to 11.8
(DVD references 18 and 47–55)

Sect 2 dense, channels very discrete—pitch/rhythm

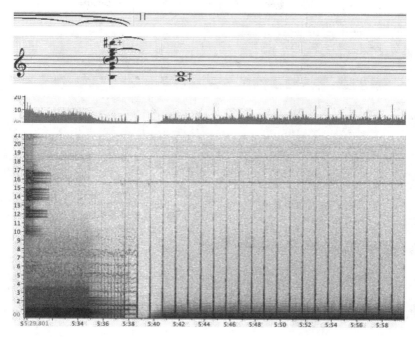

pulse breaking apart   channels very discrete

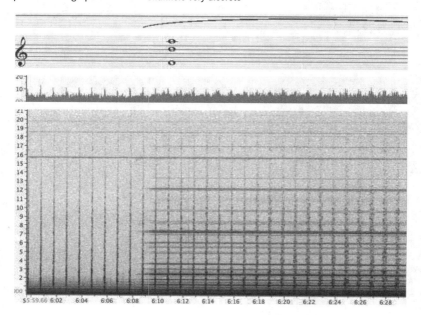

D pitch widens out to band, pulse merges into texture ch 8 roar

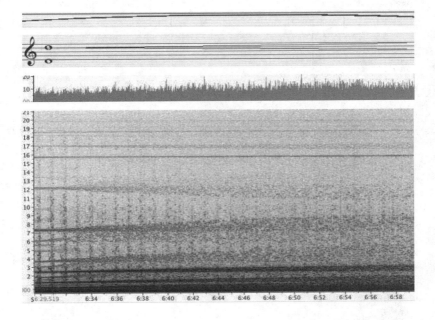

midrange larger longer grains

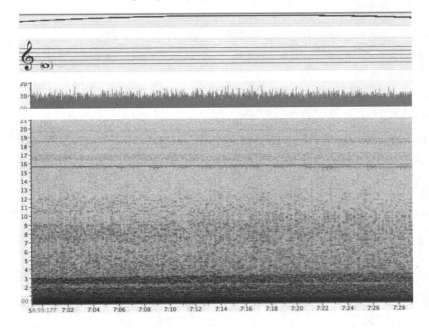

#2, #10 to 10.8 (DVD references 5 and 37–45)

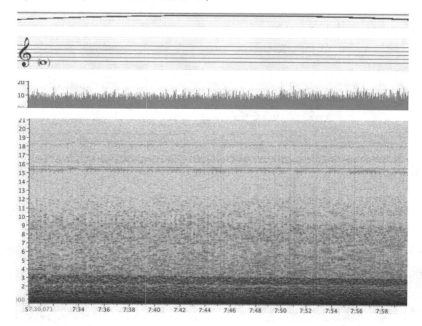

bands narrow to

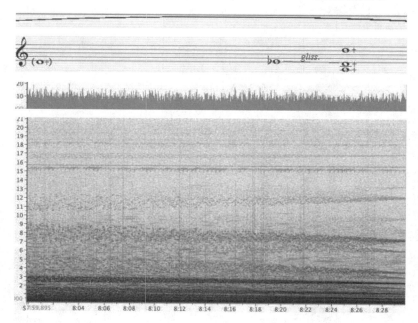

pitches   #3   Sect 3   pitches
(DVD reference 6)

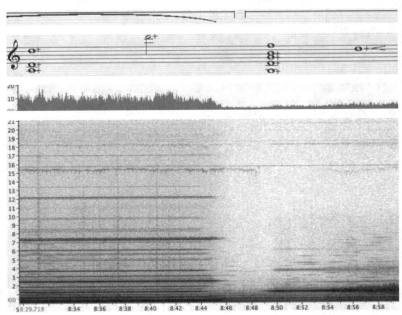

widen to bands, #3   midrange frequencies   large grains unpitched
(DVD reference 6)

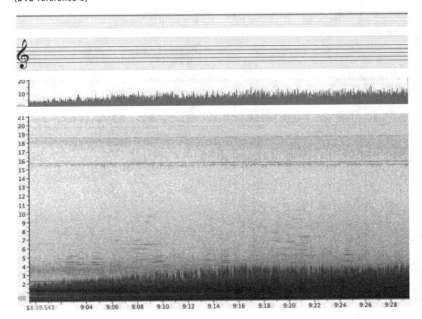

all channels have similar material

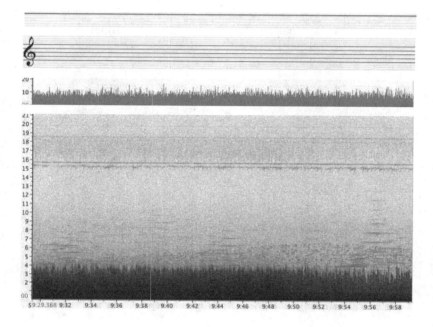

channels differing again   bands narrow to pitches

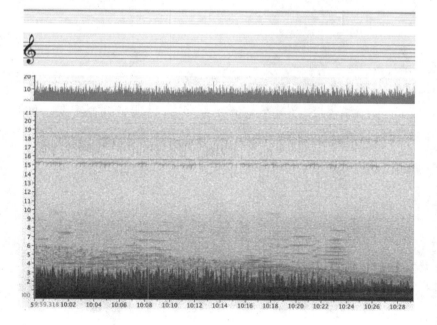

#4
(DVD reference 8)

Sect 4

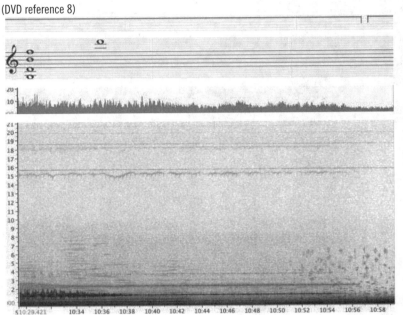

growls, high metallic

(front to back) + scratchy

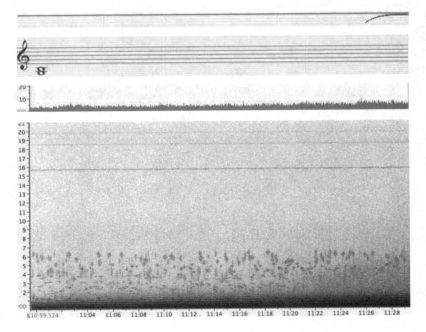

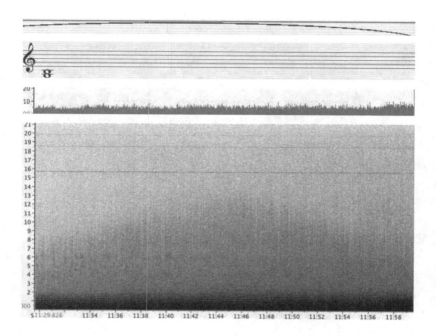

arrival on B (7.11) vocal "Ah" sound surge and fade

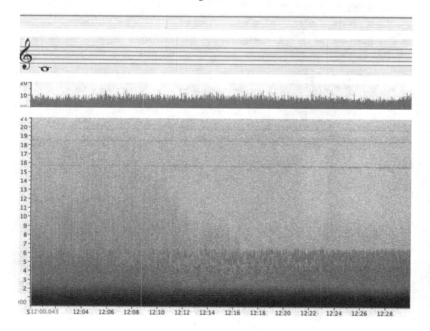

low + scratchy layers enter (low B, G)

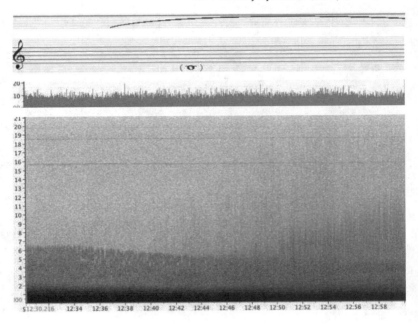

"helicopter"

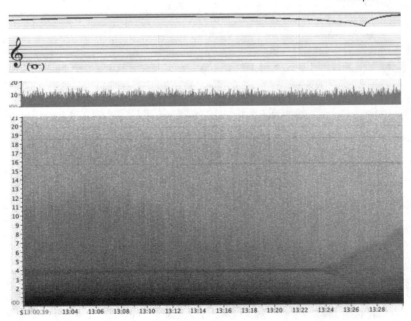

buzz   #6   descends, convergence to B
        (DVD reference 13)

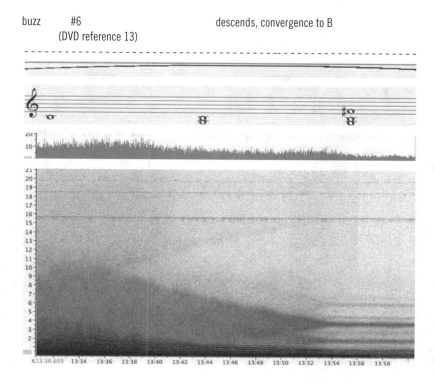

Section 5 #7 "crickets" (seq M) and low drone (seq G)

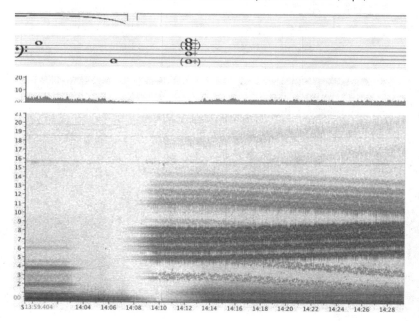

(low E roar)

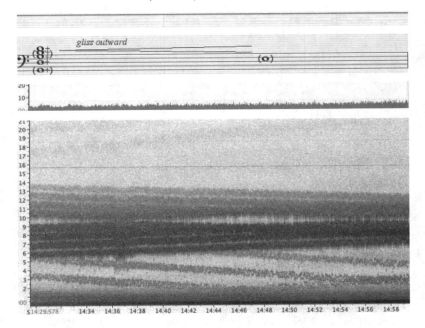

very slow glissandi

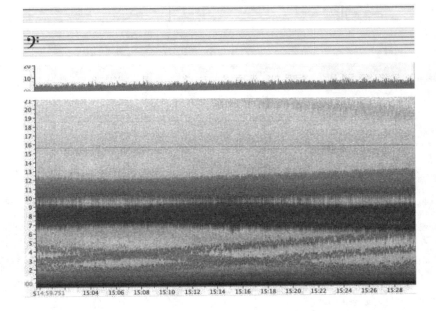

"twitter"   5th arrival

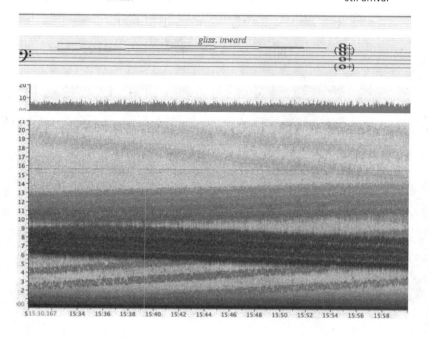

drone with solid 5th   front: pitched roar   sides and rear: higher freq. grains

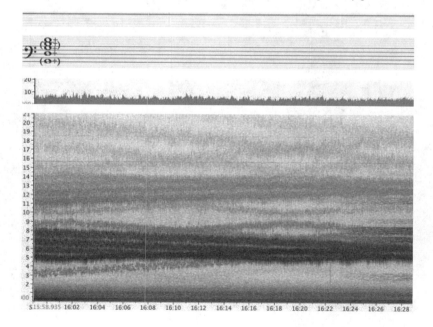

addition of lower octave D, sliding

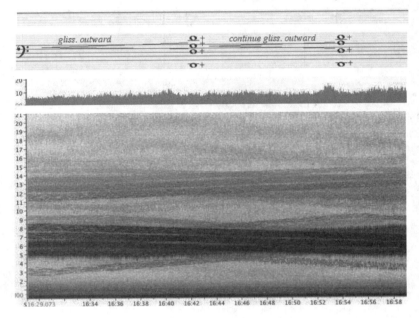

little arrival   arrival

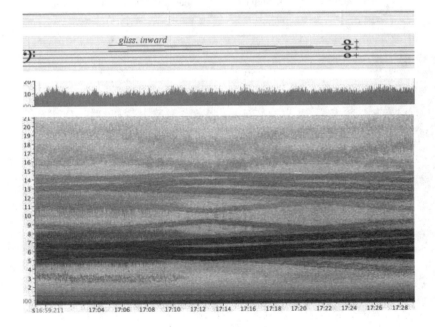

in phase 5th arrival

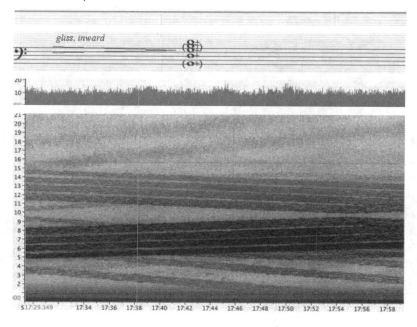

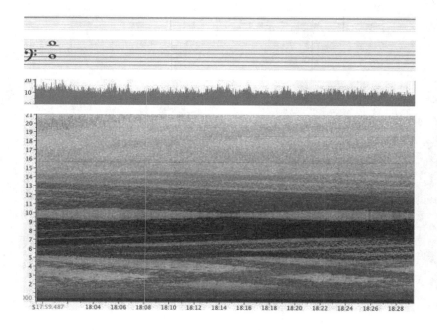

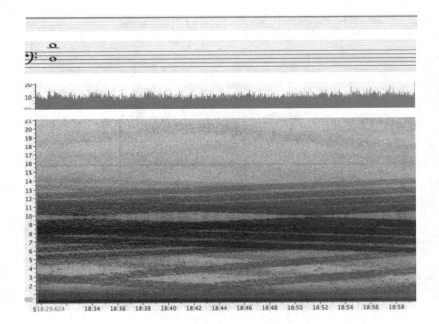

5th arrival   drone ends

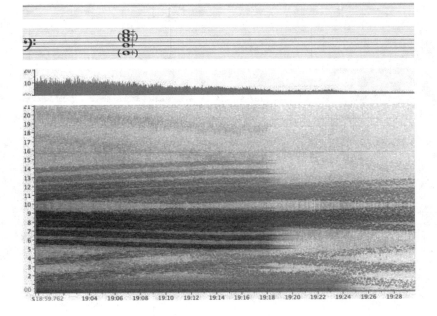

fade out of M sequence

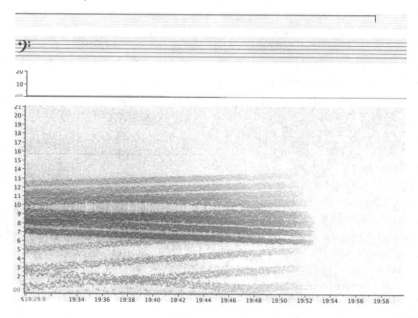

8.4. Conclusion

To fully absorb the impact of *Riverrun*, the listener perceives information on widely ranging time-scales. Granular synthesis is microlevel synthesis, and while one cannot always hear individual grains, these tiny events within random distributions make a continually changing, rich texture. Attention to the microlevel is encouraged. To understand each textural state, however, the listener must experience it for some time, and must also become aware of the slower changes. The complex but subtle changes in heard event group-ings, occurrences of long single event grains that stand out, pitch relations due to frequencies within grains or grain rates, and layering and densities form large-scale gestures that unfold over whole sections of the work. This heightened awareness to both micro- and macrolevels of the work may be somewhat similar to one's state of mind when listening to an Indian raga, which may unfold over long periods of time, but with much attention to the local improvised melodic fragments. This may also be how one listens to natural phenomena such as bird sounds: there is not a sense of goal or direction on a phrase-oriented level, but the bird sounds certainly contain much microlevel complexity and interest, and they may evolve with the bird's activity levels over the course of several hours. Neither of these sound worlds approach the microlevel complexity of granular synthesis, which may involve thousands of events per second, and invites focused listening on the most minuscule levels.

As a soundscape experience, *Riverrun* is an interaction with a river-like sound entity. Individual droplets heard in the beginning are perhaps a magnification of the remote finger of a stream beginning to descend a rocky mountain after melting from snow. The precise rhythmic point ending Section 1 may exist as an extreme magnification of lower-level microlevel grain rates, and also serve to point to the open-endedness and fluidity of its surrounding material through contrast, as well as prepare the listener for the denser textures to follow. Additional grain layerings suggest converging streams and higher waters, and build to the sounds of dense turbulent currents in Section 4 with a powerful momentum, if not a sense of goal-oriented progression. The arrival points on perfect intervals near the end may suggest points of stability, but do not drive harmonically forward to close the piece; the ending seems as though the listener simply emerges and separates from a soundscape that continues forever.

While many of the sounds in the piece may not sound like an actual river, they are clearly related to water sounds, and their transformations and variations seem meaningful and coherent in the manner of James Joyce's *Finnegans Wake's* invented words and grammatical constructions. This river is larger than life; it is capable of resembling sounds as diverse as those of machines and insects. Often this is interpreted as the ability of the soundscape to draw one in so as to hear on the highly magnified microlevels at the same time as the higher levels, perhaps hearing the regular pulsing of electronics around the nuclei simultaneously with individual water drips and the faraway sound of the vast expanses of a large river delta. This multiplicity of scales breaks down the listener/soundscape separation, so that the listener hears his or her path inside and outside the river, the river coursing near, by, and through him- or herself. This connection to the natural world creates a profound appreciation for the intensity and beauty of natural processes as well as the composition *Riverrun* for its fantastic homage to them.

Appendix

Many of the grain objects with letter names are described in the following printout provided by Truax (Figure 8.19). Parameters are listed in columns, from left to right, Object No., Frequency, Frequency RNG, Duration, Duration RNG, Delay, Ramp, Max M.I., and MI RNG. "RNG" indicates a range

RIVER. GEN

J.NO.	FREQ.	FREQ.RNG	DUR.	DUR.RNG	DELAY	RAMP	MAX.M.I.	MI.RNG
1	75	8	20	1	0	1000	5	4
2	150	8	20	1	0	1000	6	4
3	225	8	20	1	0	1000	5	4
4	300	8	20	1	0	1000	3	2
5	100	5	10	0	0	100	3	2
6	100	5	20	2	0	100	3	2
7	100	5	30	2	0	100	4	4
8	100	5	100	2	0	100	10	8
9	100	5	100	2	0	100	10	8
10	150	5	20	1	1	1000	4	1
11	125	5	8	2	0	1000	1	4
12	250	5	8	2	0	1000	1	4
13	375	5	8	2	0	1000	1	4
14	750	5	8	2	0	1000	1	4
15	0	100	20	1	1	2000	1	0
16	0	150	20	1	1	2000	1	0
17	0	200	20	1	1	2000	1	0
18	0	250	20	1	1	2000	1	0
19	250	25	50	5	1	1000	2	1
20	500	50	50	5	1	1000	2	1
21	1000	100	50	5	1	1000	2	1
22	1250	125	50	5	1	1000	2	1
23	500	5000	8	0	1000	1000	2	1
24	5000	500	50	5	1	1000	1	1
25	6000	600	60	5	1	1000	1	1
26	7000	700	70	5	1	1000	1	1
27	8000	800	80	5	1	1000	1	1
28	200	2000	8	12	0	1000	1	0
29	200	2000	8	0	250	400	1	0
30	1200	50	20	1	1	100	1	0

Fig. 8.19 *Riverrun* parameter listing. (Truax 1986a)

for the previously described average value. For example, for object no. 1 in the second list, frequency is 200 Hz, and the frequency range 10 Hz indicates that the chosen frequencies were between 195 and 205 Hz. Duration is 20 ms and with the duration range of 1 ms, this would produce durations of 19 to 21 ms The maximum modulation index produced would be between 1 and 9. Not shown, but sometimes used, was a "DELAY RNG" parameter, which could be displayed instead of "DUR.RNG" through a keyboard command. Use of a range for delay values produced effects similar to asynchronous grain streams, although the truly asynchronous granular programs he developed were written after *Riverrun* was composed.

The grain objects for sequence K, the bass ostinato, are found in the following printout.

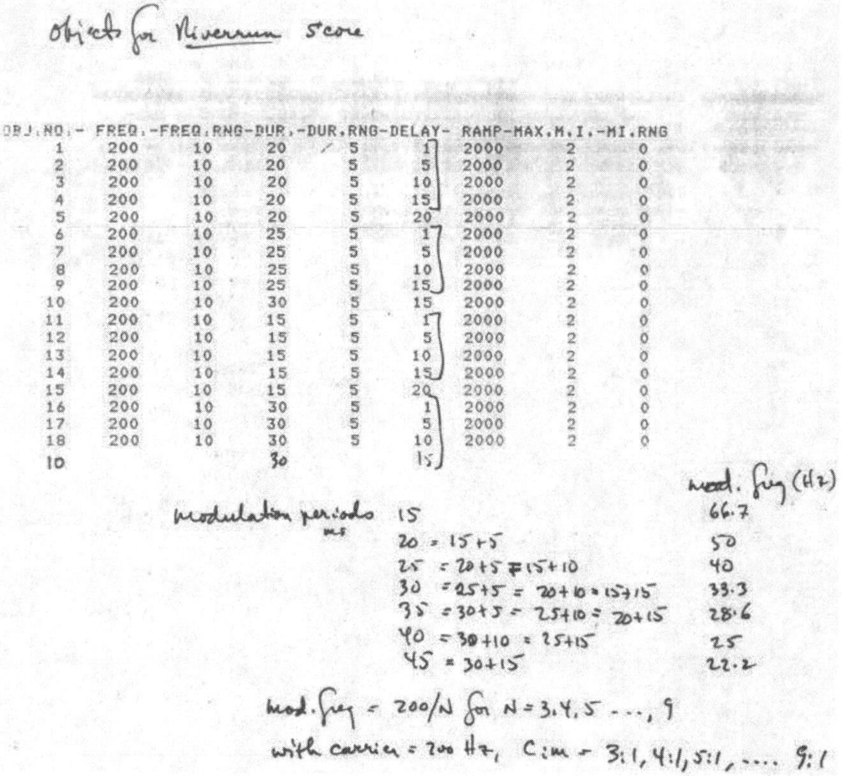

Objects for Riverrun score

OBJ.NO.	FREQ.	FREQ.RNG	DUR.	DUR.RNG	DELAY	RAMP	MAX.M.I.	MI.RNG
1	200	10	20	5	1	2000	2	0
2	200	10	20	5	5	2000	2	0
3	200	10	20	5	10	2000	2	0
4	200	10	20	5	15	2000	2	0
5	200	10	20	5	20	2000	2	0
6	200	10	25	5	1	2000	2	0
7	200	10	25	5	5	2000	2	0
8	200	10	25	5	10	2000	2	0
9	200	10	25	5	15	2000	2	0
10	200	10	30	5	15	2000	2	0
11	200	10	15	5	1	2000	2	0
12	200	10	15	5	5	2000	2	0
13	200	10	15	5	10	2000	2	0
14	200	10	15	5	15	2000	2	0
15	200	10	15	5	20	2000	2	0
16	200	10	30	5	1	2000	2	0
17	200	10	30	5	5	2000	2	0
18	200	10	30	5	10	2000	2	0
10			30		15			

modulation periods (ms)   mod. freq (Hz)

$$15 \qquad\qquad 66.7$$
$$20 = 15+5 \qquad 50$$
$$25 = 20+5 \neq 15+10 \qquad 40$$
$$30 = 25+5 = 20+10 = 15+15 \qquad 33.3$$
$$35 = 30+5 = 25+10 = 20+15 \qquad 28.6$$
$$40 = 30+10 = 25+15 \qquad 25$$
$$45 = 30+15 \qquad 22.2$$

$$\text{mod. freq} = 200/N \text{ for } N = 3,4,5\ldots,9$$
$$\text{with carrier} = 200 \text{ Hz}, \quad C{:}m = 3{:}1, 4{:}1, 5{:}1, \ldots, 9{:}1$$

Fig. 8.20 *Riverrun* objects for sequence K.

References

Cogan, Robert. *New Images of Musical Sound.* Cambridge, MA: Harvard University Press, 1984.

Cogan, Robert, and Pozzi Escot. *Sonic Design: the Nature of Sound and Music.* Englewood Cliffs, NJ:Prentice-Hall, 1976.

Dodge, Charles, and Tom Jerse. *Computer Music: Synthesis, Composition and Performance.* New York: Schirmer Books,1997, 275.

Emmerson, Simon, ed. *The Language of Electroacoustic Music.* New York: Harwood, 1986.

Gabor, Dennis. "Acoustical Quanta and the Theory of Hearing." *Nature* 159, no. 4044 (1947): 591–94.

Garton, Brad. Rev. of "Digital soundscapes." *Computer Music Journal* 15, no. 1 (1991): 60–62.

Helmuth, Mara. "Multidimensional Representation of Electroacoustic Music." *Journal of New Music Research* 25 (1996): 77–103.

Holtzman, Steven R. "The Aesthetics of Cyberspace," In *Digital Mosaics.* New York: Simon & Schuster, 1997, 83–84.

Joyce, James. *Finnegans Wake.* New York: Viking Press, 1939.

Roads, Curtis. "Automated Granular Synthesis of Sound." *Computer Music Journal* 2, no.2(1978): 61–62.

———. 1985. "Granular Synthesis of Sound." *Foundations of Computer Music.*Edited by Curtis Roads and John Strawn, 145–159. Cambridge, MA: MIT Press, 1985.

———. *Microsound.* Cambridge, MA: MIT Press, 2001.

Truax, Barry. "The POD System of Interactive Composition Programs." *Computer Music Journal* 1, no. 3 (1977): 30–39.

———."Timbral Construction in Arras as a Stochastic Process." *Computer Music Journal* 6, no. 3 (1982): 72–77.

———. "Organizational Techniques for C:M Ratios in Frequency Modulation." Rpt. in *Foundations of Computer Music,* edited by Curtis Roads and John Strawn, 68–82. Cambridge, MA: MIT Press, 1985a.

———. "The PODX System: Interactive Compositional Software for the DMX-1000 Digital Signal Processor." Computer Music Journal 9, no. 1 (1985b): 29-38.

———. Unpublished notes on *Riverrun* provided to author. 1986a.

———. *RIVERRUN.* 1986b. Available online: <http://www.sfu.ca/~truax/river.html>

———. *Digital Soundscapes.* Cambridge Street Records, 1987a.

———. "Real-Time Granulation of Sampled Sound with the DMX-1000." In *Proceedings of the 1987 International Computer Music Conference,* edited by J. Beauchamp, 138–145. San Francisco: Computer Music Association, 1987b.

———. "Composing with Real-Time Granular Sound." *Perspectives of New Music* 28, no. 2 (1988a): 120–34.

———. "Real-time granular synthesis with a digital signal processor." *Computer Music Journal,* 12, no. 2 (1988b): 14–26.

———. *Acoustic Communication.* Westport, CT: Ablex, 2001.

———. "Re: speakers." E-mail to the author. May 16, 2004a.

———. "Re: new version and more questions." E-mail to the author. July 2, 2004b.

———. "Re: Riverrun." E-mail to the author. July 4, 2004c.

———. "Re: system, etc." E-mail to the author. August 16, 2004d.

———. "Re: Riverrun essay." E-mail to the author. August 26, 2004e.

———. *Riverrun,* for eight computer-synthesized soundtracks, 2004f.

Smalley, Denis. "Defining Transformations." *Interface* 22, no.4 (1993): 279–300.

Voorvelt, Martijn. "The Environmental Element in Barry Truax's Compositions." *Journal of New Music Research* 26 (1997): 48–69.

Xenakis, Iannis. *Formalized Music.* Bloomington: Indiana University Press, 1971.

DVD References

Number	File Name	Description	Media
1	Fig.8.1TruaxC.TIFF	Picture of Barry Truax	Color TIFF
2	Fig.8.2PDPC.TIFF	Truax's PDP 11 and DMX-1000	Color TIFF
3	Fig.8.3SonoFirstC.TIFF	Riverrun sonogram, 0:00–10:00	Color TIFF
4	SoundEx1.aif	Riverrun section 1 sound excerpt, 0:20–0:25.	Stereo AIFF
5	SoundEx2.aif	Riverrun middle of section 2 sound excerpt, 7:30-7:40	Stereo AIFF
6	SoundEx3.aif	Riverrun beginning of section 3 sound excerpt, 8:49–9:05	Stereo AIFF
7	Fig.8.4SonoSecondC.TIFF	Riverrun sonogram, 10:00–20:00	Stereo AIFF
8	SoundEx4.aif	Riverrun ending of section 3 sound excerpt, 10:32–10:48	Stereo AIFF
9	Fig.8.5DiagramC.TIFF	Truax's diagram of Riverrun	Color TIFF
10	Fig.8.6DiagMHC.TIFF	Diagram of Riverrun materials	Color TIFF
11	Fig.8.7R1.02C.TIFF	Riverrun sonogram 1:02–1:08	Color TIFF
12	SoundEx5.aif	Riverrun section 1 sound excerpt, 1:02–1:07	Stereo AIFF
13	SoundEx6.aif	Riverrun section 4 sound excerpt, 13:35–14:00	Stereo AIFF
14	Fig.8.10R8.50C.TIFF	Riverrun sonogram, section 5 lower spectral activity, 0–1.9 kHz	Color TIFF

Number	File Name	Description	Media
15	SoundEx7.aif	Riverrun section 5 excerpt, 14:10–16:10.	Color TIFF
16	Fig.8.12R5.30C.TIFF	Riverrun sonogram end of section 1, 5:30–5:39	Color TIFF
17	Fig.8.13R5.39C.TIFF	Riverrun sonogram end of section 1, 5:39–5:45	Color TIFF
18	SoundEx8.aif	Riverrun end of section 1 sound excerpt, 5:35–5:45	Stereo AIFF
19	SoundEx9-8ch.aif	Riverrun section 1 sound excerpt 2:59–3:01, 8 channels	8-channel AIFF
20	SoundEx9.1.aif	Riverrun section 1 sound excerpt 2:59–3:01, channel 1	Stereo AIFF
21	SoundEx9.2.aif	Riverrun section 1 sound excerpt 2:59–3:01, channel 2	Stereo AIFF
22	SoundEx9.3.aif	Riverrun section 1 sound excerpt 2:59–3:01, channel 3	Stereo AIFF
23	SoundEx9.4.aif	Riverrun section 1 sound excerpt 2:59–3:01, channel 4	Stereo AIFF
24	SoundEx9.5.aif	Riverrun section 1 sound excerpt 2:59–3:01, channel 5	Stereo AIFF
25	SoundEx9.6.aif	Riverrun section 1 sound excerpt 2:59–3:01, channel 6	Stereo AIFF
26	SoundEx9.7.aif	Riverrun section 1 sound excerpt 2:59–3:01, channel 7	Stereo AIFF
27	SoundEx9.8.aif	Riverrun section 1 sound excerpt 2:59–3:01, channel 8	Stereo AIFF
28	Fig.8.15.1R3.00ch1C.TIFF	Riverrun sonogram excerpt 2:59–3:01, channel 1	Color TIFF
29	Fig.8.15.2R3.00ch2C.TIFF	Riverrun sonogram excerpt 2:59–3:01, channel 1	Color TIFF
30	Fig.8.15.3R3.00ch3C.TIFF	Riverrun sonogram excerpt 2:59–3:01, channel 3	Color TIFF
31	Fig.8.15.2R3.00ch4C.TIFF	Riverrun sonogram excerpt 2:59–3:01, channel 4	Color TIFF
32	Fig.816.1R3.00ch5C.TIFF	Riverrun sonogram excerpt 2:59–3:01, channel 5	Color TIFF
33	Fig.8.16.2R3.00ch6C.TIFF	Riverrun sonogram excerpt 2:59–3:01, channel 6	Color TIFF
34	Fig.8.16.3R3.00ch7C.TIFF	Riverrun sonogram excerpt 2:59–3:01, channel 7	Color TIFF
35	Fig.8.16.4R3.00ch8C.TIFF	Riverrun sonogram excerpt 2:59–3:01, channel 8	Color TIFF
36	Fig.8.17Sect2C.TIFF	Riverrun sonogram section 2, channels 1–8	Color TIFF
37	SoundEx10-8ch.aif	Riverrun section 2 sound excerpt 7:30–7:40, 8 channels	8-channel AIFF
38	SoundEx10.1.aif	Riverrun section 2 sound excerpt 7:30–7:40, channel 1	Stereo AIFF
39	SoundEx10.2.aif	Riverrun section 2 sound excerpt 7:30–7:40, channel 2	Stereo AIFF
40	SoundEx10.3.aif	Riverrun section 2 sound excerpt 7:30–7:40, channel 3	Stereo AIFF

Number	File Name	Description	Media
41	SoundEx10.4.aif	Riverrun section 2 sound excerpt 7:30–7:40, channel 4	Stereo AIFF
42	SoundEx10.5.aif	Riverrun section 2 sound excerpt 7:30–7:40, channel 5	Stereo AIFF
43	SoundEx10.6.aif	Riverrun section 2 sound excerpt 7:30–7:40, channel 6	Stereo AIFF
44	SoundEx10.7.aif	Riverrun section 2 sound excerpt 7:30–7:40, channel 7	Stereo AIFF
45	SoundEx10.8.aif	Riverrun section 2 sound excerpt 7:30–7:40, channel 8	Stereo AIFF
46	Fig.8.18Sect5C.TIFF	Riverrun sonogram section 5, channels 1–8	Color TIFF
47	SoundEx11-8ch.aif	Riverrun section 5 sound excerpt 5:35–5:45, 8 channels	8-channel AIFF
48	SoundEx11.1.aif	Riverrun section 5 sound excerpt 5:35–5:45, channel 1	Stereo AIFF
49	SoundEx11.2.aif	Riverrun section 5 sound excerpt 5:35–5:45, channel 2	Stereo AIFF
50	SoundEx11.3.aif	Riverrun section 5 sound excerpt 5:35-5:45, channel 3	Stereo AIFF
51	SoundEx11.4.aif	Riverrun section 5 sound excerpt 5:35–5:45, channel 4	Stereo AIFF
52	SoundEx11.5.aif	Riverrun section 5 sound excerpt 5:35–5:45, channel 5	Stereo AIFF
53	SoundEx11.6.aif	Riverrun section 5 sound excerpt 5:35–5:45, channel 6	Stereo AIFF
54	SoundEx11.7.aif	Riverrun section 5 sound excerpt 5:35–5:45, channel 7	Stereo AIFF
55	SoundEx11.8.aif	Riverrun section 5 sound excerpt 5:35–5:45, channel 8	Stereo AIFF
56	0000Sono.TIFF	Riverrun sonogram 0:00–0:30	Color TIFF
57	0030Sono.TIFF	Riverrun sonogram 0:30–1:00	Color TIFF
58	0060Sono.TIFF	Riverrun sonogram 1:00–0:30	Color TIFF
59	0090Sono.TIFF	Riverrun sonogram 1:30–2:00	Color TIFF
60	0120Sono.TIFF	Riverrun sonogram 2:00–2:30	Color TIFF
61	0150Sono.TIFF	Riverrun sonogram 2:30–3:00	Color TIFF
62	0180Sono.TIFF	Riverrun sonogram 3:00–3:30	Color TIFF
63	0210Sono.TIFF	Riverrun sonogram 3:30–4:00	Color TIFF
64	0240Sono.TIFF	Riverrun sonogram 4:00–4:30	Color TIFF
65	0270Sono.TIFF	Riverrun sonogram 4:30–5:00	Color TIFF
66	0300Sono.TIFF	Riverrun sonogram 5:00–5:30	Color TIFF
67	0330Sono.TIFF	Riverrun sonogram 5:30–6:00	Color TIFF
68	0360Sono.TIFF	Riverrun sonogram 6:00–6:30	Color TIFF
69	0390Sono.TIFF	Riverrun sonogram 6:30–7:00	Color TIFF
70	0420Sono.TIFF	Riverrun sonogram 7:00–7:30	Color TIFF
71	0450Sono.TIFF	Riverrun sonogram 7:30–8:00	Color TIFF
72	0480Sono.TIFF	Riverrun sonogram 8:00–8:30	Color TIFF
73	0510Sono.TIFF	Riverrun sonogram 8:30–9:00	Color TIFF
74	0540Sono.TIFF	Riverrun sonogram 9:00–9:30	Color TIFF
75	0570Sono.TIFF	Riverrun sonogram 9:30–10:00	Color TIFF
76	0600Sono.TIFF	Riverrun sonogram 10:00–10:30	Color TIFF

Number	File Name	Description	Media
77	0630Sono.TIFF	Riverrun sonogram 10:30–11:00	Color TIFF
78	0660Sono.TIFF	Riverrun sonogram 11:00–11:30	Color TIFF
79	0690Sono.TIFF	Riverrun sonogram 11:30–12:00	Color TIFF
80	0720Sono.TIFF	Riverrun sonogram 12:00–12:30	Color TIFF
81	0750Sono.TIFF	Riverrun sonogram 12:30–13:00	Color TIFF
82	0780Sono.TIFF	Riverrun sonogram 13:00–13:30	Color TIFF
83	0810Sono.TIFF	Riverrun sonogram 13:30–14:00	Color TIFF
84	0840Sono.TIFF	Riverrun sonogram 14:00–14:30	Color TIFF
85	0870Sono.TIFF	Riverrun sonogram 14:30–15:00	Color TIFF
86	0900Sono.TIFF	Riverrun sonogram 15:00–15:30	Color TIFF
87	0930Sono.TIFF	Riverrun sonogram 15:30–16:00	Color TIFF
88	0960Sono.TIFF	Riverrun sonogram 16:00–16:30	Color TIFF
89	0990Sono.TIFF	Riverrun sonogram 16:30–17:00	Color TIFF
90	1020Sono.TIFF	Riverrun sonogram 17:00–17:30	Color TIFF
91	1050Sono.TIFF	Riverrun sonogram 17:30–18:00	Color TIFF
92	1080Sono.TIFF	Riverrun sonogram 18:00–18:30	Color TIFF
93	1110Sono.TIFF	Riverrun sonogram 18:30–19:00	Color TIFF
94	1140Sono.TIFF	Riverrun sonogram 19:00–19:30	Color TIFF
95	1170Sono.TIFF	Riverrun sonogram 19:30–20:00	Color TIFF
96	SoundEx12Riverrun.aif	Riverrun soundfile—stereo mix of 8-channel version	Stereo AIFF

Notes

1. The author would like to acknowledge Barry Truax's generosity in providing the new eight-channel recording, source materials for the piece, his notes and program data, as well as answers to many questions. Cambridge Street Records has granted permission to include the sound examples included on the DVD.
2. For a more detailed description of granular synthesis see *Microsound* (Roads 2001) or *Computer Music* (Dodge and Jerse 1997).

Philippe Manoury's Opera K...[1]

MOMILANI RAMSTRUM

9.1. Overview

Philippe Manoury's opera, titled *K...* after Franz Kafka's *The Trial*, combines electronic elements with singers and full orchestra. This analysis employs an historical–cultural approach to explore the links between Kafka and Jewish mysticism, examining the technology, serial processes, musical form, and semiotics used in Manoury's *K....* Text, image, video, and score examples contribute to the analysis, which integrates both acoustic and electronic elements.[2]

While musical analyses often use audio recordings as source materials, this analysis of *K...* is based upon observations of the live performance. The analysis was completed after seeing and hearing the work over five weeks of daily rehearsals and performances and interviewing the participants. The drama and breadth of the performance milieu in the Grand Salle at the Opéra Bastille is unrivaled by any recording. In addition, while almost any performance is better live, viewing the live production of *K...* was necessary for the analysis because of the essential role of sixteen channels of spatialized audio in the staging of the opera.

Technology is integrated into the composition and performance of *K....* The technology is extensive, complex, and must be meticulously organized and rigorously monitored. Only with the commitment of the Opéra Bastille and IRCAM (The Institute for Research and Coordination in Acoustics and Music), were successful performances of this large and technologically sophisticated production achieved.

9.2. Background

Kafka's parable "Before the Law" is central to both the novel *The Trial* and the opera *K....* Kafka's parable of Jewish mysticism may be understood intuitively and experientially, though not necessarily logically. In *The Trial* the parable signifies the impossible ascent to the Throne of God. Josef K., the main character, fails to comprehend the incomprehensible. Manoury translates the parable into a dense musical palette.

The names K., K..., and *K...* are distinct. In Kafka's book the main character is referred to as Josef K. or simply K. In the opera he is called Josef K... (with an ellipsis after the letter K). When referring to the opera *K...,* the name will be in italics.

The parable "Before the Law" (Kafka 217) was published independently of *The Trial* during Kafka's lifetime. In the novel a Priest relates the parable to Josef K. in a cathedral. The parable tells of a man who comes to the gate of the Law and demands entrance. The gatekeeper tells the man he does not have permission to enter. The man decides to wait. After many years the man is about to die. The man asks the gatekeeper, *"'Everyone strives to reach the Law, ... how does it happen, then, that in all these years no one but me has requested admittance.'* The gatekeeper responds, *'No one else could gain admittance here, because this entrance was meant solely for you. I'm going to go and shut it now'"* (Kafka 215). K. and the Priest discuss the parable's meaning. Each of K.'s suggested explanations are contradicted by the Priest who relates the contrasting viewpoints of the commentators. The Priest finally states, "The commentators tell us: the correct understanding of a matter and misunderstanding the matter are not mutually exclusive" (Kafka 219).

It has been suggested that Kafka is ridiculing the reader's inclination toward rationalization and pointing out the futility of using intelligence to comprehend reality (Carroll 1999). The Priest, by relating the parable, is telling K. that he will die without knowing the Law and that his arrest and trial were not a mistake and were meant only for him. Or is the choice of waiting for entrance the significant aspect of the story? Should one enter without permission and risk the consequences? Does K. die because he accepts his death or finds he cannot live and so must die to continue? Does K. die because he loses the will to resist the Law? Does K. die because he was incapable of transcending his intellectual attempts to comprehend the Law?

Manoury once related, during an interview with the author, that he believed that all of the events of the opera were real events in the life of Josef K. The events were stretched to the edge of possible reality, but nonetheless real. Manoury said the events in Kafka's novel were like the Law—too complex to understand consciously—but that this did not necessarily imply that they weren't genuine (Jan 26). Manoury had to depict the mystical significance of the unknowable, hidden behind the frustrating exterior of the everyday. Everyone longs to approach the Throne but can never grasp or achieve the union, and sometimes doesn't even know that they are trying. Jewish conceptions of guilt lurk beneath a Christian exterior to further aggravate the challenge of portraying Kafka's novel. Manoury's work is labyrinthine and intricate. The opera was completed though the novel was not.

The struggle between reality and transcending reality is the subtext of the opera. Musically, the struggle is experienced through the tension between acoustic and electronic elements. Manoury believes that bodily exhaustion is an important part of the encounter with extended works. The embodiment of fatigue can be directly related to the evolution of the character of Josef K… in the opera. The personal existential experience of the audience becomes a metaphor for the transformative journey of the main character.

Philippe Manoury composed *K…* from 1998 to 2000. With the help of musical assistant Serge Lemouton, Manoury programmed and generated the electronic components of the opera during the same period at IRCAM. The opera premiered in 2001 at the Opéra Bastille and was restaged in 2003. In *K…*'s three acts and twelve scenes, fourteen singers perform nineteen roles (five roles are doubled for political coherence). A nine-member girls' chorus sings in only one scene. The orchestra is large and features an extensive percussion section. See Table 9.1 for the orchestration used in *K…*.

How could Kafka be turned into an opera? The answer is, in part, found in Manoury's compositional methods. Philippe Manoury favors serial processes as a foundation to his compositional work using multiple melodic and rhythmic rows to generate musical elements of the opera. The multiplicity of these materials corresponds to the lack of focus on one God. Instead there exist a multiplicity of perspectives that manifest as confusion and chaos and culminate in death.

9.3. The Analysis

The handwritten score includes a German libretto, French musical directions, and precise notation of the acoustic and electronic elements of the opera. The diagrammatic representation of the electronics are notated in the score, with numbers under each electronic event. Manoury illustrates the electronic part with pitches, rhythms (standard notation and graphic representations), or words to describe specific events. Manoury feels that notating precise electronic events is essential for the evolution of the art. The initial acoustic sounds of the opera—a bass drum roll (Gr. Caisse—*Grand Caisse*) and a pedal on note D in the violoncellos (D is rearticulated fourteen times by the cellos in the first ten measures)—are shown on the first page of the three-foot high

Table 9.1 Orchestration in *K*...

3 flutes, 1 piccolo
3 oboes, 3 English horns
3 clarinets in Bb, 2 clarinets in Eb, 3 bass clarinets in Bb
3 bassoons, 3 contrabassoons4 French horns
3 trumpets
1 bugle in Bb
3 trombones
1 tuba
4 tympani (1 timpanist)
3 percussionistsI.

    I.   crotales, vibraphone, snare drum, glass chimes, tam-tam (small) 2 gongs (1–2 high), tubular bells

    II.   bass drum, xylophone, tam-tam (middle), 2 gongs (3–4 middle), triangle

    III. 2 theater gongs (or slip-gongs, 1 ascending, 1 descending), 6 cow bells, 3 suspended cymbals (small, middle, and large) tam-tam (large), 2 gongs (5–6 large)

1 piano
1 MIDI clavier
1 celesta
2 harps
14 violins I
12 violins II
10 violas
8 cellos
6 double bass

---

score in Figure 9.1. The notation of the electronic part is found in middle of the full score. A closer view of the electronic part is found in Figure 9.2.

The first electronic sounds of the opera are a tuba sample, a cymbal sample, and a six note fortissimo chord synthesized by Phase Aligned Formant Synthesis (PAFS), a technique for the synthesis of vowel formants that change over time (Puckette 1995, 40–47). Manoury believes that a real-time system is the only way to preserve expressivity when combining electronic and acoustic instruments. When human musicians follow a recorded electronic part, they lose a significant interpretive dimension because the tempo is fixed. Small adjustments in tempo are a means of musical expression and vary according to the size of the performance space, the mood of the music, and the nature of the musician's responses to the music. These microtemporal changes are possible with a real-time based performance strategy.

Fig. 9.1 The first page of Manoury's full score of *K....* The opera opens with electronic and acoustic sounds. The electronic part is found in the middle of the score; the circled numbers refer to event numbers. The first electronic sounds include a tuba and cymbal sample and six synthesized notes. The cellos play the note D and the bass drums play a roll.

During a performance of Manoury's opera, each part of the electronic music system requires adjustments by human technicians or musicians. The system can be divided into the areas of input, monitoring, triggering, processing, connections, and output. With the exception of the short duration

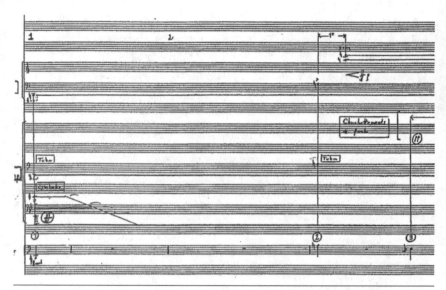

Fig. 9.2 An excerpt of page 1 of the score of *K...* showing the notation of the electronics. The electronics begin with a loud cymbal and tuba sample and six synthesized notes, followed by a downward glissando. Electronic events are circled numbers. At event 2 the tuba sample is resounded along with the synthesized sounds after a delay of one second. At event 3 the crowd sounds begin (*Chuchotements de foule*).

of an electronic event, there is no time in the opera when the technology runs by itself. Continuous human interaction allows for the adaptation of the technological components to the natural performance rhythms of the conductor, singers, and orchestra players.

9.3.1. Use of Technology

The real-time system used in *K...* is diagrammed in Figure 9.3. The flow of information follows the arrows, with each event beginning with the clavier player in the orchestra pit. A musician in the orchestra pit follows the conductor and plays single notes on a clavier that trigger electronic events such as a sample playing or sound spatialization. The clavier plays a note that is sent to the back of the opera hall via an optical signal to avoid degradation and dropout. The pitch of the note is never heard though the note number and timing-onset information are converted to a MIDI signal and sent to a Silicon Graphics computer (SGI) in the machine room at the back of the hall. The computer begins spatialization, synthesis, transformation, or sample events in response to the MIDI trigger. Up to sixteen channels of digital audio are sent via an optical signal to the digital audio mixer in the sound booth. The sounds are equalized, amplified, and sent to thirty of the Opéra Bastille's 200

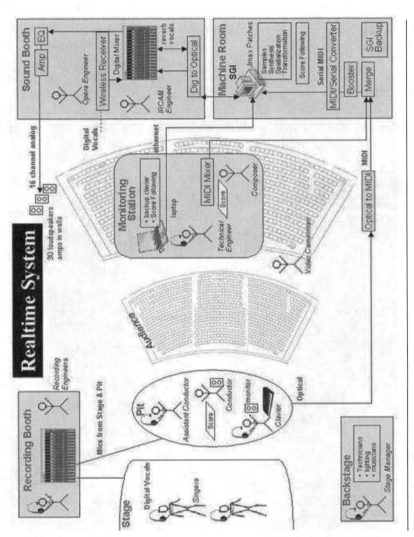

Fig. 9.3 The real-time system used in *K*….

loudspeakers. The composer sits in the first balcony and manually controls the levels of the electronic sounds during rehearsals and performances. The musical assistant is also seated in the first balcony and checks the progress of the computer against the score, making adjustments as necessary. Four singers are amplified in three scenes to balance with strong orchestral and electronic parts. Vocal parts are captured using wireless microphones attached to the head of each singer. The signal from the wireless microphone is received in the sound booth and routed to a digital mixer. In one scene, the vocals are sent to the computer for reverberation and spatialization. During two of the three scenes when there is amplification, vocal sounds are sent to loudspeaker 16, which is located in the scenery onstage close to the singer's location, to create a focused sound. The layout of the loudspeakers in the Grand Hall of the Opéra Bastille is shown in Figure 9.4.

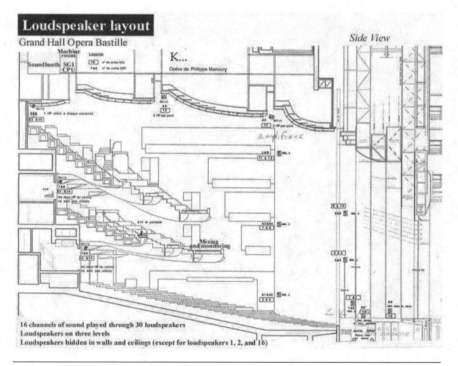

Fig. 9.4 Layout of the loudspeakers used in the Grand Hall of the Opéra Bastille. There are three levels of loudspeakers. The numbers in the boxes correspond to the sixteen audio channels. Audio channels 1–12 are sent to one loudspeaker each. Audio channels 13–16 are sent to multiple loudspeakers. Channels 13 and 14 are heard on three loudspeakers each: three levels on either side of the back of the hall. Channel 15 is heard from multiple locations on the ceiling and channel 16 is placed in the scenery onstage.

Piano/Clavier MIDI

Fig. 9.5 Excerpt of the clavier part at measure 1857 in the third section of Scene XI.

In the opening Prologue, a violin sample is triggered by the clavier player many times. The violin sample is spatialized and harmonized by the computer. The electronic sounds are triggered by notes played on the clavier that are rhythmically timed to precisely accompany the orchestra and singers. The pitch of the notes played change to facilitate score following by the computer. In score following, the computer monitors what note is played by the clavier and the time elapsed in milliseconds from the beginning of a section to the onset of that note. A MIDI signal, comprised of the note number and the elapsed time since the note onset, is sent from the clavier to the computer. Figure 9.5 is an excerpt of the score performed by the clavier player at measure 1857. The number above each note refers to the number of the electronic event within a section of a scene. For example, events 7 to 10 in Figure 9.5 are in measure 1857 in the third of four sections in Scene XI.

The software used in the real-time system of K... executes approximately 2000 preset electroacoustic events. These electroacoustic events include sampling (orchestral samples and concrète samples of everyday sounds), synthesis (PSOLA and PAFS), transformation (harmonizer, reverberation, and Leslie Effect), and spatialization (spatial conditioning and spatial articulation).

Samples are prerecorded sounds. Manoury uses over 500 samples in the opera to amplify events, to simulate events for symbolic meaning, and to create a virtual orchestra. Throughout the opera, Manoury creates a virtual orchestra using short orchestral samples as echoes as well as spatial and timbral counterpoint to the orchestra. These samples begin with orchestral sounds that seem to be transformed and spatialized, moving provocatively around the hall. Table 9.2 is a partial list of the samples used in K.... Each sample is used in the opera in one or more places. Some scenes have a strong component of electronics. Scene IX takes place in an artist's atelier that is overrun with young girls. Nine girls are laughing and yelling on stage as samples of birds, spider monkeys, and girls' cries and laughs are processed and heard moving around the opera hall.

Table 9.2 A partial list of the samples used in *K...*

Cloches/jan1.aiff (cathedral bells)	1.04 sec
Cloches/jan2-processed.aiff	1.08 sec
Fillettes/cri1.aiff (girls crying)	0.94 sec
Fillettes/rire1.aiff (girls laughing)	1.94 sec
Konkret/antique_keys.aiff (typewriter)	0.35 sec
Konkret/steam_train.aiff	52.77 sec
Konkret/telephone.aiff	6.01 sec
Konkret/whip.aiff	19.93 sec
Oiseaux/black_bird.aiff	1.50 sec
Oiseaux/blue_jay.aiff	1.36 sec
Oiseaux/monkey_spider.aiff	2.60 sec
Pas/escalier1.aiff (steps/stair)	0.11 sec
Pas/palier1.aiff (steps/landing)	0.21 sec
Voix/foule1.aiff (voices/crowd)	59.87 sec

Manoury digitally synthesizes sounds in *K...* using the synthesis methods PAFS (Phase Aligned Formant Synthesis) and PSOLA (Pitch Synchronous Overlap-Add). PAFS was developed by Miller Puckette and Norbert Schnell in 1989 for Manoury's *La Partition du Ciel et d'Enfer* for orchestra and electronics. PAFS allows the synthesis of specified fundamentals and formants, and their changes over time; vowels are defined by the presence of formants at particular frequencies and strengths. This method produces a complex, speechlike sound in real-time and is most effective when combined with other instruments. In Figure 9.2 the notes E, D, A, and C-sharp are all created with PAFS. PSOLA is a process that enables the transposition or time stretching of a sound sample, independent of pitch, speed, and timbre. PSOLA is used to create a virtual choir and to transform choral voices into sounds not possible with live singers. The virtual choir is generated from 200 recorded samples of chorus members singing ten Czech phrases written by Daniela Langer and composed by Manoury. With PSOLA, each sample is deconstructed so that each waveform is equal to a pitch period. Segmentation into voiced and unvoiced segments, pitched notes, phonemes, words, and phrases is also carried out. Waveforms may be summed with repeated waveforms and inserted to increase the length of a sample. Skipping alternate waveforms contracts the total duration. The only constraint is recording in a nonreflective room; for example, these chorus samples were recorded in the Espace de Projection at IRCAM, which is configured for nonreflective sound (Schnell et al. 2000, 6). Researchers found that PSOLA does not work well for very high-pitched vocal samples (Schnell et al. 2000, 5). PSOLA was used most prominently during scenes with crowds or suggested crowds onstage. The superhuman singing creates a powerful effect, while the crowd never sings. Figure 9.6 shows an example from the score of the PSOLA part at the beginning of Scene IV. The text of the Czech poetry is shown in the center of the page underneath the notes of the synthesized choral parts. In this example, three phrases are heard simultaneously from the virtual choir: "Ten pa'n, Kdo je ten pa'n, Dlouhou chodbou, nekonecnou, clovece" (pronounced Taine paan, ge-dan iê taine paan, Dloou ho-ou shod-bo-ou, nê-kon-êtci-noou, Tchlo-vié-tchi).

Fig. 9.6 An excerpt of the score showing the use of PSOLA. The Czech text is shown under the notes of the synthesized chorus in the center of the page. *Bruit de Foule* are samples of noises of a crowd.

Transformation involves the alteration of a sound's spectral, pitch, or timbral characteristics using signal-processing techniques. The harmonizer transposes an audio signal without changing the duration or timbre, allowing a buildup of harmonic textures from a single sound source. In Manoury's opera, the use of the harmonizer is often followed by a glissando. Manoury creates the illusion that sounds are in motion through spatialization via successive intensity panning of loudspeakers. Another spatialization technique is Leslie Effect—sound emanates from a loudspeaker while the loudspeaker rotates. This technique is simulated in $K...$ using filtering. Manoury also creates an illusion of spatialization through the use of Leslie Effect, simulating movement in space and movement of loudspeakers in one loudspeaker. The result is an increase in dissonance and a changing of timbre over time.

Spatialization is the simulation of the movement of sound in space. In $K...$ spatialization articulates form, contributes to the recognition of materials, and creates a sense of atmosphere. Spatialization is conjoined with metaphoric movement in the music for a powerful effect. Music is often thought to have metaphoric movement, as notes seem to lead from one to another, from high to low, or to gain momentum and rush upwards. In $K...$, sounds move around the room and simulate virtual spaces using the acoustic characteristics of the space. One consequence of the use of spatialization in $K...$ is the engendering of sonic objects. In $K...$ the audience is immersed in a sonic bath as objects rush around them creating the perception of a sound that has self-movement and sensation. The movement is more than metaphoric, as in traditionally presented music; here the perceived movement is seen as real. The impact is unsettling and unusual in the context of a classical opera and the result is the conferring of a new perceptual model or schema for contemporary opera.

With the creation of spatial sonic objects, the listener is given a unique immediacy with the opera in which the listener is allowed to have a physical and social relationship with sound. If something moves near us, it is not socially neutral. As Trevor Wishart has detailed in his book *On Sonic Art* (1996) there are environmental, psychological, aesthetic, and social connotations to our perceptions. "In front" and "behind" have different social implications for humans (108). In a conversation or any social interaction, sound is usually in front of us. When sound is behind us, we are usually overhearing someone else's conversation or being given a command, situations that are not a part of reciprocal discourse. Sounds in back of us are invisible, ungraspable, and threatening. Thus, the social implications of sounds coming to us from the front are those of a mutual interchange in which the participants are publicly empowered, while sounds from behind produce a discourse of domination and stealth.

The use of reverberation in *K...* contributes to sound spatialization and simulates virtual spaces. Reverberation is the acoustic environment that surrounds a sound and is the component of sound that arrives to the listener after the direct sound via a reflective surface. If a sonic object is far away, there will be more reverberation as compared with the level of the direct sound which comes from the sound source directly to the listener. Direct sound always travels a straight-line path; so, in almost all cases it will reach the listener before sound that reflects off walls (early reflections) or reverberated sound (late reflections). Reverberation is composed of a series of tightly spaced echoes; there is no reverberation in an outdoor concert, but there is a lot of reverberation in a large enclosure such as a cathedral. The number of echoes and the way that they decay play a major role in the perception of acoustic space. The dimensions of a space (length, width, and height) and the materials of construction (hard or soft walls, carpets, draperies, or bare walls) can be perceived aurally by evaluating the nature of the reverberation in that space.

It is also possible to synthesize reverberation to imitate natural and supernatural environments. For example, one could create the reverberation of a room fifty feet long and five feet wide, with a four-foot ceiling, which gradually expands into a stadium. The synthesis of reverberation by digital signal processing usually attempts to mimic real acoustic spaces, simulating early reflections, the compounding of echoes, and the decay of high versus low frequencies.

Reverberation level and the ratio of reverberated to direct sound help the listener determine distance in an enclosed environment. The localization of a sound is also achieved by the listener's perception of distance cues embedded in the sound. Three acoustic qualities of the sound create distance cues for the listener—timbre, loudness, and reverberation. When reverberation is combined with spatialization in *K...*, sounds appear to originate from far away, have self-initiated movements, and exist in virtual locations. One of Manoury's aims is to create changing virtual expanses through the modification of distance cues embedded in the electronic tones. Movement through a cathedral is simulated by altering the amount of reverberation in sonic events (sounds repeatedly return to listeners by bouncing off of virtual stone walls) while adjusting its spectral content (higher frequencies are attenuated with distance and continued reverberation). During a scene toward the end of the opera, a cathedral is acoustically simulated. The audience sees the scenery of the Courtroom while hearing the singers and the electronic accompaniment in a cathedral. During this scene, the Priest and Josef K... wear wireless microphones to capture their voices, which are sent to the computer, spatialized, and reverberated in real time.

Table 9.3 Two Electronic Events in *K*...

Electronic event C: Crowd sounds appear from around the opera hall and are then spatialized or given Leslie Effect. As the whispering of the crowd is transformed with timbre and position changes, the social nature of the experience is manipulated. Initially the murmuring appears to come from other audience members. As the electronic nature of the crowd sounds becomes more apparent, the result is a shift in signs.

Electronic events E1 and E2: The virtual orchestra, concrète sounds, and vocal sounds enlarge the drama and are spatialized and harmonized. Orchestral samples create a spatially distributed virtual orchestra. Sonic trajectories of sounds simulate virtual movement.

There are sixteen types of significant electronic events in *K*.... These electronic events have been cataloged and given letters; related events are grouped by the same letter. There are about 2,000 electronic events in the opera. Two of the electronic events are described in Table 9.3; their placement in the opera is shown in Figure 9.12. The use of crowd sounds, either spatially placed or with Leslie Effect, is called event C and occurs in the Prologue, Scene IV, and Scene VII. Figure 9.2 shows the first appearance of the sounds of the crowd.

Event E1 (orchestral samples) and E2 (concrète samples) are samples that are played and then distorted timbrally or spatially. There are hundreds of orchestral samples (Event E1) played in Scene I forming the virtual orchestra as seen in Figure 9.7. In this scene, samples of brass instruments are placed around the opera hall as a spatial and timbral counterpoint to the actual orchestral sounds. Above each electronic event in Figure 9.7 are letters and Roman numerals referring to chordal harmonies algorithmically generated by Manoury. Events E1 and E2 are the most frequently occurring electronic events in *K*.... In other parts of the opera, samples of yelling, shouting, crying, laughing, and applauding are heard amplifying acoustic and dramatic events. The initiation and cessation of the electronics provide sonic markers at turning points in the opera. When a character begins to relate a story, or when the opera turns from inner to outer life, the electronics are removed with a noticeable effect and structural impact. The use of spatialization and samples create salient features in the opera that could not have been duplicated by other means. Samples enlarge the dramatic impact and spatialization produces an aural image in conflict with visual stimuli. The electronics heighten the confusion surrounding the reality or unreality of dramatic action.

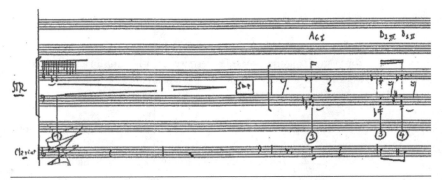

Fig. 9.7 The virtual orchestra in Scene I is created using samples of brass instruments. The samples are spatially placed around the opera hall. The letters and Roman numerals refer to chordal harmonies algorithmically generated by Manoury.

9.3.2. Serial Processes

Serial processes generate materials that are adapted according to the needs of the drama or music (Manoury 2003b) to form a foundation that is not consciously perceivable to the listener. Beginning with four generative melodic series, Manoury used the program Open Music (see Agnon et al. 1998) to automate the generation of note structures in *K....* Algorithmic processes were used to generate harmonic, melodic, rhythmic, and ornamentation materials, which were printed out and bound into notebooks. As Manoury composed, these were the raw materials upon which he drew. In *The Trial* and *K...*, everyone desires to know the Law. Although it is accessible to all, no one has ever seen its higher workings. The opera is appropriately serial; Manoury's music, with its algorithmic and serial structures, is complex, belies immediate understanding, and yet, has a substantial organization. The opera, like the Law, has integrity because of what we do not know. There are many forms of the Law latent in the opera: man's law, moral law, legal law, religious law, spiritual law, natural law, Kabbalistic law, Jewish law, and personal law. *K...* feels guilty, though he and the listener never know what law has been broken or invoked. Manoury's music is engaging and coherent, though the listener doesn't always know what structures have been engaged or transformed. Using serial pitches, chords, rhythms, and ornaments, Manoury's music imparts meaning without apparent hierarchy and structure. The musical impact and the creation of a sense of the transcendent are in inverse relationship to the listener's engagement with materials without being able to directly identify structures. Twenty-nine musical motives and recurrent elements have been identified in *K....* Two of the motives are described in

Table 9.4 Two Musical Motives in *K*...

Motive 1: Long Note String Motif

Prologue—Violins I and II play the notes of generative series 1 in unison and are followed by an electronic tail that changes timbre and is spatialized.

Scene VII—The motive is played by the entire string section, which changes notes in unison.

Scene VIII—The motive is played by the strings and woodwinds. The changing of notes is rhythmically staggered.

Scene XI—A very abbreviated form of the motive occurs at the opening of this scene. It is cut short after the first two notes by a dense and dissonant fortissimo chord in the orchestra.

Scene XII—The form of the motive from the Prologue is reprised by violins I and II with an electronic tail.

Motive 2: Death Motif, Bugle solo

Scene IV—Opening the scene the offstage bugle plays through generative series 2. The bugle motive returns throughout the scene.

Scene VIII—As Josef K... discusses the Judge with Leni, the bugle motive returns, this time from the orchestra pit.

Scene XII—The bugle motive returns preceding the execution of Josef K...

Table 9.4. Both motives recur repeatedly throughout the opera. Their placement in the opera is shown in Figure 9.12.

Manoury created four generative series of notes as the foundation of the opera. The first of the four series, shown in Figure 9.8, forms the notes of motive 1, a series of notes sustained in the string section, which recurs five times in the opera—in the Prologue, Scene VII, Scene VIII, Scene XI (a short reprise), and Scene XII leading up to the climax where Josef K... is killed. Each time the motive returns there is a growing complexity and then a return to simplicity in the finale. Figure 9.9 shows motive 1 as it appears in the Prologue played by the violins. Figure 9.8 depicts generative series 1, which is the algorithmic foundation for much of the opera as well as comprising the notes of motive 1.

Motive 2 is derived from the second of the four generative series and is shown in Figure 9.10. Motive 2 is played by an offstage solo bugle and is

Fig. 9.8 Generative series 1 is the algorithmic foundation for much of the opera as well as comprising the notes of motive 1.

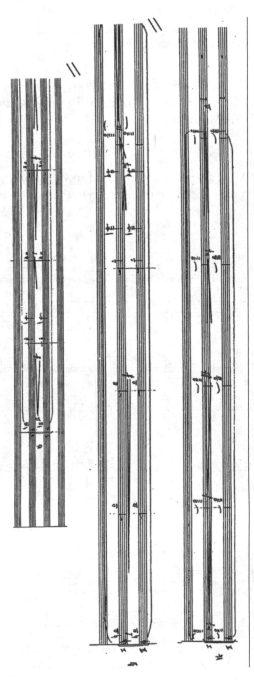

Fig. 9.9 Motive 1 from the Prologue of *K…* is played by the unison violins I and II.

Fig. 9.10 The notes of generative series 2 comprise the notes of motive 2.

heard in Scene IV, Scene VIII, and Scene XII. Motive 2 is heard at the end of Scene XII at the same time as motive 1 preceding the execution of Josef K… . Figure 9.11 shows Motive 2 in Scene IV.[3]

9.3.3. Musical Form

To assess the form of *K…*, it is necessary to identify pivot points in the drama and music. The opera is divided into three acts; yet, the work is continuous

Fig. 9.11 Motive 2 is played by an offstage bugle at the opening of Scene IV. Motive 2 is found in three scenes of the opera. The example above is from the reduced piano score created by Manoury for rehearsals.

and is performed without breaks, making for a seamless flow. Upon closer examination, it can be seen that there are, in fact, logical fractures in the flow of the story corresponding to the division into acts. The opera can be segmented in terms of the mental progress of the central character Josef K.... In Act I, from Scenes 0 through IV, K... is confused but defiant about his arrest. In Act II, Scenes V through VII, K... is uneasy and weakening, crumbling under the weight of his accusation and his personal sense of guilt. In Act III, Scenes VIII through XII, the emotional evolution of K.... is repeated—from defiance and confusion, to unease and fear, and finally to K...'s acquiescence to the power dominating him. The structural diagram of the opera is shown in Figure 9.12. K...'s mental progress, motivic materials, pivotal events, interactions with women in the opera, Blackouts, and scene symmetries can be seen in this reduction of K.... Each of these components, including the numbers and letters of the motives and electronic events in K... is described below.

The overall level in the structural diagram indicates the relative mental state of Josef K... as he changes from confused to defiant to fearful to acquiescent. It is K...'s acceptance of his guilt that leads directly to his execution.

There are symmetries present in the formal organization of the opera. Except for Scene IX, each scene can be paired in opposition with another. See Table 9.5 for a list of scene symmetries.

K...'s meeting with Titorelli in Scene IX alone represents a way out of his situation. However, Josef K... rejects Titorelli's options. The Prologue and Scene XII can be paired as the thought of death and its enactment. In the Prologue, Josef K... is confused by a nightmare that portrays his thoughts of death. In Scene XII he succumbs to the pressures surrounding him, accepts his own dissolution, and is slaughtered.

Scenes I and VII represent K...'s dealings with the Court. In Scene I he is arrested and his life begins to break down. In Scene VII he visits the Offices of the Court and collapses as the bad air and his agitated emotions physically incapacitate him. This scene is an important turning point in the story.

Table 9.5 Scene Symmetries in *K...*

Prologue: K...'s Nightmare—Scene XII: The Punishment
Scene I: The Arrest —Scene VII: The Offices of the Court
Scene II: Fraülein Bürstner—Scene VI: Return to the Courtroom
Scene III: The Bank—Scene V: The Chastisement
Scene IV: The Tribunal—Scene XI: The Cathedral
Scene VIII: At the Lawyer's—Scene X: Return to the Lawyer's
Scene IX: At Titorelli's (DVD references 1–8)

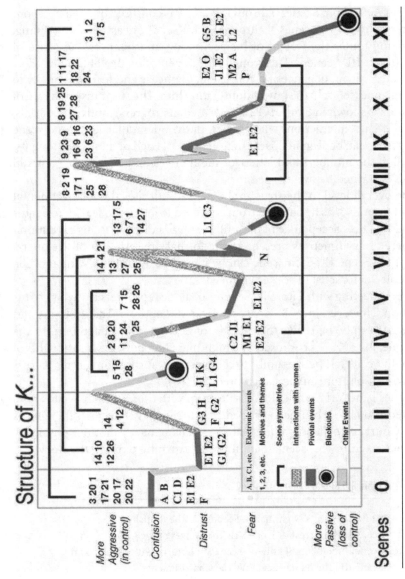

Fig. 9.12 Structural diagram of *K. . . .*, showing motives (see above for descriptions of motives 1 and 2), electronic events (see above for descriptions of electronic events designated by letters C, E1, and E2), the mental state of Josef K. . . ., and significant events of the opera by scene. (DVD reference 9)

Scenes II and VI are representative of his dealings with women. In Scene II he is the invited aggressor of his neighbor Fraülein Bürstner. In Scene VI he loses the Bailiff's Wife to the law student Bertold, which is his first apparent loss in the realm of the Court.

Scenes III and V both take place in the workplace of Josef K.... At the bank in Scene III, K... receives a call and summons to an interrogation. K... is disturbed though still in control of his emotions. In Scene V, K... comes upon Franz and Willem being whipped. He is overcome by their cries and fearful that someone else will hear, representing another breakdown for K....

Both Scenes VIII and X take place in the Lawyer's house, though they are inversions of each other. In Scene VIII, K... is brought to meet the Lawyer Huld by his Uncle Albert. K... encounters Huld's mistress Leni and is seduced to the detriment of his case. In Scene X, K... returns to reject Leni and fire his lawyer, representing his rejection of assistance from family and friends.

Scenes IV and XI represent his direct dealings with the Court. Both scenes are musically very complex and dense, with the virtual choir playing a prominent role. The transformed human voices are transcendent yet shrill and oppressive. In both scenes, K... has reached an end point and makes a momentous shift. In Scene IV, K... defies the Judge and the Tribunal with an accusatory speech and his precipitous departure. Scene XI takes place in the cathedral, where he converses with the Priest who is also a part of the Court. The scene marks the end of K...'s defiance and his acceptance of the immanence and inevitability of his death. The music climaxes in its complexity in Scene XI and then returns to simpler textures in Scene XII, showing that once the choice is made, even if it is death, the path is simple.

Sonic trajectories are treated as structural markers in *K*.... In each act, there are brief moments when there are interruptions in the action, the internal emotional processes of K... are highlighted, and K... glimpses his execution. Manoury terms these episodes "Blackouts." These dramatically tense moments function as structural turning points in the narrative and are accompanied by a suspension of time and a fast moving trajectory of the synthesized chorus on consonant harmonies. These transient sonic events have dramatic and fleeting trajectories and effectively refocus the listener's perception from the static nature of the sound to its motion; they also presage the final sonic episode of the opera. During the Blackouts, the spatial trajectories begin at the back of the opera hall going toward the front, dashing right and left like "sonorous flashes," then plunging toward the floor near the orchestra pit (Manoury 2001, 121). The third of the Blackouts is the last sound in the opera. The electronic noise starts at the back, zigzags forward, and then appears to leave through the roof of the hall.

In *K*..., the musical whole fuses even when the parts are disjunct. As the sound moves around the hall during the Blackouts, the listener becomes aware of its objectlike nature. The Blackouts draw the listener out of the dramatic flow of the opera, effectively stopping dramatic time. In each Blackout, K… has a change of mental state and becomes physically and emotionally weakened. As the Blackout ends, the drama restarts in time, and K… is closer to the acceptance of his death. The result is an awareness of a sonic object through the progressive stopping, compressing, and then restarting of time. While the elements of drama, music, time, and spatial pathway are disparate, they fuse into a quixotic statement with manifold proportions. The outcome is a sort of musical Stroop Effect[4]—difficult to pull apart because of the incongruence of the components.

There are four marked Blackouts in the opera, though only three are actually performed. The Blackouts occur in Scenes III, VII, and XII. Manoury hopes that, rather than the nature of the sounds themselves, the striking spatial trajectories are most notable (Manoury 2001, 121). Here Manoury strives for thematic function with the spatialized sounds.

The first Blackout is in Scene III at the bank, the workplace of K… . He has just finished a telephone call with officials of the Court regarding regular interrogations, and he is still puzzled as to the time of his hearing. The sound of the virtual choir is heard moving quickly through the opera house. K… stops, looks up, and sees two men looking at him intently and showing him a gleaming knife. The external manifestation of his sense of guilt or desire for death pauses the action and the music. K… is slightly shaken as the music resumes and work continues busily around him at the bank. See Figure 9.13 for a diagram of the spatial pathway and denouement of Blackout I.

The second Blackout is marked near the end of Scene VI after the Bailiff's Wife is carried off. Manoury stated that due to director André Engel's objection the Blackout was replaced with silence (2002).

The third Blackout is in Scene VII and takes place in the Offices of the Court. K… becomes weak and dizzy, and feels faint when the Bailiff turns on a film of Franz and Willem being whipped. A significant turning point in the opera occurs during this Blackout when K… is physically shaken, as if he has had a blow to the heart. The sounds of the synthesized choir are heard with a spatial trajectory as in Blackout I. After the Blackout in Scene VII, K… becomes physically subdued by the events of his arrest. The music of the scene features high harmonics on the strings, which sound eerily electronic.

The last Blackout differs in sonic character from the other Blackouts, though the spatial trajectory is similar. The sound is a noisy hiss with an ascending, forward-moving, spiraling pathway. The last Blackout is also the final sonic event of the opera and prompts the listener to reflect on earlier instances of the same sonic motion.

The Blackouts are placed at points in the story when the events have a profoundly negative impact on K… . There is a contrast between the dramatic

Blackout I in *K*...

BEFORE THE BLACKOUT
At the opening of Scene III Josef K... is on the phone with the Office of
the Law. The clerks dash around him at his bank office. K... hangs up the
phone and is disturbed by the call.

DURING THE BLACKOUT
As the Blackout begins the action and music stop. The consonant harmonies
of the virtual choir are dramatically spatialized. Two men appear carrying a big knife.
As they gaze intently at K... and flash the knife he looks up. The two men walk
slowly away.

AFTER THE BLACKOUT
Josef K... is flustered by the vision of his death. Gradually the office activity and
orchestral music return to continue the steady pace.

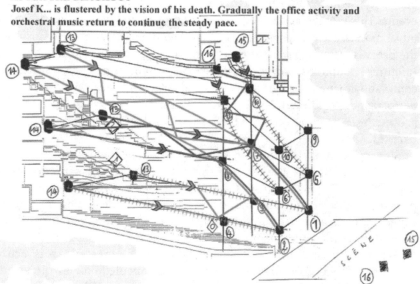

Fig. 9.13 Blackout I in Scene III. The numbers refer to audio channels. The sound moves in a zigzag
forward then plunges downward to the orchestra pit. (DVD reference 10)

tension at each Blackout and the relative consonance of their harmonies.
When the dramatic tension at each Blackout is combined with the consonant
sounds and the energetic release of their spatial pathways, the result is a para-
doxical moment in the opera when the drama, music, and spatial pathways
pull in different directions. The effect is an accumulation of momentary
discontinuities that rupture the fabric of the opera as the arrest has done in
the life of Josef K... the ultimate discontinuity is death.

9.3.4. Semiotics

The semiotic process in music is like a string of oddly shaped beads. Semiotics is a sequential process in which the mind perceives the music and then
the sign, then develops the sign, which leads to another sign, then to a more
developed sign, and so on. The beads may be separated by centuries and

continents, but are somehow connected in the mind of the listener. If the composer is successful, the beads form into a necklace at conclusive points in the music, and the listener glimpses the whole in a revelatory gestalt experience. The revelation in the listener produces a release and a considerable feeling of satisfaction. For example, during a performance of "The Star Spangled Banner" a listener might feel patriotic or be moved to stand. In the mind of the perceiver, an equivalent or more developed sign might be created in an infinite relay of meaning, such as when she or he has stood up before to listen to the "The Star Spangled Banner" in school or at sporting events. This might lead to thinking of other times the person has stood for music as in church or synagogue, thereby extending, in an unlimited fashion, the process of semiosis. Most everything becomes a sign and signs can be "pictures, symptoms, words, sentences, books, libraries, signals, orders of command, microscopes, legislative representatives, musical concertos, [and] performances of these"(Pierce quoted in Liszka 1996, 20). In the semiotic process, the meaning of a specific sign arises with an interpretation in a particular context.

Shifting semiotic processes in $K\ldots$ are created by the transformation of musical signs through the use of technology. The transformation of signs begins in the Prologue. Motive, with it's strange electronic behaviors, is played by the string section and is first heard here. The audience shifts its expectations to adjust to the music of the opera. The motive returns three more times during the opera without electronics. When the motive recurs repeatedly without strange electronic transformations, the audience is secure in the belief that the string motive will be accompanied only by orchestral timbres. When the motive returns a final time in Scene XII, the spatial behaviors and timbral shifts are even more extreme than during the Prologue. The audience is startled into a new shift of perspective as the sound of the violin is transformed into flying sonic projectiles. When combined with the onstage tension, Josef K.'s stress, and the intervening conflicts in the dramatic narrative, the agitation is intensified until culminating in death.

At the end of the opera, a significant revelation occurs for the listener when the first notes of generative series 1 (which have been heard repeatedly in the long string motive), reveal themselves out of the dense textures of Scene XI and coalesce into the death march of Scene XII. The march dies away and the long string motive returns along with the executioners.

On one level, the musical signs in the finale of $K\ldots$ continue to portray real objects (the bugle, the orchestral instruments, the voice). On another level, the music transforms to the unreality of the violin timbres and behaviors and then back to reality with the roll of the drums before $K\ldots$'s execution. As the signs twist from the actual to the improbable and then back, the impact is like an agogic accent of signs and the chilling return of reality that results in death.

The result is a resounding accent of signs coming together to agree and inform the listener of a climatic moment. The climax of the opera is followed by the death of the central character—an orgasm and then death. The listener experiences a release and a sense of the whole; it is a very satisfying experience and a powerful way to end the opera.

9.3.5. Music Structure Discovery

The examination of the opening and the closing scenes of *K*... begins with signal analysis using a program called Music Structure Discovery (MSD) developed by Geoffroy Peeters at IRCAM. The program creates a visual rendering of an audio recording by searching for acoustic self-similarity over time. The audio file becomes a square with time running both from left to right and bottom to top of a visual display. Similar regions are red (darkest in the black and white rendition) and most dissimilar regions are blue (also dark in the black and white rendition). Intermediate relations are lighter and range from orange to yellow to green to light blue to dark blue. A main diagonal represents the most similar regions (Foote and Cooper 2001). Self-similar regions become blocks providing a structural overview of the audio recording independent of traditional symbolic notation (Peeters 2004, 142–65). Peeters ran the MSD analysis for *K*... and provided the author with the results.

MSD is most helpful in analyzing music that has no explicit generating text, such as a score in traditional music, because the analysis is based on the aural result not the written representation. Self-similarity analysis can show sectional and structural relations in music that have surface differences. Areas that have similar properties will appear on the diagonal axis as red. The X and Y-axes are time in a musical selection. The center diagonal will be entirely similar as each musical event is being compared with itself. Moving farther away from the center diagonal results in comparisons of each musical event with all other parts of the selection.

The Prologue opens the opera and lays the foundation for the musical and narrative progress of the work. The Prologue is 340 seconds long, features a strong component of electronics, and is clearly divided into six sections: Scenes 0A–F. (The electronics of the Prologue can be heard in DVD reference 13.) The MSD analysis of the Prologue provided in Figure 9.14 shows a clear division into six segments. When comparing from 0 seconds to a little before 50 seconds on the Y-axis, with 0 seconds to a little before 50 seconds on the X-axis, there is a dark block showing a high degree of self-similarity for this region. The times beginning each blocked segment correspond exactly with each Prologue section (0 seconds, 40 seconds, 73 seconds, 146 seconds, 192

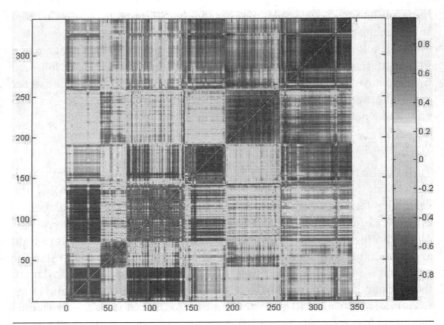

Fig. 9.14 Music structure discovery from signal analysis: Prologue. (DVD reference 11)

seconds, 201 seconds). The MSD analysis also shows the bracketing between sections 0A and 0B, the similarities between 0A and 0D, 0C and 0F, and a less strong connection between 0A and 0E, and 0A and 0D. In addition, the first 70 seconds are seen as closely linked to the opening 10 seconds.

As the opera opens, the stage is dark. The Prologue begins with a massive, dissonant, bass cluster, which descends spatially and harmonically. The audience hears the sounds of a cymbal, a tuba, and a synthesized cluster of notes. The recorded and synthesized notes begin on the ceiling and spiral downward five stories and two octaves. In the second measure of the opera, a strongly contrasting high violin consonance plays the notes D and A, which are the first two notes of one of the generative series underlying the entire opera (see Figure 9.8). The shift from moving bass dissonance to static high consonance produces a shifting of signs from the improbable to the possible. In the second measure, the electronic sounds begin sliding around the hall in a slow spiral descent in space and pitch. The result is stirring and suggests a powerful moving mass of instruments.

The sounds of murmuring appears around the hall. (In Figure 9.2 the circled number 3 in the middle of the electronic score plays a recording of a crowd whispering—*Chuchotements de foule*). The listener is unsure if the murmuring is from members of the audience expressing their disapproval of the opening sounds, or is part of those sounds. The ambiguity of the sound source creates social dissonance; that is, a social setting characterized by conflict and contradiction. As the murmuring increases in volume and density, its source becomes at once apparent and concealed. It is clear that the people in the hall are not the cause of the sound, but the source is hidden as the loudspeakers in the opera hall are embedded in the walls and ceiling.

As the Prologue continues, the cellos, harps, and horns support the string consonance on the same notes. The consonance is disturbed by spatially distributed samples of people murmuring and muttering, as well as by ornamentation figures in the violins and violas producing disjunct rhythms with *col legno battuto*. The murmuring of the crowd continues to appear from varying locations around the hall throughout the Prologue.

The relative calm is pierced by the harsh, high dissonance of the crotales on A, A-sharp, and B. A sample of three piccolos are spatialized, playing the notes E, F-sharp, and G, and are harmonized with a downward glissando over the next four measures. The timbres are harsh and dissonant and their spatial behavior is unexpected. In the first 40 seconds of the opera, the signs shift rapidly between coherent and in agreement, to divergence, creating a confused and unpredictable presentation.

With the exception of the first section, Scene 0A, all others begin with a seven note figure consisting of 64th note samples of timpani and cymbals. Section 0B begins with the same timpani/cymbal figure, as seen in Figure 9.15. As the section continues the clarinets add a second ornamentation figure. Both clarinet and string ornamentations were generated algorithmically from one of Manoury's generative series. The piccolo and crotale dissonances are retriggered at a slightly higher cluster, followed by an extended and more complex harmonizer glissando.

Section 0C begins with the timpani and cymbal accent along with the stopping and restarting of the clarinet ornamentation. Oboes are added in a similar, though rhythmically disjunct, pattern of ornamentation. The string ornamentation continues and the tam tams are added with a staggered surging sound. The piccolo and crotale dissonances, joined by the xylophone, are heard once more at measure 25. The high clustered sound is followed by a harmonizer glissando sequence that is the longest and most complex of the Prologue, and which continues (with only one stopping point at the end of section Scene 0D and the beginning of Scene 0E) throughout the rest of the Prologue. In Section 0C, the notes E-flat and A-flat are also played, tremolo, in the high register on the xylophone and violins. The acoustic notes become audible when the electronic part diminishes at the end of the section, when they appear as an acoustic prolongation of the electronic distortions. The aural result signifies a momentary return to normality. The xylophone and violins

Fig. 9.15 Seven-note figure delineating sections in the Prologue—64th note samples of timpani and cymbals.

build up the texture, playing additional ornamental figures and adding to the rhythmic dissonance. Key motivic material is first presented in an abbreviated form and then recapitulated with elaborated texture and length.

There is a dramatic transformation at the end of the Prologue from nightmarish, rhythmic disorder, to the regularity of the waking life. Josef K…'s nightmare is characterized by the instability of the ornamental figures and harmonic dissonance that resolves to 4/4, 16th notes, with all the strings pulsing on the note E-flat. Beginning at measure 79, the harmonizer becomes striated with uniform palpitations with Leslie Effect rotations at 2400 per second. In measure 81, the strings and woodwinds articulate a varied quintuplet figure. By measure 87, the woodwinds have faded out and the strings have speeded slightly in tempo but are articulating unison 16th notes on E-flat. The impact is order out of chaos. The instruments walk up chromatically but end on the same repeated E-flat note, creating an acoustic transcription of the auditory illusion known as Shepard tones.

The ground bass provides an underpinning to the work that stabilizes each section in which the bass remains the same. The sections of the Prologue are distinct due to five factors: (1) the unifying ground bass, which remains the same within a section; (2) the timpani/cymbal sample, which delineates the beginning of each section; (3) the ebbing and surging in pitch and volume of electronic elements within a section; (4) the changing of background elements in subsequent sections; and (5) the overall increase in density, pitch, and volume.

The Prologue contrasts very high and very low sections, building density and texture with phrases that are developed by increasing their complexity and length. The bass line is an exact copy of the most prominent generative series but drawn out over three minutes so as to be unrecognizable, analogous to the talea of an isorhythmic motet. The bass line returns in Scenes VII, VIII, and XII in the strings and woodwinds.

The boundary between electronic and acoustic sounds is blurred as orchestral samples originate from loudspeakers located approximately where the player of that instrument is located. Often the acoustic sound begins and the sound is finished by a sample of that instrument with an unusual spatial behavior. The perception is familiar, but the behavior is twisted. The first sounds of the Prologue are obviously electronic. Soon afterwards, the boundaries are blurred with orchestral sounds flying around the room. Material is recognizable by the repetition of exact pitches embedded in dense harmonic and rhythmic dissonances. Large accents of signs, drama, rhythm, and music are deceptively finalelike but make way for the resurgence of the primary materials with greater harmonic dissonance and complexity. The spatial and timbral dissonance challenges many of the opera listeners' expectations within the first six minutes. The opening music is confrontational and subverts expectations with a visceral impact on the audience. The result is a tightly integrated and powerful opening statement creating both interest and incomprehension for the listener.

The Music Structure Discovery analysis for Scene XII is shown in Figure 9.16. There are no longer clearly delineated sections as found in the Prologue. Instead there is a gradual drifting from one musical texture to the next with more diverse components. The opening of Scene XII (XIIA) is rhythmically striated, showing the definitive beats of the death march that emerges out of the dense orchestral textures of Scene XI. The second section of Scene XII (XIIB) begins at 76 seconds after the first section has faded out. Scene XIIB is characterized by longer tones and irregular smaller sections. It is in the end of Scene XIIB that Josef K... sings his last words to his executioners. The last section begins at 170 seconds and is characterized by more rapid

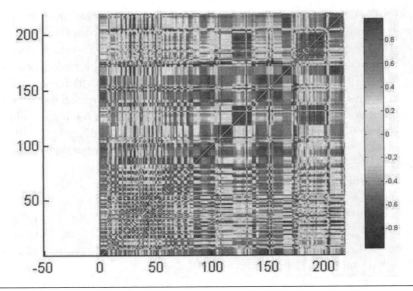

Fig. 9.16 Music Structure Discovery from signal analysis: Scene XII. (DVD reference 12)

shifts in texture. Scene XIIB is sparsely orchestrated and culminates with the solitary sounds of the last Blackout.

Scene XII is an harmonic release from Scene XI. At the onset of Scene XII, large bell samples are played on the first, second, third, and fourth beats of consecutive measures. Immediately, Scene XII begins building tension, dissonance, and tempo. There is a measure of rest for the bells and the pattern repeats. At the same time, the dynamics and dissonance increase in density through the addition of chromatic ornamentation figures in the woodwinds and brass sections of the orchestra. There is a reprise from the Prologue; the piccolo sample goes to the harmonizer followed by a descending glissando. The texture builds, ornamentation is added, and then fades out.

The next section reprises the string motive that has recurred in the Prologue and Scenes VII, VIII, and XI. In Scene XII the string motive has predominantly unison harmonic changes with a spatialized electronic echo that reinforces, and redistributes the orchestral sounds. The string motive continues until just before the cutting of K...'s throat. K... falls down dead, and the last Blackout of the opera sends an electronic sound (PAFS with added noise to localize the sound) zigzagging forward with an accelerating spiral upward.

Near the end of the opera, a bugle call is heard in the background. The musical material representing K...'s trial recurs with the same melodic line, texture, and timbre. The orchestral accompaniment in the strings is high, sustained, and harmonically consonant. The string motive has occurred prominently at five places in the opera. The sounds themselves are string sounds associated with familiar orchestral sounds. As the strings are sustained they are transformed electronically: the sound of the strings is distorted and their spatial behavior becomes unfathomable as they fly around the room. The transition is achieved smoothly and subtly, and the audience is unaware of the shift. The consequence is an incongruity between sound and sight as sonorities shift and the listener is unaware of the cause. As the executioner grabs Josef K..., all music stops except for a bongo drum, which sounds as a drum roll before an execution. K...'s throat is slit with a swift motion, and he gasps, "*Wie ein Hund!*" (Like a dog), and collapses to the ground.

9.4. Summary

The aesthetic experience of technology and music in *K...* is intimately bound with the experience of the acoustic portions of the opera. The impact of the use of technology becomes most dramatic when sonic events are spatialized and at the boundaries between electronic and purely acoustic music. When the electronics in *K...* are removed from the sonic textures, the result is a humanizing of scale, bringing the audience closer to the performers, just as when someone whispers, the listener leans forward to hear better if she or he is sufficiently engaged with what the whisperer has been saying. Manoury first captivates his audience with a dazzling and dense palate; then, by simplifying the design, he allows the listener to lean forward both cognitively and emotionally.

The temporal experience of *K...* is shaped by the use of technology during the Blackouts. The Blackouts are a series of electronic events that function as structural markers and prefigure future events in the opera that lead to the destruction of the hero. Why include the Blackouts? After all, the Blackouts were not in Kafka's story. In the novel, Josef K. undergoes radical internal shifts described by the narrator. In the opera, the Blackouts depict these moments of change. Through the use of electronics and music, Manoury allows the audience to understand these shifts on a nonintellectual or emotional level.

Through exposure to popular culture, listeners are disposed, habituated, and accustomed to technology in music. For some listeners, technology makes opera more accessible because reverberation and spatialization of sound create an immersive cinematic experience. Although Manoury was not striving to obtain a cinematic experience, the result is gripping.

In Kafka's story, the reader is always with the hero Josef K., inside his head and hearing his thoughts. This interior view allows the reader to understand the events of the story as a series of occurrences happening to Josef K. In a theatrical dramatization, an internal point of view is impossible without a narrator explaining what is inside of K...'s head. Manoury only uses the spoken dialogue of the book for the opera. Thus, the audience is distanced from the events as compared with the reader of the novel. Spatialization engulfs the listener in sound, giving a proximity to the world of Josef K..., filling the opera house with self-motivated sound, and drawing the audience into a more interior experience of the drama. Spatial polyphony combined with PSOLA creates the illusion of a virtual choir, producing spatial counterpoint and texture. The sounds swirl around listeners, allowing a closer identification with, and simulating the tumultuous experience of Josef K.... Most operas have a large sound that fills the opera hall. In K..., sounds fill the opera hall but seem to be self-animated. The movement of sound is significant to the listener's understanding of the work. Spatialization defines narrative sections, creates specific virtual locations, and constructs sonic objects. The motion of a sound creates a perceptual objectification of that sound. As the sound moves around the hall, its behavior becomes a recognizable object and the listener may attribute to the sound such physical qualities as touch, density, and dimension. Thus, sound with spatial trajectories changes the experience of opera.

Reverberation simulates virtual settings by changing the listener's sense of space and architecture on a subconscious level. The processing of sounds to create reverberant characteristics other than those of the Opéra Bastille place the listener in the acoustic space where the action occurs. The use of technology conveys turmoil. In the Prologue, there is a restart and heightening to the horror of Josef K...'s nightmare and the electronics ebb and surge to intensify the terror. A distant groaning in the electronics suggests an unknown fear on the edge of consciousness. The effect is made stronger by the strangeness of the timbres and the twisting manner in which they move. Technology also expands the dramatic and musical impact of the opera through the use of samples. Samples in Scene VI and Scene XII are church bells, which have numerous associations in music with death. In Scene V the sound of a bullwhip accompanies the onstage whipping and cries of Willem. The change in the timbre and the decorrelation with the action produces a shifting of signs throughout the scene. The result is the destabilization of semiotics and a swelling of the dramatic action. In the Prologue and the final scene, samples extend, distort, and twist the spatial behavior of orchestral instruments. In Scene I, the orchestral samples are heard as a spatial and timbral counterpoint to the orchestral music. The virtual orchestra subverts the dramatic flow by pulling the listener's attention away from the stage. The virtual orchestra also strengthens the musical presentation by redirecting the sound back at the stage in articulated, virtual movement.

Philosopher Wolfgang Welsch, in an article entitled "Aesthetics Beyond Aesthetics," discusses the phenomenon of global aestheticization whereby an aesthetic fashioning of reality is conveyed by media (1997, 7). According

to Welsch, the refashioning of reality by contemporary media produces an extensive restyling of bodies and behaviors. Welsch feels that the contemporary understanding of reality includes a "derealization of reality," which is consequent from a media projected and conveyed reality. When the normative mode is for all visual objects to be subjected to distortions by electronic media, our daily reality is created, transmitted, and perceived through media manipulation.

Aesthetic philosopher Roger Scruton states that metaphors about space, movement, and animation are implicit in our experience of music (1997, 80). When we listen to music, we create meaning for ourselves through a process of identification with our own internal schemata about music. These internal schemata are related to our schemata of our bodies. In *K. . .*, image schemata are disrupted by the use of technology—changing semiotic signs to create unsettling subconscious disruptions.

Metaphoric movement in music is an element of the music that is ascribed a particular meaning. The metaphoric movement can be a melodic line that jumps or moves from high to low that leads convincingly from one to another (Scruton 1997, 49). Feeling in music can resemble actual feelings by distilling and transforming emotion into a symbol. In *K. . .*, metaphoric movement is experienced as embodied and genuine. Sometimes, elements of music are linked to enhance metaphoric movement in the music, such as a rising melodic line that is linked to its spatialization. The sophisticated linking of metaphoric movement with technological elements of the music is critical to the perception of meaning.

Dowling and Harwood state that expectations and resolutions about music are mostly subconscious. Listeners accumulate structural schemata their entire lives, though they are unaware of the exact outlines (Dowling and Harwood 1986, 219). Meaning is produced by a process of identification with and absorption in an aural experience that stimulates a physical response, and produces in the listener's mind the awareness of a host of corollary reactions and responses. As philosopher Schopenhauer stated, music is meaningful and eloquent because it accesses feelings that go beyond words.

Technology in music challenges the primacy of vision. Welsch believes our sense of hearing is being reevaluated due to an "essentially social character in contrast to the individualistic execution of vision, and because of its link with emotional elements in opposition to the emotionless mastery of phenomena through vision"(7). Welsch points out the proximal, emotional, and social aspects of our experience of sound. Sound plays a profoundly important role in the listener's assessment of meaning. In Manoury's opera, the social nature of the experience is manipulated using sampled crowd sounds in the Prologue. The hall is dark, hiding other audience members. Recessed speakers hide the sound sources, so the listener concludes that the other audience members are dissatisfied and talking. The social impact is unsettling and disturbing. As the Prologue progresses, the electronic sounds becomes more apparent resulting in a shift in signs.

Manoury's opera is dense and complex. Yet, the listener is absorbed by the experience and comes away feeling satisfied. There are several reasons why the listener is musically and dramatically satisfied:

1. The spatialization of sonic objects enhances the listener's ability to relate to the music.
2. The returning string motive and the Blackouts create recognizable motivic elements that return at structural points in the opera.
3. Four generative series unify the work by forming harmony, melody, ornamentation, and a ground bass.
4. The return of Prologue materials in the Finale constitutes a recapitulation.
5. The shift between real and virtual through the use of technology decorrelates the music from the drama, clouds the perception of the drama as actual events, and causes a shifting of signs.
6. In Scene XII, the emergence of the death march out of the chaos of Scene XI yields a harmonic, textural, and melodic release of tension.
7. The semiotic agreement of signs coincides with the execution of Josef K… and the end of the opera.

The end of Manoury's opera is more conclusive than that of the novel. By selecting only the novel's spoken dialogue, Manoury could not use the last words of the novel. In Kafka's work, K.'s last gasped words before dying, "*Wie ein Hund*," are followed by, "it seemed as though the shame was to outlive him"(231). Why was K. shamed? Was he shamed by his guilt, shamed that he had to prove himself, that he couldn't prove himself, that he couldn't get a real acquittal, shamed by his death, by the manner of his death, by his inability to carry out his own death, or his inability to fight it off? In the opera, K…'s death may be interpreted as the acceptance of the inevitable, transcendence of the pettiness of life, being crushed by modern life, or a step into a higher existence. In the novel, the idea of shame is placed in the foreground and the number of diverse interpretations of K.'s execution are increased. In the opera, the noisiness of the Blackout, the last sonic event of the opera, swarms forward and ascends in spirals to the roof. The movement evokes the idea of rising up after death and transcendence. The trajectory of the Blackout is swift and the sound quality is machinelike, not the consonant vocal harmonies of the earlier Blackouts. There is ambiguity in the shift from human to mechanical sounds; yet, there is more definitiveness in the trajectory of ascent of these sounds compared to previous sounds. The last event of the opera has no shame. The sense that the sound of the Blackout outlives the hero, is not one of shame. The conclusion of *K...* is a depersonalization of the hero, not a personification of shame as in Kafka's novel.

Kafka's novel has many interpretations. When a production is staged, many of these interpretations become actualized due to the nature of stage performance. In the novel, the reader questions if the events are real or in the mind of the main character. In an opera, the audience witnesses events, and sees that these events are real. The physicality of the staging renders the story more conclusive. Manoury's music challenges the drama through shifting signs, causing the listener to be dislocated and off-balance. The termination of the opera is musically conclusive but dramatically inconclusive. The listener never knows if *K...* is truly guilty. Yet, on another level, the drama is very conclusive, considering the death of the main character. The discontinuity of these elements facilitates the equivocality of the experience.

The listener is satisfied with the resolution of the musical ending. Is the musically satisfactory ending a mismatch with Kafka whose writings are puzzling and inconclusive? The music is a *semiotic* complement to the story. Without the technology and music, Kafka's novel could not have been effectively staged.

Manoury's opera animates Kafka's novel of Jewish mysticism. While the libretto is not a sacred text, neither is it simply a tale of a man enmeshed in the bureaucracy of the modern world. Central to the story is the parable of the unlearned who agrees to sit and wait, unworthy to challenge the gatekeepers. Kafka wrote the "Parable of the Law" with the message that everyone wants to ascend to the Law. To stop and wait is a choice. Manoury expresses the unattainable mystery beyond consciousness that Kafka posits for the world—the unknown and unknowable.

References

Agon, Carlos, Gérard Assayag, Mikael Laurson, and Camilo Rueda. "Computer Assisted Composition at IRCAM: PatchWork & OpenMusic." *Computer Music Journal* 23, no.3(1999): 59–72.

Carroll, John. "Franz Kafka." *Encounter*. Producer: Sarah Kanowski. Radio National, Australian Broadcasting Corporation, November 21, 1999. <http://www.abc.net.au/rn/relig/enc/stories/s70778.htm>.

Dowling, W. Jay, and Dane L. Harwood. *Music and Cognition*. San Diego: Academic Press, 1986.

Foote, Jonathan, and Matthew Cooper. "Visualizing Musical Structure and Rhythm via Self-Similarity." In Proceedings of the International Conference on Computer Music (ICMC). *Havana, Cuba, 2001*.

Kafka, Franz. *The Trial*. 1925 (in German). Translated by Breon Mitchell. New York: Schocken Books, 1998.

Liszka, James. *A General Introduction to the Semiotic of Charles Sanders Peirce*. Bloomington and Indianapolis: Indiana University Press, 1996.

Manoury, Philippe. *Va-et-Vient: Entretiens avec Daniela Langer*. Paris: Musica Falsa Societé de Presse, 2001.

———. Personal Interview. December 20, 2002.

———. Personal Interview. January 26, 2003a.

———. Personal Interview. February 10, 2003b.

Peeters, Geoffroy. "Deriving Musical Structures from Signal Analysis for Music Audio Summary Generation: 'Sequence' and 'State' Approach." *Computer Music Modeling and Retrieval, International Symposium 2003* in Montpellier, France. Series: *Lecture Notes in Computer Science* 2772. Edited by Uffe Kock Wiil, 142–165. Berlin: Springer, 2004.

Puckette, Miller. "Formant-based audio synthesis using nonlinear distortion." *Journal of the Audio Engineering Society* Vol. 43, No. 1 (1995): 40–47.

Ramstrum, Momilani. *From Kafka to K…: A Multimedia Exploration of Manoury's Opera K…* Paris: Opéra Nationale de Paris, IRCAM, 2004.

Schnell, Norbert, Geoffroy Peeters, Serge Lemouton, Philippe Manoury, and Xavier Rodet. "Synthesizing a Choir in Real-Time Using Pitch Synchronous Overlap Add (PSOLA)." Proceedings of the International Conference on Computer Music (ICMC). San Francisco: International Computer Music Association: 2000.

Schopenhauer, Arthur. *Works.* Translated by Thomas Bailey Saunders, Richard Burdon Haldane, and John Kemp; edited by Will Durant. New York: Simon & Schuster, 1928.

Scruton, Roger. *The Aesthetics of Music.* Oxford: Oxford University Press, 1997.

Welsch, Wolfgang. "Aesthetics beyond Aesthetics." *Undoing Aesthetics.* London: Sage, 1997.

Wishart, Trevor. *On Sonic Art.* Edited by Simon Emmerson. Chur, Switzerland: Harwood, 1996.

DVD References

Number	File Name	Description	Media Type
1	01scene3b.mpg	Movie of Scene 3	MPEG (DVD ROM partition)
2	02scene4a.mpg	Movie of Scene 4	MPEG (DVD ROM partition)
3	03scene5a.mpg	Movie of Scene 5	MPEG (DVD ROM partition)
4	04scene5b.mpg	Movie of Scene 5	MPEG (DVD ROM partition)
5	05scene6f.mpg	Movie of Scene 6	MPEG (DVD ROM partition)
6	06scene7e.mpg	Movie of Scene 7	MPEG (DVD ROM partition)
7	07scene8d.mpg	Movie of Scene 8	MPEG (DVD ROM partition)
8	08scene12b.mpg	Movie of Scene 12	MPEG (DVD ROM partition)
9	07structuralDiagram withElectros copy.tif	Structural Diagram	600-dpi color TIFF
10	13BlackoutI.tif	Blackout I in Scene 3	600-dpi color TIFF
11	16MSDScene0Color.tif	Music Structural Description Image Scene 0	600-dpi color TIFF
12	14MSDScene12Color.tif	Music Structural Description Scene 12	600-dpi color TIFF
13	180.aiff	Electronics in Prologue	Stereo AIFF

Notes

1. The author would like to thank Miller Puckette for setting things in motion, Philippe Manoury for sharing insights into his work, and Serge Lemouton for assistance and information. The author is grateful to Vincent Puig at IRCAM for supporting her work and Pierre Moitron at the Opéra Bastille for allowing this research to go forward. Also, she would like to thank all the performers, without whom there would have been no opera, for their willingness to allow the author to film them. The author thanks her husband, Gunnar Ramstrum, for his help, support, laughter, and love.
2. For the full analysis see Ramstrum (2004).
3. For audio recordings, scores, descriptions of function, and locations of each motive see "Motivic Materials" in Ramstrum (2004).
4. The "Stroop Effect" was named after J. Ridley Stroop who discovered the phenomenon in 1935. Subjects took longer to name a word that was incongruent with its appearance. For example, if the word "red" is written in green ink, it is harder to name than if it is written in red ink.

Annotated Bibliography

Boulez, P. *Boulez on Music Today*. Cambridge, MA: Harvard University Press, 1971.
  The book gives an insight into Boulez's views on music analysis and composition through an active process that involves observation, the search for musical coherence, the interpretation of the work, and the psychology of the compositional process.

Brindle, R. S. *The New Music*. New York: Oxford University Press, 1987.
  The book gives a concise description of selected musical works of the avant garde (1945–86). Discussion includes music after World War II; the influence of Webern; pointillism; integrated serialism; free twelve-note music; indeterminacy, chance, and aleatory music; improvisation including graphic and text scores; concrete music, electronic music; jazz; theatrical-performance music; extended performance techniques (instrumental and vocal); and the avant garde and society. The author provides an overview of music from 1945–75 and 1975–86 that is useful for readers who seek a broad historical context for electroacoustic music. The last section of the book is a summary of notational systems that have developed during the time period covered by the book and would serve as an excellent resource for composers.

Chadabe, J. *Electric Sound: The Past and Promise of Electronic Music*. Upper Saddle, NJ: Prentice-Hall, 1997.
  The author presents an enjoyable and extensive history of electronic music suitable for readers who are new to the field as well as seasoned practitioners. The book includes many photos and quotes of historical significance.

Cogan, R. *New Images of Musical Sound*. Cambridge, MA: Harvard University Press, 1984.
  This influential book introduces the application of sonograms to musical analysis.

Dodge, C., and Thomas A. Jerse. *Computer Music: Synthesis, Composition, and Performance*. New York: Schirmer Books, 1997.
  The book provides an introduction to three main fields in computer music: synthesis, composition, and performance. Chapters 1 through 10 are a thorough presentation of the fundamentals of computer music including acoustics, psychoacoustics, signal processing, basic synthesis techniques, and analysis–resynthesis techniques. Chapter 11 provides an overview of approaches to algorithmic composition. Chapter 12 is a cursory overview of real-time performance techniques.

Dunsby, J., and A. Whittall. *Music Analysis in Theory and Practice*. New Haven, CT: Yale University Press, 1988.
  The audience for this book is musicians who are not expertly trained in music analysis. The book is not intended to serve as a textbook but instead to convey thought processes about the analysis of music. Part 1, chapter 2, entitled "The History of Theory and Analysis: A Short Survey," is a succinct chronology of theoretical treatises and opinions on music analysis. Part 2 has

chapters on Schenker, Tovey, and Schoenberg. Part 3 discusses elements of atonality specifically harmony, voice leading, symmetry, pitch class sets, and twelve-note composition.

Eargle, J. M. *Music, Sound, and Technology*. New York: Van Nostrand Reinhold, 1995.
   The author presents a thorough introduction to acoustics, psychoacoustics, tuning systems, the acoustics of traditional instruments (strings, woodwinds, brass, percussion, and keyboard instruments), the evolution of musical ensembles, sound reinforcement, sound recording, electronic musical instruments, room acoustics, and noise control.

Ernst, D. *The Evolution of Electronic Music*. New York: Schirmer Books, 1977.
   The book discusses early genres of electronic music including music for solo tape, music for performers and tape, and live electronics. The introduction is an extensive survey of the history of music theory and artistic movements that have shaped the history of electronic music and concludes with a chronological list of pre-1948 events that influenced the development electronic music.

Fiske, H. E. *Music and Mind: Philosophical Essays on the Cognition and Meaning of Music*. Lewiston, NY: Edwin Mellon Press, 1990.
   The author discusses a framework for constructing a theory of music through three axioms associated with music cognition: music cognition is unique to human brains, identification of patterns is limited to tonal and rhythmic relationships, and music cognition requires time and effort. Chapters are presented on the structure of the music decision-making process, musical meaning and communication, and why music is not a theory of emotion.

Forte, A. *The Structure of Atonal Music*. New Haven, CT: Yale University Press, 1977.
   This influential book codifies a theoretical framework for the processes underlying atonal music through a rigorous mathematical classification of pitch-class sets. The first part of the book is an exposition of the analytical procedures of atonal music using set theory. The second part of the book purports a structural model of atonal music by citing a number of musical excerpts. Appendix 1 gives the prime forms and vectors of pitch-class sets of three through nine elements.

Licata, T. *Electroacoustic Music*. Westport, CT: Greenwood Press, 2002.
   This book begins with a thought-provoking forward by Jean-Claude Risset that aptly sets the tone for this edited volume. Analyses of compositions by Stockhausen, Xenakis, Koenig, Nono, Laske, Risset, Dashow, and Yuasa are presented in each chapter. A wide array of analytical techniques and graphic representations are employed including sonograms.

Mathews, M. V. *The Technology of Computer Music*. Cambridge, MA: The M.I.T. Press, 1969.
   This important historical work provides an introduction to digital audio, synthesis processes using the Music-N model of sound generation, and the "Music V Manual." The book includes annotated subject references and problems at the end of each chapter. Appendix A contains definitions of terms used in psychoacoustics. Appendix B includes pertinent mathematics used in digital signal processing.

Nattiez, J-J. *Music and Discourse*. Princeton, NJ: Princeton University Press, 1990.
   The book presents a theory of musical semiology that considers practical, methodological, and epistemological views of a work.

Paynter, J., Tim Howell, Richard Orton, and Peter Seymour, eds. *Companion to Contemporary Musical Thought*. Vol. 1. London and New York: Routledge, 1992.
   Part I is entitled "People and Music." Part II of Volume 1 is entitled "The Technology of Music" and includes contributions from Richard Orton, F. Richard Moore, Peter Manning, Barry Truax, Curtis Roads, Craig R. Harris, Joel Chadabe, David Kershaw, Hugh Davies, Denis Smalley, Bruce Pennycook, Trevor Wishart, and Jean-Claude Risset.

Paynter, J., Tim Howell, Richard Orton, and Peter Seymour, eds. *Companion to Contemporary Musical Thought*. Vol. 2. London and New York: Routledge, 1992.
   Part III is "The Structure of Music" and covers a wide range of topics with notable contributions from Jonathan Harvey. Part IV is "The Interpretation of Music."

Perle, G. *Twelve-tone tonality*. Berkeley and Los Angeles: University of California Press, 1996.
   This book provides a liberal and expanded interpretation of Schoenberg's serialism. A collaboration between George Perle and Paul Lansky from 1969–73 influenced Lansky's doctoral dissertation "Affine Music" (Princeton University, 1973).

Rahn, J. *Basic Atonal Theory*. New York: Longman, 1980.
The author provides an accessible approach to the theory and analysis of atonal music for music theorists and composers. Chapters include exercises to enhance listening and analytical skills.

Roads, C. *Microsound*. Cambridge, MA: M.I.T. Press, 2001.
The book is a diary of the author's research in granular synthesis, using both time-domain and frequency-domain representations. The book is accompanied by an audio CD that presents historical examples, musical excerpts, and sound examples that document the author's experiments in synthesis and transformation.

Truax, B. *Acoustic Communication*. Westport, CT: Ablex, 2001.
Barry Truax applies an interdisciplinary framework of communication to the human perception and interpretation of an acoustic environment. This thought-provoking book explores a continuum of three major systems of acoustic communication: speech, music, and soundscape. The book is accompanied by the CD-ROM "Handbook of Acoustic Ecology" by Barry Truax (Cambridge Street Publishing, 1999) that contains definitions of over 500 terms, graphics, and sound examples.

Wishart, T. *On Sonic Art*. Amsterdam: Harwood, 1996.
This book is an expansion of lectures given by the author during a six-week residency at the Queen's University, Kingston, Ontario. Although the book presents synthesis methods, it is essentially about music composition, specifically, the organization of sonic events in time. The author challenges prevailing assumptions regarding music analysis and composition. The book includes an audio CD with a wealth of musical examples ranging from concrete sounds to complete compositions.

Xenakis, I. *Formalized Music: Thought and Mathematics in Composition*. Stuyvesant, NY: Pendragon Press, 1992.
This book is an historical landmark documenting Xenakis' views on compositional processes that utilize free stochastic or Markovian stochastic processes.

Glossary

acoustics — the study of the physics of sound.

algorithm — a series of steps used to complete a task.

ambient music — a genre of electroacoustic music that creates an acoustic environment intended to take the listener through a soundscape journey. For an example of ambient music, listen to Brian Eno's "Ambient1: Music for Airports" (EG Records, Ltd., EEGCD 17, 1978).

amplitude — in acoustics, the peak amount of atmospheric displacement of a sound measured in Newtons per square meter. In a time-domain representation amplitude is the vertical, or Y-axis.

amplitude modulation — in sound synthesis, the process of periodically altering the amplitude of a sound. An example of amplitude modulation is a string player's tremolo, when the movement of the bow alters the amplitude of the vibrating string.

attenuation — a reduction in magnitude of the physical quantity of a sound.

bandwidth — the measurement in Hertz of the width of the region of a filter where frequencies are either passed or attenuated.

cardinality — in set theory analysis, the number of pitch-class elements in a set. For example, the pitch class set 0, 1, 3, 7 has four pitch-class elements and, thus, has a cardinality of 4.

chromagram — a time-frequency analysis technique that wraps all frequencies of the same pitch class to one row in a time-frequency image. For example, the frequencies 110 Hz, 220 Hz, 440 Hz, and 880 Hz would be represented on four different rows in a conventional spectrogram. However, for a chromagram, these four frequencies are mapped to the same pitch class, the pitch class A.

constant-q — in sound synthesis, the process of altering the bandwidth of a filter so that the Q of the filter remains constant over a frequency range. Q is calculated as the center frequency divided by the bandwidth of the filter. For example, two band-pass filters, one with a center frequency of 500 Hz and a bandwidth of 100 Hz and the other with a center frequency of 2,500 Hz and a bandwidth of 500 Hz, have a Q of 5.

cross-synthesis — in sound synthesis, the process of applying the analysis of one signal to the resynthesis of another. Examples of cross-synthesis include phase vocoding and linear predictive coding.

decibel (dB) — in acoustics, a unit of relative measurement used to compare the intensity or amplitude of two sounds on a logarithmic scale.

delay — a signal processing technique that makes a copy of an audio signal and alters its playback time.

diffusion — the distribution of sound pressure throughout a space. If sound pressure is uniformly distributed throughout a space, the sound is considered to be well diffused.

diffusion score — the notations that plot the movement of sound pressure in a space over time.

dramaturgy — in theater, the contextualization of a work or the interpretation of a performance.

envelope — in sound synthesis, a single-event, time-variant control signal. An envelope may be applied to amplitude to create an amplitude envelope when the amplitude of a sound changes over time in direct relation to the shape of the envelope. Envelopes may also be applied to other attributes of sound such as frequency, pitch, or the bandwidth of a filter.

equal loudness contour — in psychoacoustics, a plot of frequency (X-axis) vs. loudness (Y-axis) that compares the subjective loudness of pure tones of varying frequencies with the loudness of a 1kHz tone. The equal loudness contour shows that the ear is most sensitive in the region of 3 to 3.5 kHz and becomes increasingly less sensitive as frequency decreases. Equal loudness contours have been created by Fletcher and Munson and further refined by Robinson and Dadson.

equal temperament — a tuning system in which all twelve tones of the chromatic scale are divided into equal frequency ratios. The frequency between adjacent notes in the chromatic scale is $2^{1/12}$ or 1.05946.

filter — in signal processing, a device or algorithm used to affect certain parts of a spectrum by either attenuating, amplifying, or passing certain frequency regions.

formant — the amplified frequency region of a spectrum that minimally changes with respect to the fundamental frequency. A formant is a fixed resonance. Examples of formants are vowel sounds that have amplified frequency regions that remain static regardless of changes in the fundamental. Formants in vowel sounds contribute to our perception of the vowel and are an important auditory cue in our perception of timbre.

Forte numbers — in set theory analysis, a system codified by Alan Forte that identifies each pitch class set with a unique name and interval vector.

Fourier Transform — a mathematical operation for translating a time-domain signal, such as an acoustic pressure wave from a musical instrument, into the frequency-domain. The Fourier transform decomposes the signal into a (possibly infinite) list of sine waves, so that the original signal can be represented as a linear combination of sine waves.

frequency modulation — in sound synthesis, the process of periodically altering the frequency of a sound. An example of frequency modulation is vocal vibrato.

frequency-domain representation — a graphic representation of a spectrum as a linear combination of sine waves in which frequency is the horizontal, or X-axis, and amplitude is the vertical, or Y-axis.

fundamental — the lowest frequency component in a spectrum.

granular synthesis — the use of a large number of sonic grains to create a timbre. Based on the work of Dennis Gabor, Iannis Xenakis hypothesized that every sound could be understood as an assembly of a larger number of elementary particles or grains. Curtis Roads automated granular synthesis of sound.

harmonic — a frequency that is an integer multiple of a fundamental frequency. For example, the frequencies 100 Hz and 200 Hz are in a harmonic relationship.

harmonic series — a succession of frequencies that are positive integer multiples of a fundamental frequency. For example, the first five harmonics in the harmonic series that begins on 100Hz are 100 Hz, 200 Hz, 300 Hz, 400 Hz, and 500 Hz.

Hertz (Hz) — a unit of measurement for frequency that represents the number of repetitions per second of a periodic waveform.

inharmonic — a frequency that is not in an integer ratio with another frequency. For example, the frequencies 100 Hz and 120 Hz are in an inharmonic relationship.

interval class — in set theory, the difference between two pitch classes reduced to the interval of a tritone under inversion. For example, the difference between C-sharp (pitch class 1) and C (pitch class 0) is 1 (1 – 0 = 1). Since the interval 1 (a minor second) is less than a tritone, no inversion is required. The difference between A (pitch class 9) and D (pitch class 2) is 7 (9 – 2 = 7). Since the interval 7 (a perfect fifth) is greater than a tritone, the interval is inverted to a perfect fourth (interval 5).

interval vector — in set theory analysis, an ordered array of numbers enclosed in square brackets that represents the total possible number of occurrences of any intervallic dyad of a pitch class set arranged in increasing order from the minor second to the tritone. For example, set 6-Z26 is comprised of pitch classes 0,1,3,5,7,8 with an interval vector of [232341]. The interval vector indicates that all possible pairings of the pitch classes in set 6-Z36 result in 2 minor seconds, 3 major seconds, 2 minor thirds, 3 major thirds, 4 perfect fourths, and 1 tritone, or their intervallic complement.

intonation — a slight modification to a tuning system.

Leslie Effect — an effect caused by rotating a speaker during the playback of sound.

microtonal — in a tuning system, the practice of modifying intervals so that they are smaller than one-half step.

MIDI — an acronym for Musical Instrument Digital Interface. The MIDI 1.0 specification details a communications protocol to be used by MIDI-compatible devices such as computer interfaces and electronic keyboards.

musique concrète — the use of found sounds in music composition. Pierre Schaeffer is considered the pioneer of music concrète through his use of both disk recordings and magnetic tape.

nexus set — in set theory analysis, a pitch class set that is a superset of other pitch class sets.

noise — white noise is all audible frequencies at random instantaneous amplitudes. White noise creates a uniformly flat distribution.

normal order — in set theory analysis, a particular permutation of a collection of pitch classes in ascending order.

Nyquist frequency — the frequency that is precisely one-half of the sampling rate. The Nyquist theorem states that the highest frequency that may be theoretically represented without distortion by a digital audio system is one-half the sampling rate. For CD-quality sound, the sampling rate is 44.1 kHz; therefore, the Nyquist frequency is 22.05 kHz.

overtone — a frequency component of a spectrum that sounds above the fundamental and may be categorized as harmonic or inharmonic. The first frequency component sounding above the fundamental is identified as the first overtone.

partial — a frequency component of a spectrum that sounds above the fundamental and may be categorized as harmonic or inharmonic. The fundamental of a spectrum is identified as the first partial.

pedal tone — a sustained tone.

periodic — a phenomenon characterized by repeating cycles. Sound waves that repeat in the range of 20 cycles per second (20 Hz) to 20,000 cycles per second (20 kHz) are within the range of human perception and contribute to the sensation of pitch.

pitch — the highness or lowness of a note. Pitch is the human perception of frequency.

pitch class — in set theory, one of the twelve equal-tempered pitches designated by the integers 0–11. For example, the pitch C has a pitch class of 0, the pitch C-sharp or D-flat has a pitch class of 1, etc.

pitch tracking — a computer algorithm that analyzes a digital audio signal in real time and determines the fundamental pitch during a certain time interval.

prime form — in set theory analysis, a set in normal order transposed so that the first pitch class is 0.

psychoacoustics — the study of the human perception of sound.

Q — a measure of the selectivity of frequencies that pass through a filter. Q is defined as the center frequency divided by the bandwidth.

real-time — a characteristic of a process such that the time it takes to complete the process is perceptually instantaneous between the input to and the result of the process.

resonance — the spectral peak or an amplified frequency region in a timbre.

sampling frequency or sampling rate — the speed at which a digital audio system can output discrete amplitude values to describe the time-domain representation of a waveform.

score following — an algorithm whereby software stores an abstraction of a score and real-time input to the software, generally by a human performer, is analyzed and compared against the stored abstraction of the score. The computer follows the score of a human performance.

segmentation — in set theory analysis, the process of identifying a collection of events that may be characterized as a set.

semiotics — relating to the observance and meaning of signs.

serialism — a compositional process that orders members of an element of music into a series and uses that series in the realization of the music. Arnold Schoenberg applied serial techniques to pitch by forming the tone row—a succession of twelve notes, none of which are omitted or used more than once. Serialism has also been applied to other elements of music such as rhythm or dynamics.

set complement — in set theory analysis, a set derived through set subtraction. The elements of a given set are subtracted from the universal set to form the set complement. For example, set 4-1 is comprised of pitch classes 0, 1, 2, 3. Subtracting set 4-1 from the universal set 0, 1, 2, 3, 4, 5, 6, 7, 8, 9, 10, 11 returns pitch classes 4, 5, 6, 7, 8, 9, 10, 11. These pitch classes may be reduced to the prime form 0, 1, 2, 3, 4, 5, 6, 7 or set 8-1.

set complex relation — a set of sets associated by inclusion.

set theory — a field of mathematics that Alan Forte applied to the analysis of atonal music in order to study the relationships among collections of pitches.

Short-Time Fourier Transform (STFT) — a modification to the Fourier Transform to enable the analysis of time-varying spectra. The conventional Fourier Transform is computed over all time; hence, changes in spectral content over time are not represented in the Fourier Transform. The STFT applies a finite window function to the signal prior to computing the Fourier Transform, yielding separate spectra for each window.

sideband — in sound synthesis, a frequency in a spectrum that is created as a result of modulation.

signal processing — the study of generating and analyzing signals.

sine wave — a waveform with a spectrum containing one frequency component.

sonogram — a spectrogram computed from an audio signal (also refers to an image generated by ultrasonography).

soundscape — the aggregate of all sound energy in a given context that creates a sonic environment with consideration for the human perception of that environment.

spatialization — the process of placing sound in a space.

spectralism — the quality or behavior of spectra.

spectrogram — a graph of a spectrum generated from the magnitude component of the Short-Time Fourier Transform. Time is the horizontal, or X-axis, and frequency is the vertical, or Y-axis.

spectromorphology — the form or structure of spectra.

spectrum — the distribution of acoustic energy in a timbre.

stochastic — involving random variables, chance, or probability.

synthesis — in digital synthesis, the realization of sound by means of a computer.

tape piece — a genre of electroacoustic music that does not include a human performer.

temperament — a tuning system that relates frequencies to pitches. Examples of temperaments include the Pythagorean tuning system, just intonation, mean-tone temperament, and equal temperament.

timbre — the tone color of a sound.

time-domain representation — a graphic representation of the acoustic pressure of a waveform in which time is the horizontal, or X-axis, and amplitude is the vertical, or Y-axis.

time-frequency analysis — a signal-processing technique that estimates the spectral content of a signal at successive moments in time, yielding a representation of the time-varying spectra of the signal.

universal set — in set theory analysis of atonal music the universal set contains all twelve pitch classes: 0, 1, 2, 3, 4, 5, 6, 7, 8, 9, 10, and 11.

Contributors

Mary Simoni holds a master's degree in music composition and a Ph.D. in music theory from Michigan State University. She completed post-doctoral studies at the Center for Computer Research in Music and Acoustics, Stanford University; the Center for Computer Music, City University of New York; and the Electronic Music Studios of Mills College. Dr. Simoni serves as Professor of Music Technology, Associate Dean for Technology Initiatives, Director of the Center for Performing Arts & Technology, and Department Chair at the University of Michigan School of Music in Ann Arbor. Her music and multimedia works have been performed in Asia, Europe, and widely throughout the United States and have been recorded by Centaur Records, the Leonardo Music Journal published by MIT Press, and the International Computer Music Association. The Kellogg Foundation, the National Science Foundation, and the Michigan Council for the Arts and Cultural Affairs have funded her work. Dr. Simoni has appeared as a pianist using live electronics in the United States, Europe, and Asia. She currently serves as Associate Editor of the journal *Organised Sound* published by the Cambridge University Press. Her service to the International Computer Music Association includes at-large Director and board member (1994-2004), Publications Coordinator (1996-2000), and President (2000-2004). In addition, she has authored an e-book, *A Gentle Introduction to Algorithmic Composition,* published by the University of Michigan Office of Scholarly Publishing.

Norman Adams holds B.S. and M.S. degrees in electrical engineering (with highest distinction) from the University of Virginia in Charlottesville. He is currently a Ph.D. candidate, researching signal processing applications for music and acoustics in the Electrical Engineering and Computer Science Department at the University of Michigan, Ann Arbor. Concurrently, he is pursuing a M.A. in the Media Arts in the Department of Performing Arts Technology at the University of Michigan School of Music. His technical research interests include binaural sonification, music information retrieval, and time-frequency analysis. He also is interested in stochastic composition and his compositions have been included in a 60 by 60 Vox Novus concert/CD and a regional SEAMUS concert.

Leigh Landy earned his B.S. and M.A. at Columbia University and a Ph.D. at SUNY, Buffalo. He worked at the University of Amsterdam before moving to the UK, where he currently directs the Music, Technology, and Innovation Research Centre at De Montfort University. His work is both creative and scholarly. The former involves a number of collaborative projects with other artists and art forms including extensive work with video artist, Michel Jaffrennou; playwright, Heiner Müller; composer-performer, Jos Zwaanenburg; and choreographer, Evelyn Jamieson. Landy currently directs the performing arts company Idée Fixe—Experimental Sound and Movement Theatre, with Ms. Jamieson. In the 1980s, he was also the first composer in residence for the newly formed Dutch National Theatre company. He is widely published including three books with one in progress. He also edits *Organised Sound* (Cambridge University Press) and is on the editorial board of *Avant Garde* (Rodopi). His writings focus on issues of access in the experimental arts both in terms of appreciation and providing opportunities for people to become involved with innovative creativity. He initiated the ElectroAcoustic Resource Site (EARS) and is founding member of the Electroacoustic Music Studies Network. Landy has received grants from the Fulbright Foundation, British Council, Dutch Ministries of Science and the Arts, and many others. He has been a visiting professor in China and a keynote speaker in Brazil (and a few places in between). His work has been performed around the globe, although a disadvantage of electroacoustic music is that he is not always needed to be present.

Benjamin Broening's compositions have been widely performed and broadcast across the United States, as well as in Europe and Asia. He has composed works for many media including orchestral, choral, chamber, and electroacoustic music. Recent commissions include a work for clarinet and piano commissioned by the Band and Orchestral Division of Yamaha Corporation of America for Arthur Campbell, a work for clarinet and electronics for F. Gerard Errante, and choral/instrumental works for the Choral Arts Society of Philadelphia, the James River Singers, the Connecticut Choral Society and the Grace Choral Society of Brooklyn, as well pieces for pianist Daniel Koppelman and Eighth Blackbird. Other recent commissions include a cantata for the Charlotte Symphony and the Oratorio Singers of Charlotte, a clarinet concerto for the Interlochen Arts Academy Wind Ensemble, a multi-media cantata for Hampton-Sydney College, chamber works for Quorum Chamber Arts Collective and Currents new music ensemble, three choral works for the Virginia Glee Club, an orchestral piece for the Ricciotti Ensemble (Netherlands), music for theater and dance, as well as numerous solo works for performers around the country. A recipient of the Presser Music Award, Broening has also received recognition and awards from the American Composers Forum, the Norfolk and Bowdoin Chamber Music Festivals, as well as from Yale, Christ's College, Cambridge, the University of Michigan, and the University of Richmond. His music has been recorded on the Centaur, Equilibrium, MIT Press, and SEAMUS labels. Broening is founder and artistic director of Third Practice, an annual festival of electroacoustic music at the University of Richmond, where he is an Assistant Professor of Music. He holds degrees from the University of Michigan, Cambridge University, Yale University, and Wesleyan University.

Michael Clarke is Professor of Music at the University of Huddersfield in England, where he has been Director of the Electroacoustic Studios since 1987. He studied at Durham University, England, earning a B.A. (Honours Music) and later a Ph.D. in composition. He has made extended visits to major studios abroad, spending eight months at EMS, Stockholm (1983-4) and six months at IRCAM, Paris (1988) and spent shorter periods working at Simon Fraser University (1995) and, most recently, at SARC, Belfast (2004). As a composer, he writes both acoustic and electroacoustic works, often combining these media. Clarke's compositions have been performed around the world and have been awarded a number of prizes, including the CIM France Prize at Bourges in 1983 for *Soundings*, the Chandos Prize in Glasgow in 1984 for *Uppvaknande,* and the Musica Nova prize in 1997 in Prague for *Tim(br)e*. Four of his works are available on the CD *Refractions*. Professor Clarke is also involved in the development of software for sound synthesis and transformation. He added unit-generators to MIT's Music 11 (later Csound) and more recently, in collaboration with Xavier Rodet of IRCAM, added objects to Max/MSP. Three times he has led teams that have won European Academic Software Awards (1994 for SYnthia in Heidelberg, 2000 for Calma in Rotterdam, and 2004 for Sybil in Neuchâtel). Clarke has also written about various aspects of music technology, for example contributing to *The Csound Book* (MIT Press) and to journals such as *Perspectives of New Music* and *Organised Sound*.

Andrew May is currently Assistant Professor of Music and director of the Center for Experimental Music and Intermedia at the University of North Texas. A composer, computer music researcher, violinist, and improviser, May also co-founded two contemporary music series, Atomic Clock Music Events and Pendulum. May's compositions have been performed in Japan, Korea, Singapore, Greece, Switzerland, Germany, England, and widely in the United States. SEAMUS and EMF Media have released recordings of his music. As a violinist, he has performed across the United States and has been recorded on CRI. His compositions have been supported by grants from the American Music Center and the Center for Research and Creative Work at the University of Colorado, as well as by numerous commissions. He is an Americas Regional Director as well as Secretary and Treasurer for the International Computer Music Association. May holds a Ph.D. in composition from the University of California, San Diego; an M.F.A. from the California Institute of the Arts in composition and violin; and a B.A. summa cum laude in music from Yale University. He completed the Stage d'Informatique Musicale at IRCAM in 1998. His teachers include Roger Reynolds, Mel Powell, and Jon Berger in composition, and Miller Puckette in computer music.

Mara Helmuth composes for computer and acoustic instruments, often using her own software. She is an Associate Professor in Composition and the director of (ccm)², the College-Conservatory of Music Center for Computer Music, at the University of Cincinnati. She holds a D.M.A. in music composition from Columbia University, a B.A. and M.M. from the University of Illinois at Urbana-Champaign, and has taught at Texas A&M University and New York University. She has had numerous performances in the United States and internationally. In addition, Helmuth has served as International Computer Music Association member of the board of directors (1998-2001), *Array* newsletter editor or co-editor (1998-2003), and Vice President for Conferences (2004-2005). Her tape music includes *Abandoned Lake in Maine* (1997), based on loon sounds; *Mellipse* (1989,1995), which won third prize in the 1990 NEWCOMP computer music competition; and *bugs and ice: A Question of Focus* (2002). Collaborations for percussion and computer with Allen Otte are heard on the Electronic Music Foundation compact disk *Implements of Actuation* (EMF 023) and in the first Internet2-streamed opera, *Clotho: the Life of Camille Claudel*. Recent work includes the interactive *Staircase of Light* installation for the Sino-Nordic Arts Space in Beijing. Helmuth's software includes *Patchmix*, a Cmix/RTcmix graphical code-generating instrument builder; *StochGran*, a granular synthesis composition application; and *Soundmesh*, for Internet 2 network improvisation. Her writings have appeared in the monograph *Audible Traces* and in the *Journal of New Music Research, Computers and Mathematics with Applications*, and *Perspectives of New Music*. She also plays the qin, a Chinese zither.

Momilani Ramstrum holds a B.S. in biochemistry from the University of Massachusetts at Amherst, a master's degree in music composition from San Diego State University, and a Ph.D. from the Critical Studies and Experimental Practices area of the Department of Music at the University of California, San Diego (UCSD). Her areas of research include computer music, the philosophy of technology as applied to music, and electronic opera. A year-long residency (2002 – 2003) at IRCAM, Paris was funded by grants from the French Embassy in Washington D.C. and UCSD. Working as a writer, videographer, musicologist and producer she created a DVD-ROM exploring Philippe Manoury's electronic opera *K*.... Dr. Ramstrum returned to IRCAM in 2004 for three months to finish the DVD-ROM entitled *From Kafka to K...*, which was published by IRCAM in 2004. She is a multimedia composer and has created works for varied instruments, singers, electronics, and animation that have been performed throughout the United States. She has developed and taught courses in world music, music theory, aural skills, electronics in popular music, and computer music at UCSD, San Diego State University, San Diego City College, Southwestern College, and Mesa College. Her current projects include documenting the role of women in the development of electroacoustic music, and creating an interactive documentation of the compositional, theoretical, and performance creations of Trevor Wishart. A continued interest in interactive music has led her to work that facilitates music-making in audiences of all ages.

Index

Page numbers in italic indicate tables or figures.

291